Hope Beyond Healing

A Cancer Journal

Dale Aukerman

Brethren Press®

Photographer: Ken Koons, *Carroll County Times*
Cover Design: Cedar House Design Company
Cover photo: D. Jeanene Tiner

Library of Congress Cataloging in Publication Data
Aukerman, Dale.
    Hope beyond healing: a cancer journal / Dale Aukerman.
        p.   cm.
    ISBN 0-87178-023-2
    1. Cancer--Patients--Religious life. 2. Aukerman, Dale--Diaries.
    3. Cancer--Patients--United States--Diaries. I. Title
BV4910.33 A72 2000
248.8'6196994'092--dc21
[B]

                                                               99-059737

Manufactured in the United States of America

Dedication

So many people have supported us in this time, both by caring for our day-to-day needs and by helping us sustain our faith. They have offered rides, run errands, baked bread, tended the garden, and kept up the homestead. They have prayed with us and for us. Their acts of love and service and their outpouring of compassion have borne us up in this time. Some are mentioned here, and many more are not. So many kindnesses have become part of the routine of our lives. I dedicate this book to all those friends and loved ones who have eased my walk through the valley of the shadow of death, and who have helped me keep my eyes on the One who walks this path with me.

Dale Aukerman
September 2, 1999

Contents

Foreword

The day Dale Aukerman died, following a three-year battle with cancer, was the day we baptized our one-year-old son, Luke. As Luke began his life in the Christian community, Dale ended his on this earth. In the service for Luke, I invoked the memory of Dale as a role model for my son and for all of us. I said I didn't know any Christian who cared more about living consistently and persistently as a disciple of Jesus Christ.

Dale was a long-time writer, activist, and companion of Sojourners, and became a personal friend as well. His first article appeared in our magazine in March 1978 and his last in January–February 1998. In the years I knew and worked with Dale, I had the blessing of many talks with him, of planting trees with him at his beloved Maryland farm, of being arrested with him in Washington, D.C., for acts of peacemaking. Our Peace Ministry held retreats at his farm in Maryland, and we often had the joy of worshiping with Dale and his wonderful wife, Ruth, and their children, Daniel, Miriam, and Maren, in the Sojourners Community.

Dale Aukerman had a great mind, a warm spirit, and a big heart, which made him one of our best teachers and writers. Who will forget the insight and intensity of his books like *Darkening Valley* or *Reckoning with Apocalypse* or, for that matter, any conversation with Dale? It seemed that each time I talked with him he had a new insight into the gospel vision of peacemaking. He saw the life of Christian peace witness not as optional, but as the essence of following Jesus—that "the response of faith involves putting oneself and all one's living under the Lordship of Jesus Christ, who taught and exemplified what human life should be."

Hope Beyond Healing— this journal of Dale's final years—deepens his legacy and adds a resounding affirmation to his life and death. The entries are moving, inspiring, at times painful to read, but filled with his abiding faith in God. While he deeply desired and prayed for physical healing, his faith also told him that God's will may not always be that physical miracle. He writes, "Jesus says to me, 'Go in peace'—into whatever is ahead." And to the end, Dale went in peace.

Following Jesus was the passion of Dale's life, and he did it with a faithful single-mindedness rarely seen in the church today. In his last article, published in the July 1999 issue of the Church of the Brethren *Messenger*, Dale writes: "It's not just that I am convinced in my mind that Jesus is risen. I have found again and again that this living Lord comes to me. I have not seen the risen Jesus with my eyes or touched him with my hands as the disciples did. But throughout my life he has met me. . . ." On the morning of September 4, Dale finally saw the risen Lord with his eyes and was welcomed home with a loving touch.

At his memorial service, I said that for Sojourners Community "Dale was always a friend, often an inspiration, sometimes a challenge, and consistently a prophetic witness to the gospel of Jesus Christ."

Rest in peace, my friend.

—Jim Wallis

1996

Monday, November 4.

My wife, Ruth, had been urging me for weeks to go to Dr. Caricofe, my primary care physician, to have him check my nagging cough. I thought of the cough as a minor symptom. But finally I went. I was given a TB test and sent to Westminster for chest x-rays.

Tuesday, November 5.

I got an early call from Dr. Caricofe's office that he wanted to see me. I had been scheduled to come in tomorrow to have the TB test read. So right after the call I pretty much figured out what I would hear—lung cancer. I didn't mention that to Ruth; but we both saw the call as ominous. Ruth said, "Whatever comes, we will face it together."

Before going in, I turned to Psalm 116. Not that this psalm came to my mind; it was relatively unfamiliar to me. But I was checking a cross-reference from a footnote to a New Testament passage, and in that way the psalm was given to me. "The snares of death encompassed me" (v. 3). "For thou hast delivered my soul from death" (v. 8). In verse 15 the Revised Standard Version has "Precious in the sight of the Lord is the death of his saints." Weiser in his commentary has "It is too hard in the eyes of the Lord when his godly ones die and are no more."

Dr. Caricofe came in with the x-rays in his hand and said in his monotonal way, "We have a problem, and it's going to be a major problem." Then he had me read the written report: a mass on the left lung "strongly suspicious for pulmonary carcinoma." We talked about the next step. He spoke of finding a pulmonary specialist or thoracic surgeon in Frederick.

After I told Ruth of the tentative diagnosis, she was able to reach Dr. Frauke Westphal in Rockville, a close friend of ours. Frauke said that I should have a CT scan of the chest and abdomen and recommended that I see a pulmonary specialist in her office. She made arrangements for me to have the CT scan in Westminster.

Most of us have had a telephone call that brings grim news or have at times imagined the possibility of such a call. Now we needed to make that sort of call to our children. When we reached Maren in Phoenix, she was so evidently devastated. In addition she and Ruth and I needed to deal with a big question. Maren, a bilingual teacher, had flight bookings to bring twelve Hispanic schoolchildren and one other chaperon to Washington for a week, to arrive on Saturday. In her grant applications, Maren had written that the group would receive free food and lodging on a farm in rural Maryland— that is, our four-acre homestead with log house. Now, faced with this huge crisis, should we go ahead with things as planned? I would be having further tests. I needed to be very careful to avoid picking up any respiratory infection. We decided to go ahead.

Miriam is in St. Petersburg with her Russian friends, Mark and Larissa. We decided against trying to reach her there and ruining the visit. We called her husband, Chuck, in New York. He will send her an e-mail message at the Ford Foundation office in Moscow where she works.

Daniel is in his first year of medical residency in Augusta, Maine. He told Maren on the phone, "I have so much I still want to learn from my father."

Thursday, November 7.

I had the CT scan on Wednesday. This afternoon Ruth took the day off from her teaching job and we drove to Rockville for a consultation with Dr. John Saia, a pulmonary specialist. He thinks I quite probably have lung cancer. But only a biopsy will indicate that for certain. The scan shows lesions on my liver. Ruth held up her hand, with thumb and index finger a little apart: "How long do we have?"

Dr. Saia replied, "It's not that short." But he would not say anything more in terms of length of time.

Two or three times earlier in my life when I thought I might have cancer, I was quite apprehensive. This time, when it seems I have one of the quickest kinds, I'm not feeling any fear or apprehension, no inner constriction. Such grace there is in that. I read from Colossians 3:15: "And let the peace of Christ rule in your hearts, to which indeed you were called in the one body. And be thankful." That rule has come. Of course, I may veer out of it at times.

There is irony in how this tumor or cancer has made its stealthy growth in my body. A grandmother, my sister Jane at fourteen, my mother, and then my father all died of cancer. My surviving sibling, Ann, has had breast cancer, now in remission. With so much cancer in my family, I have tried to

2

be on my guard, going for various checkups. Last January I had my yearly physical with Dr. Caricofe—probably a little too early for him to detect any problem with the left lung. In the spring Ruth was concerned about my coughing. I didn't know that coughing could be a symptom of lung cancer. During the summer I didn't seem to be coughing much. In the fall I was noticing some shortness of breath at times, but I figured this came with growing older. In spite of all my concern and caution in relation to the cancer threat, this tumor had grown to an imposing size before being detected.

Saturday, November 9.

Friends close by have been responding remarkably to help us receive Maren's Hispanic group from Phoenix. The Palsgroves and the Mastalerzes offered their vans. Brenda Palsgrove and I drove the vans to Washington National Airport to pick up the fourteen. The children, former students of Maren, who are now sixth and seventh graders, were all excitement as they spread out in our log house. They look at me with puzzled concern, probably wondering, Is he going to die so very soon? Some of them have sniffles, so I will stay in my third-floor office most of the time when they are here. We had some food already prepared. But friends have brought in a lot.

Sunday, November 10.

I slept through the night rather well. Still in bed I asked Ruth how she had slept. She said, "I was awake till 3:00, but it was so beautiful listening to you sleep and breathe."

As we took our morning walk to the end of Stem Road, I asked Ruth about her father's exact words, near the time of our wedding in Germany, regarding our task. She said in German, *"einander in den Himmel bringen* [bringing each other into heaven]."

She and I have hugged each other again and again. We've shed tears together. In the night I sometimes get choked up as I lie thinking and praying. There is sadness over the likely departure, but as Ruth has said, "also an incredible joy." All that we have had together and all that we have together now becomes amazingly more precious than before. There is such fullness and wonder in the interaction between us.

An Australian friend, Jamie Edgerton, called just before he left for Africa where he works with the World Bank. He had shared the word about me in the Sojourners service. The text was from Job, and the message dealt with why bad things happen to good people. Jim Wallis, leader of the Sojourners Community, saw what has come upon me as evoking that riddle. When Jim gave Jamie the bread in the communion, he said, "The body of Christ broken for you, Jamie, and for Dale."

I have not asked the question, Why me? But I've been thinking about the narrative in Job 1 and 2. Satan is the one who brings on evil—with God's permission. He seeks to tarnish God's honor, but that honor triumphs. "I had heard of thee by the hearing of the ear, but now my eye sees thee" (42:5). God does not will cancer, but he takes each cancer or other illness into his purposeful willing in relation to the stricken human being and the whole, just as a world master in chess would take a threatening move by an upstart player into his strategy and design for triumph in the game.

Later in the day I went to my computer and composed the following letter to friends:

November 10, 1996

After the first Peace Pentecost prayer vigil in the Capitol Rotunda, about one hundred twenty of us men were packed into two holding cells. We sang and prayed far into the night. With marvelous intensity God's Spirit moved in our midst. Jim Wallis offered the comment, "We are not worthy of the grace we are experiencing here."

These past several days I've thought at various times of that night. I had had a cough for a while. On Monday I went to my family doctor to have him check it. On Tuesday I learned that I have a large mass on my left lung. That lung is partly collapsed and has fluid under it. CT scans on Wednesday gave a fuller picture and showed that there are also a couple of lesions on my liver. I'm to have some biopsy procedures done on Tuesday. But it seems virtually certain that I have lung cancer. The mass is so centrally located that it cannot be removed surgically.

Ruth and I find ourselves so borne up by the love and peace of Christ and by the love and help of friends. I've written and preached on 2 Corinthians 1:8-10 in relation to the nuclear threat: setting one's hope in God for deliverance even when feeling under a sentence of death. Now the text takes on another depth of meaning for me. But this morning I took in verse 11, which I'd given little attention to before: "You also must help us by prayer, so that many will give thanks on our behalf for the blessing granted us in answer to many prayers." That blessing has come to us so much already.

Each day and each loving relationship are such amazing gifts, far more precious than before. One's outlook changes remarkably as to what is important enough to give time and energy to, when time left may be very limited.

God gives us life through the life, death, and rising of Jesus. Even with this incursion of death within my body, life in such deepened intensity is being given me. God's gracious will for life is going to win out. We can stake our living and our dying on that.

Monday, November 11.

When Miriam called us after her return to Moscow, she was crying. She even asked whether there might be such a thing as transplanting a lung. She said she hopes to come home for Thanksgiving rather than having her husband, Chuck, fly to Moscow as they had arranged. Ruth and I are so touched that each of the children is ready to come home to help.

There have been calls upon calls from friends. Cliff Kindy, peacemaking activist in Indiana, encouraged me to write about all this "for the rest of us." He offered that he and his family could come out to help if needed. I told Cliff I had thought of him in relation to my circumstances. He had been face to face with death a number of times, doing Christian Peacemaker Teams work in the Gaza Strip and Hebron.

Yvonne Dilling, a dear friend who was based in our spring house for three years, called from Massachusetts, spoke of her schedule, and said she would be glad to come and be house hostess for a time—getting food on the table and coping with visitors. I was moved by this readiness on her part.

When I called Paul Grout, longtime friend and pastor in Vermont, to tell him, I mentioned that my life has a certain completeness in a number of ways. He replied, "Then start something new."

I've told some people, "There must be an easier way to get a lot of people to pray for you." We have felt the power of all those prayers so much, helping the peace of Christ to rule in us. Rather often there is a buoyant sense of all that prayer pressing toward me. If the prayers of so many do not turn back this onslaught of death, those prayers, nevertheless, will have weight against the powers of death that otherwise seek to lay us low.

Tuesday, November 12.

John Witiak, a friend living nearby in Union Bridge, drove me to Suburban Hospital in Bethesda for the biopsy procedures. As the surgeon started to prep me for draining fluid from under the right lung, I said, "I take it this is to be for the left lung."

He asked, "What am I doing over here?" That's precisely what I was wondering. He drained off 700 cc's, about .7 of a quart. According to the report, the fluid did not seem to contain malignant cells. But the biopsied tissue from the tumor on the lung was malignant as expected—non-small-cell lung cancer.

God breathed into the nostrils of the human being the breath of life (Gen. 2:7). That breath of life comes to my attention far more now. Breathing will likely become more and more of a struggle for me. But God still gives each breath.

Wednesday, November 13.
Frauke and Heiner Westphal bought us a fax machine as an early Christmas gift. They thought we needed it for dealing with the medical reports.

I have no sense of being rushed or of needing to rush. I can take my time through each good hour and day that is given to me. But I must certainly make the best possible use of what may be a very short time ahead of me.

Thursday, November 14.
When we woke up this morning, there was about an inch of snow on the ground. Maren's children had never seen snow before. They were ecstatic as they romped around in it and scooped up handfuls for snowballs. The boys also had a splendid time splitting firewood.

These children here in our home for the week seemed to come at such an inopportune time. Yet they have been so thoughtful and considerate toward me. The girls sit in a circle each evening saying the rosary for me. I wonder whether the rosary was ever said for me before.

Friday, November 15.
Ruth took me to Rockville for the appointment with Dr. Saia. He changed his approach: The spots on the liver might not be cancerous; this needs to be determined. If they are not, there may be some chance that the left lung with the mass can be removed. But there would be no point in operating "if it's out of the barn," or "out of the pasture," as I said to Daniel on the phone, on account of our history with steers. He called Dr. Dick at Suburban Hospital about checking the spots on my liver. He was able to set up an appointment for later in the afternoon.

Frauke Westphal, who is in the same office as Dr. Saia, told Ruth, "I never prayed harder in my life than when you were with Dr. Saia. You are like family, and we are ready to help financially or in any way needed."

On the drive back, Ruth began singing with strong emotion: *"Trotz dem alten Drachen. . . . Jesu, meine Freude* [In spite of the old dragon. . . . Jesus, my joy]."

Maren drove me to Suburban Hospital for the 4:00 p.m. appointment. As we pulled into the visitor parking, she pointed to the two spots "Reserved for Clergy" and asked playfully, "Are you included?"

The time with Dr. Dick was brief. He looked at the CT scans of the liver: "If I had to guess, I would say they are hemangiomas [benign masses]."

Saturday, November 16.
It has been a beautiful, sunny day. Most helpful friends of ours, Ken, Stephanie, and Ry Koons, Mark Yount, and John and Ted John Witiak, were here cutting and splitting wood. They stacked outside of the kitchen most of what I think we will need for the winter. In the early spring before Miriam's wedding, our neighbor to the south brought us logs and branches out of a tree line he took down, right up the hill from our place. I did the brush work and paid him for bringing the wood to what became a really big pile in the corner of our hay patch. Now the cancer has dashed my plans for working up that pile during the winter.

Ken, a photographer with the *Carroll County Times*, asked whether he could do photos of me at various stages of what is coming. He would start next week, taking photos of my doing regular work around the place. The photos would also be available for our family. I told him I would be glad for him to do this.

Maren and her children bade us goodbye and headed to the airport in the two vans.

Sunday, November 17.
This is the day we decided on for the service of anointing for healing. I had invited some close friends to join us. Though a few were unable to come, Mabel Braune and her daughter Donna, Bill Heltzel, Paul and Phyllis Dodd, Dave and Ruth Fitz, and our pastor, Scott Duffey, were here. Ruth Fitz sang "My life flows on in endless song." That touched me deeply and still echoes in my spirit. Scott read the James 5 passage about anointing and had an opening prayer. He asked me to share confessionally or otherwise. I said I

had told several people I have felt more wholeness in me since the news hit than for the period of time before. "As I see it, I wasn't doing very well seeking God's kingdom first, putting his work first in my life. I was giving too much priority to what needed doing in the garden and around the place. I wasn't doing very well in my devotional life. I wasn't giving God that much attention. But God has ways of getting our attention."

Scott knelt beside me. The others formed a circle around me. Scott asked in his prayer, "Drive out what is foreign." Most of us said a spoken prayer.

It was a time full of peace and blessing. David Fitz said afterward, "There was healing for us all in the service."

Later I told Ruth in bed, "All these loves are around me, and especially the love of the children. But among all the human loves bearing me up, yours is central."

Monday, November 18.

We must not focus on the disease, but on God and God's grace. Ruth said on our walk this morning, "I was beginning to focus on the possibility of an operation rather than on God."

So many people have been calling. Dale Brown, retired seminary professor, commented, "It says something about the church and how close-knit it is that word like this gets around so fast."

Chalmer Faw, another retired seminary professor, said to me, "May God give you healing—or something better." Ruth responded to that comment, "Dying might be better for you, but it's hard to see how that would be better for me."

Kermit Johnson, retired Chief of Chaplains of the U.S. Army, called right after he received my letter. (Some years ago he contacted me after reading *Darkening Valley*, and our lively friendship developed.) He said, "Eternal life is a miracle."

Roman Catholics turn to saints to intercede for them. In the New Testament the term *saints* is applied not to an extremely select group, but to all Christians. I have a great many saints interceding for me.

Tuesday, November 19.

My father would say when my sister Jane was battling cancer, "If I could only take it on myself and she would not have it." Ruth has said a number of times, "If only I could take it myself."

I was sitting in the red rocking chair by the fire. Ruth sat down beside me, put her arm around me, and sang that song of my childhood:

There is a happy land far, far away,
Where saints in glory stand bright, bright as day.
Oh, how they sweetly sing,
Worthy is the Savior King;
Loud let their praises ring, forevermore.

Our folk singer friend Steve Kinzie had learned that song from Old German Baptist (plain-clothed) cousins of mine the evening he and I spent with them near Modesto, California, in 1964. His liking the song so much revived it for me.

Ruth said to me, "I wouldn't miss this time with you for anything."

I replied, "This is still more beautiful than our engagement time."
She nodded.

Wednesday, November 20.

Daniel has taken a month's leave of absence from his medical residency in Maine and is here with us. Ruth and I are so grateful for this sacrifice of his. One great help is that he can take over the medical calling and proceed with making appointments.

Is there nostalgia beyond this life for the earth and what has filled our lives here? As I look around me and marvel at what I see, I think that in the interim beyond I could be nostalgic.

We live here in such incompleteness. We should feel so keenly the "eager longing" of Romans 8:19 for what is not yet, but we may not very much. In the clarity of the beyond, we could recognize ourselves as still incomplete, even though "at home with the Lord" (2 Cor. 5:8). But the perceived incompleteness would be more in relation to what is ahead than to what is past.

Thursday, November 21.

Daniel drove me to Suburban Hospital again for testing of the masses in my liver. Larry Fourman, a pastor friend from Ohio, went along. He and his wife, Ann, are here with us. Again and again I was put into the CT scanner. Dr. Sterelli, the surgeon, made three liver "passes" to get biopsy tissues. I was put back into the scanner each time to see if the needle was positioned correctly. Then she said, "Mr. Aukerman, I don't think they are hemangiomas."

She went out to talk with Daniel as I was wheeled back to the prep location. When Daniel came in, I looked at him: "The places are metastases?" He nodded. It was far too late for an operation to take out my left lung. I lay there for the two hours allotted for recovery, tears coming at times, thinking of scriptures and praying. Daniel asked whether he should bring Larry's Bible for me. But it was better to receive the verses that came to mind.

When Ruth returned home from school, I had to tell her, "The places are malignant." She burst into sobs. In the evening we called Miriam and Maren and told them.

At the end of the day Ruth read Christoph Blumhardt's evening prayer for this day: "*Lass im Leben und im Sterben, in allem Dein Licht leuchten* [In life and in death, in everything, let Your light shine]."

Saturday, November 23.
I turned to Revelation 1 this morning, but my eyes fell on the words in Revelation 2:10: "Do not fear what you are about to suffer." That imperative echoes within me.

Even though I have not yet had long bouts with extreme pain, I recall at times what Stella Foskey, an elderly member of the Bethany (Delaware) Church, would tell me about coping with the terrible pains in her legs: "I would just think about Jesus and how he suffered so much worse pain for me." So should I remember.

In our living room I looked at Daniel with his laptop computer and asked, "Is your cold worse?"

He replied, "No, I'm crying."

"You're writing your Christmas letter?"

"Yes."

Chuck came to Baltimore from New York to meet Miriam, arriving from Moscow. When she got home here, she was all tenderness and tears. As we were sitting in the living room, Ruth said to me, "Are you all right?"

I said, "Yes. I'm just taking everything in." And I was.

Tuesday, November 26.
In a visit today, my cousin Dean Miller commented that in the Brethren feetwashing, as part of the reenactment of the upper room story, we do an act of service but also symbolize our readiness to accept being served. I said, "Ruth and I are experiencing so much in the way of having our feet washed."

Wednesday, November 27.
Last evening as we lay in bed, Ruth said, "I can't imagine life without you. I love to hear your voice when you read."

After 5:00 a.m. or so, I found myself lying in bed praying, thinking, tears falling over my face—a blessed time.

Thursday, November 28, Thanksgiving.

It's been so hard for Miriam. But when she can throw herself into baking, that helps. Miriam and I sat in my office and talked. She was choking up when she came in: "I will miss you so much."

Maren arrived late this afternoon. As we sat down to our evening meal, I felt so keenly the pathos of the occasion: This would likely be our last Thanksgiving all together. I was so overcome that I could hardly say the prayer. Ruth said later, "We all felt that."

Friday, November 29.

We went to Pipe Creek Cemetery just across the valley and picked out two lots. There is a beautiful view out over the valley with just a glimpse of our log house through the trees. Becky Arbaugh went with us. She and her husband, Johnny, longtime friends and neighbors of ours, are in charge of the cemetery. Afterward I asked Johnny what the requirements are for burial. For most of my adult life I've been interested in simple burial without the big expense typical of funerals. A couple of years ago I'd even written to the Memorial Society we are members of to try to get more information, but the reply was not that helpful. Johnny said that burial in a box without a funeral director or embalming would be all right. The family would need to order a concrete vault and the box would be placed in it. They would need, of course, to proceed with the burial rather quickly.

I was quite relieved, even elated, to learn this. At lunch I said, "It made my day to find out about the burial possibilities." Everyone laughed.

Miriam commented, "That sentence has probably never been said in the English language before."

A bit later Ruth pointed through the kitchen window toward the cemetery on the crest of the hill and said, "One can see up there quite well."

I added, "One can probably see better from here than from up there."

Miriam said, "There will be more seeing from here than from up there."

Saturday, November 30.

I've thought a number of times of the account in *The Idiot* in which a man is being led to execution, and he takes in everything with marvelously acute perception. There is a stay of execution, as there was in a parallel situation for Dostoevsky himself. After that narrative there is a conversation about the inability to live such intensity of perceiving day by day in ordinary circumstances. But I am given something of that heightened perception. How precious each view of this valley is to me.

I think of the room in St. Petersburg where Dostoevsky died. He was fifty-nine and planning to continue the story of Alyosha begun in *The Brothers Karamazov*.

A little before Miriam and Chuck left for her return flight to Moscow, I read the passage from *The Idiot* about the execution, the reprieve, and living each moment to the full. I could hardly finish reading the account.

The time seems possibly too short for turning to anything except such particularly relevant passages by the greatest writers. Also in the Bible I read mainly passages that have more obvious relevance to what I am facing.

Monday, December 2.

Daniel, Maren, and I went to Dr. Arthur Serpick, an oncologist in Baltimore recommended by Dr. James Holland, the oncologist father of a friend of Miriam's in Moscow. For occupation I put down "Writer, pastor." He asked about my writing, what I had written. When he looked at my hands, he said, "These are not a writer's hands." I explained about work around our place.

Dr. Serpick recommended chemotherapy but only presented part of the picture. Of people comparable to me who take chemotherapy, fifty percent receive some benefit. Statistically someone in my condition has a fifty percent chance of living four months. Chemotherapy, if there is a response, may add several months. The one-sidedness of Dr. Serpick's presentation of the option inclined me against it.

Daniel had found an article about lung cancer. A chart showed that for advanced (stage IV) lung cancer, which is what I have, there is a main survival range of from two to six months.

Our Australian friend, Julie Edgerton, tells about Ginny Ernst of Circle Community in Washington and her terrible experience with chemotherapy for lung cancer. Julie, a nurse, does not think that chemotherapy makes sense unless there is a good prospect that the cancer can be eliminated. As I've thought about the alternatives, it seems good not to go the chemotherapy route. I will be doing the alternative nutritional things. I don't have high hopes for them though. They didn't stop the cancer in my mother or Jane. I feel at peace with the decision not to turn to chemo. Ruth, Daniel, and Maren are so supportive. They see it as congruent with the way I have lived my life.

I looked out my skylight this evening at the Northern Cross. I've never seen the Southern Cross.

Tuesday, December 3.
This morning I called and was able to get an afternoon appointment with Dr. Marc Hirsh, an oncologist in Hanover who was recommended by a friend. He took much time with us. I had understood that he was more into "alternative" therapies. But he too offers mainly chemotherapy. Because Dr. Hirsh was much more up front about the dangers of treatment, I feel I have a better basis for making a decision. He said that some people die from it, some are really miserable and are not helped, and others are helped a lot. He sees chemo, when it works, as contributing to the quality of life.

I came away with an inclination toward giving chemotherapy a try. The consultation was a most important one from that standpoint. If the cancer really begins to take over, my quality of life can decline abruptly, quite apart from bad side effects of chemotherapy. Frauke Westphal said a few days ago, "Your present quality of life is very much in jeopardy." Frauke also said that the cancer patients who really go down fast are those who say, in effect, "It's all over." I don't want to have that attitude in the least.

Wednesday, December 4.
Dr. David Fouts, a good friend of ours in Baltimore, called. I gave him the background. He said that he knew chemo patients who had been helped a lot and others who had only been made miserable. But on the basis of what I said, his comment was, "It's tempting to try it."

Just as Daniel was leaving to take Maren to the airport for her return to Phoenix, Dr. Bruce Johnson called back. Heiner Westphal had contacted him at the National Cancer Institute and Daniel had been trying to reach him. Daniel came back in to talk with him. They have a lung cancer study unit. Out of a group of seventy lung cancer patients, about half responded to the chemotherapy in the earlier study. It seems that I will probably be accepted as a patient. We are supposing that the program covers the costs.

A nurse called back after Daniel and Maren left, and I took a consultation appointment for December 12.

Maren said to me before she left, "I have much of you in me. And that is good to have."

This study by the National Cancer Institute is based in the Naval Hospital. I had supposed the study would be within the National Institutes of Health as such. When Kermit Johnson, retired Chief of Chaplains of the U.S. Army, called this evening, I said, "I chuckled when I told Ruth that I might end up going to the Bethesda Naval Hospital. That would be strange."

Kermit replied, "Your country owes that to you."

Today I finally reached Shirley Fike, a nurse in Indiana who gives nutritional counseling to cancer patients. I ordered various vitamins and supplements. I want to continue on that track also.

Thursday, December 5.
Daniel and I went to Johns Hopkins Hospital for an appointment with Dr. Kleinberg, a radiation oncologist. He emphasized that my general good health gives me considerably better odds for not suffering a great deal from the chemo and for getting a good response. He made the quite significant point: If one looks at the mean survival without chemo and the mean survival with chemo, it may seem that not much is gained—and for many this is the case. But with chemotherapy as in the National Cancer Institute study group, there is also the prospect that for a significant percentage there may be an extension of life for a year-and-a-half or two years. One may be inclined to take the risk, undergo what is involved, and hope for that longer survival.

Phyllis Bosler called this evening. Her husband, Bill, a Brethren pastor in Miami, Florida, was murdered in 1986. I've become her main prayer project. She prays for me several times each day with the fervent hope that the doctors will do tests again and find everything clear. She's been enlisting any "prayer warrior" she can find to pray on my behalf.

Friday, December 6.
Pastor friend Larry Fourman called from Ohio. He is rereading my book *Reckoning with Apocalypse: Terminal Politics and Christian Hope.* Over the phone he read me a passage from page 142 that I had not thought of in relation to the cancer:

> A friend may be very ill. In the usual human perspective, this person is going to die sometime. But one would be wrong to jump to the conclusion that this particular illness will cause death and nothing should be done toward preventing that. Even for what is diagnosed as a terminal illness in oneself or in someone else, one should hope and strive against death and for life.

The context deals with the death of history and the imperative to strive against all that presses toward such a death. The passage certainly has relevance with regard to chemotherapy.

In letters or otherwise, so many friends have expressed their high regard for me. I should give little attention to such praise and should be more prepared for deflecting expressions of esteem. I know how flawed I am. I should not be center stage for people. I hope for a memorial service that points to Christ rather than one that's centered on me. Now, when I am still alive, I should also seek to point to Christ when praise is expressed to me. Yet there is a place in life for giving others our thanks and for praising them, as Paul did in his letters. But one must always recognize that everything in view has its source in God. A key verse: "But we have this treasure in earthen vessels, to show that the transcendent power belongs to God and not to us" (2 Cor. 4:7).

Saturday, December 7.
There is individual sowing and reaping, as with getting lung cancer from smoking. There is the collective sowing and reaping—as with the spreading of carcinogens in the environment and some people getting cancer from them. I've tried to live counter to such sowing, but to some extent I've been part of it and bear a measure of responsibility for it. Those who are the worst in what they sow may not reap accordingly.

I try not to use the words "my cancer" or "my lung cancer." It's not mine but an alien intruder.

Sunday, December 8.
Daniel has been such a helper and encourager here. This afternoon he laid down his water-warped copy of *Darkening Valley: A Biblical Perspective on Nuclear War* and proudly announced, "I've just completed reading your book." I expressed my hearty appreciation. Then he read me a passage I had thought of after the diagnosis, though I had not turned to it:

> Physical illness generally results from a malfunction of some part of the body or from something like an alien attack by germs, viruses, harmful substances. But cancer is remarkable as an uprising from within the body against the coherence of the whole. A cell begins its wild multiplication, and that initial and most intimate dominion a person has in his own body is slowly lost. The pollution of the environment stemming from the

human quest for power brings to more and more persons the excruciating loss of that most basic and precious dominion. Man's rebellion recoils in blighted matter to become cancer's insurgency. A nuclear war would climax the rebellion and enormously increase that insurgency.

As we drove by the Pipe Creek meetinghouse this morning, I said, "Up there is the cemetery. I feel a quite different relationship to the cemetery than I did before."

Ruth smiled and nodded, "I do too."

Monday, December 9.

Our family made an outing to Robert Young's nursery to select and buy a balled Norway spruce. We've never had a cut tree but always one that would continue to grow. This will be the first really shapely Christmas tree we've had in a number of years. Ruth's creativity has always masked the deformities of our struggling spruces. Ruth said to me, "This is your tree." We have several trees that grow as reminders of special occasions.

I said, "Yes, it is Christmas '96." We think of the looming likelihood that this will be my last Christmas.

I was so moved by a homemade card with short get-well messages from eleven men on death row in Holman Prison in Alabama. Dealing with something such as lung cancer does have strong analogies to being on death row. One's day to die is coming near, but there may be a reprieve. After the diagnosis I've come to feel a new bond with friends facing execution.

> My hopes and prayers are with you.
> Leroy White

> May your faith give courage to brave these medical problems and allow you to get well soon. God bless.
> Darrell Grysn

> May God comfort you and provide for every need that you and your family may have at this time. My prayers are with you. God bless.
> Ward Gentry

> I pray God's comfort will rest upon you at this time. 2 Cor. 1:3-5; Is. 53:5; Ps. 107:20. God bless you,
> Gary Brown

"God heals the brokenhearted and binds up our wounds" (Ps. 147:3). I pray that God provides you with peace and comfort and that you get well soon.
  Ronald B. Smith

All of my thoughts and prayers are toward you and your family at this time.
  Kenny Smith

Lord, give us your strength in our weakness. I pray that the Lord will give you strength to get well soon.
  Love in Jesus,
  Bo

During this time look upon the healing powers of Jesus, also for the comfort of knowing friends and family beside you. My prayers are joined!
  Hank Hays

My thoughts are with you and your family. Look to the heavens and God will bless you.
  Mark A. Jerkir

May the Lord be with you in your time of need, and may He bring you the peace that only He can give.
  Jeff Rieber

Faith in God, Love from God, will guide you and heal you. Be strong. Our prayers are with you.
  Love,
  Brian Baldwin

The last regular sermon I preached was in an October service of the Pipe Creek congregation. The text seemed to be given to me: "But grow in the grace and knowledge of our Lord and Savior Jesus Christ" (2 Pet. 3:18). As a closing example, I told about the last visit Ruth and I had with Madeline Geiman, an elderly friend of the family. She was in the hospital with "galloping" leukemia. She must have known that the end was near, but she had such gladness of spirit, almost a hilarity. When I called the hospital a day and a half later to ask about our children coming to play their musical instruments for her, she had just died. Since the diagnosis I've thought a number of times of Madeline and that glowing, joyous spirit of hers. She remains a model for me.

Another model I think of often is Ronnie Dunkins and his last day of life before his execution in the Alabama electric chair just after midnight on July 14, 1989. His stories had us laughing. He said to me a number of times, "I know where I'm going when I leave here. . . . 'For me to live is Christ, and to die is gain.' "

Wednesday, December 11.

Paul Grout, pastor of the Genesis Church, arrived from Vermont in time for lunch. I told him that at whatever time I do die I would like for him to preach in the memorial service and that the focus should be on Christ and not on me. He put his hand over his face and said nothing for a long period. Then he made the comment, "You might have my service sooner."

I asked Paul about differing beliefs with regard to faith and healing. He told me "not to strive for intensity of faith that you will be healed, but for faith that nothing can separate you from the love of Christ." But he said he will continue to pray for my healing.

Paul wanted to have a laying on of hands. I sat in the red rocker. Ruth and Daniel put their hands on my shoulders. Paul cupped his large hands over my head. His hands were not at rest but in slight motion. At first he prayed hardly audibly in a tongue but then aloud in English. I felt an almost physical flood of God's peace and love. How wonderful it would have been to be able to keep those moments on and on. And to a small degree they remain with me. I told Paul, "That was an anointing service without oil."

Ruth remarked to me as we were going to bed, "You have better friends than Job had."

Thursday, December 12.

Paul drove off in his rented car at 5:30 a.m. When we got up, we found that he had left a small triptych painting of Jesus setting his face toward Jerusalem, the cross, but also the New Jerusalem. We had seen the painting in larger format when we visited the Grouts in Vermont last summer. I had told Paul on the phone that this picture of his often came to my mind. We were so moved that he painted it in small format for me.

For me this was the big day in Bethesda at the hematology/oncology clinic in the Naval Hospital. I had blood drawn by a Navy technician. The study unit I am entering is partly sponsored by the Naval Hospital, but also by the National Cancer Institute, which is the biggest agency within the

National Institutes of Health. Here I was, in a small office, talking with a Navy doctor in uniform. On the wall was a reproduction of a newspaper front page with headlines on the Normandy invasion, and next to it was the Iwo Jima flag-raising photo with the word PEACE imposed over it.

I would be glad if everything were simply civilian. But I can accept and affirm that through such a study and the oncological treatments, the Navy is doing something life-serving. As I've tried to think the matter through, I don't see it as ethically questionable to be in such a study. One could say, though, that by participating I am helping the Navy present itself as an agency that serves human well-being. On the other hand, it would splendid if the armed forces could yield to more and more such peace conversion.

We have pretty much decided that I will go into the study group. There seems to be no obstacle to their accepting me. It's as if God has opened a door. I may start next Wednesday or even on Tuesday. That means that I will likely be feeling lousy over Christmas. For the first cycle of chemotherapy, I will be an inpatient for five days—ninety-six hours on taxol (made from the bark of the Pacific yew tree) and then cisplatinum on the fifth day. For most patients the main side effects come during the following few days.

There are to be five more five-day cycles of the chemotherapy. But for these I am to be an outpatient, carrying a portable pump at my waist and going to the clinic on four successive mornings for a twenty-four-hour supply of taxol, before getting cisplatinum on the fifth day.

The earlier Phase I study established the best dosage level. The present Phase II study is to determine the efficacy of this mode of administering the drugs. Dr. Georgiadis said that studies comparing the standard regimens of chemo with the best supportive care without chemo show little advantage in taking the chemo. They believe their mode of treatment with the low dosage of taxol over a rather long period is doing considerably better. The median survival is eleven months. But Dr. Georgiadis emphasized that medically there is no cure. At whatever time the arrested tumor starts growing again, there is little that can be done. Some people want to try anything that might help, but there is not much chance that anything will.

When I asked about costs, Dr. Georgiadis said, "There are no costs. You have been paying taxes all these years."

Daniel said to me afterward, "If he only knew." With my semi-volunteer jobs and war tax resistance, the federal taxes we've paid have been largely on Ruth's income.

Dr. Georgiadis had no problem with the various nutritional supplements on my list.

Frauke Westphal has been afraid I will turn away from this opportunity. The only other reasonable option, it seems, is to choose no chemotherapy and go the route of best supportive care with alternative nutritional supplements.

Jim Davis, a lawyer friend in Westminster, called me. He told an anecdote he had read in *Sojourners*. His recollection of it went like this. Daniel Berrigan, peace activist priest, was leading a retreat. A young man with AIDS was there. Dan noticed him and said, "You don't look well. Are you all right?"

"I'm dying."

Dan looked him in the eye and said, "That's exciting." The comment was a turning point for the man.

Friday, December 13, Ruth's birthday.

This evening we had the birthday table for Ruth. Psalm 90, which we usually read following Ruth's family tradition, had never been so starkly relevant before. Ruth commented that it seems we may not have the "threescore and ten." She said, "Will these tears ever end?" I picked up the Bible and turned to the last two verses of Psalm 126, our engagement psalm. I was so overcome that I could not read them, but I pointed to them and asked Daniel to read. When he had read them ("May those who sow in tears reap with shouts of joy!"), we hugged each other.

Ruth's brother Gottfried, a professor of philosophy in Konstanz, Germany, called before we opened the gifts. Maren lightheartedly had a consolation gift for me, a wild berry anti-oxidant bar. Daniel read her beautiful letter: "I'll sing with you all the way from Phoenix, *'Denke daran, was der Allmächtige kann* [Ponder anew what the Almighty can do]' "—and we sobbed some more. Miriam called from Moscow last evening before she left for Perm and the former Soviet prison camp there.

This afternoon I wrote a birthday letter to Ruth, the first letter I had written her in quite a long while.

December 13, 1996

My Dearest Ruth,

What a lover you are, my lover in such a fullness of ways. Through thirty-one and a half years, our love has deepened and been tempered. Now in this crisis time you embrace me, still more than before, body, mind, and spirit with your kaleidoscopic loving. How unbelievably blessed I am with you as my wife, also now in this time.

There is much that is so lovably predictable in you. But in you too is such marvelous unpredictability, spontaneity, and openness. Without you I would probably have become older in personality by now than I am.

We are borne up by thankfulness for our children. But from your body (and mine) these children have come. As parents we both failed in many ways, but the good in them is from God's shaping through you at least as much as through me.

I see our marriage, unlike that of some of our friends, as so symmetrical—not a match with the one spouse so remarkable and the other as a dutiful helper. You have not pushed for your place, but you have it as the one so fully and winsomely matched to me in creativity, Christian commitment, spiritual insight. Your weaknesses may show more than mine, but you know mine more than anyone else on earth, and you love me still.

From time to time I have said tenderly that I want to be a more loving husband. Now with all the purposefulness I am given strength for I pledge myself to be that. How much time we will be given together we don't know, but we are given the marvel of one love-filled day after another.

My dear, dear Ruth,
Dale

I added a sheet with two promises: to make a couple of autobiographical tapes as soon as I can get to it and to take her to a play when I'm out of chemotherapy and feeling well enough. Ruth read my letter, then looked at me tenderly: "Where can I put this that I won't lose it?"

I said, "I'll make a couple of extra copies."

Ruth reflected, "This is my most wonderful birthday ever."

In his last years, Vater (Ruth's father) would say, "*Dass ich das noch erleben darf* [To think that I'm allowed still to experience this]." I had sometimes quoted this, applying it to myself, especially around the time of Miriam and Chuck's wedding. Since the diagnosis the comment comes to me on special occasions.

Saturday, December 14.

Daniel's one-month leave of absence from his residency program is nearly at an end. He got his stuff together and set out for Maine. Ruth and I worked outside at eavespout cleaning and other pre-winter tasks for a couple of hours this afternoon.

The German theologian Karl Heim has influenced my thinking so much, especially for seeing God as holding each particle and each creature in existence. I contemplate that for the two walnut trees in front of our house. Then the time comes when this upholding by God ceases. The powers of dissolution win out. But is not God like a juggler? One hand lets me fall toward the abyss, but his other hand catches me up.

All this love, attention, and prayer I've received is such a testimony to the preciousness of a single life. But really it intimates how precious each human life is before God. Each person should be showered with all that has been showered on me. How shall I view the fact that some people as sick as I are relatively alone while I am so surrounded and embraced? What I am given is far beyond any deserving.

Sunday, December 15.

I composed our Christmas letter for the year.

> Hebrews 2:9-18 may hardly ever be turned to as a Christmas text; yet it probes the depths of the incarnation of Jesus Christ: "But we see Jesus, who for a little while was made lower than the angels, crowned with glory and honor because of the suffering of death, so that by the grace of God he might taste death for every one. . . . Since therefore the children share in flesh and blood, he himself likewise partook of the same nature, that through death he might destroy him who has the power of death, that is, the devil, and deliver all those who through fear of death were subject to lifelong bondage. . . . For because he himself has suffered and been tempted, he is able to help those who are tempted." What the last verse does not make explicit is this: Because Jesus entered to the uttermost into human suffering, he comes with that as part of who he is, to be with any and each of us in our suffering; because he has borne that burden, its weight for any of us now is lightened. The pioneer of our salvation was made "perfect through suffering," and in a correlating way he tempers those who are his in bringing them "to glory." Jesus Christ has vanquished death, even though it continues its concluding rampages.
>
> The high point of the year came with the wedding of our daughter Miriam and Charles Pazdernik on May 25. The service

was in a small Brethren meetinghouse near here. The pre-wedding party and the reception were held at the Aukerman homestead. We did nearly all the food and most of the hosting. There were three major house projects to complete before the occasion. But everything came together—and a remarkable configuration of family circles and friends. It was a beautiful and grace-filled time.

Miriam and Chuck have a little apartment in Brooklyn. Chuck is writing his thesis in a doctoral program in classics at Princeton. In late September Miriam left for a three-month assignment in the Moscow office of the Ford Foundation. She has been able to fly back to be with Chuck and with her family for the Thanksgiving week.

Daniel received his M.D. in May from the University of New Mexico School of Medicine. He was placed in the Maine-Dartmouth residency program for family medicine in Augusta, Maine, and began there in June. It was hard for him to leave his many friends in New Mexico. He was with us from mid-November to mid-December for a month's leave of absence so as to be able to help out at home.

Maren is in her third year of bilingual teaching of Hispanic children in Phoenix. She spent several weeks in Mexico studying Spanish. This year she has more than thirty students in a four-five combination. She was able to get some grant money to bring twelve Hispanic children to the East for a week, November 9-16. Nearly all of them had been students of hers from earlier. Some don't speak much English. They stayed at our place and made day trips to Washington and other places.

Ruth and Dale were in Albuquerque for Daniel's graduation. They made two trips to Maine in the summer and visited Miriam and Chuck in New York City. Ruth held a workshop at the Maryland State Art Teachers' Convention in Baltimore in October. Dale was a member of a study committee that wrote a statement, "Nonviolence and Humanitarian Intervention," which was adopted by the 1996 Church of the Brethren Annual Conference. In July he completed a year and a half of interim pastoral work with the Bethany Church in Delaware.

On November 5 we learned, after chest x-rays, that Dale has a large mass on his left lung. Further tests showed that the mass is malignant and that metastases have formed in the liver. Till now (mid-December) Dale has little in the way of bothersome symptoms. It seems rather definite that he will soon begin chemotherapy as part of a lung cancer study unit of the National Cancer Institute in Bethesda, Maryland. From a medical perspective there is virtually no prospect for a cure. But our hope is in God and his gracious purposes for each human creature. As Paul wrote in Philippians 1:19, "Yes, and I shall rejoice. For I know that through your prayers and the help of the Spirit of Jesus Christ this will turn out for my deliverance."

I've begun writing a personal message on each of these letters in response to the many letters and cards that are coming to us.

Monday, December 16.
I spent much of today having radiology tests in Westminster—bone scan, x-rays of the hip, CT scans of the chest, abdomen, and pelvis. In the pictures we were given to take to doctors at the National Cancer Institute, Ruth and I could see a dark area at the right hip. I am to be admitted Wednesday morning to begin the initial inpatient cycle.

Today as I walked from the shed and looked at the house, I thought: Much as we have been drawn to it, we've always said we want to be ready to leave this place if God calls us elsewhere.

When our pulmonary specialist, Dr. Saia, called, Ruth asked him, regarding chemotherapy, "What would you do if you yourself were in this situation?"

He paused for several seconds and replied, "Probably nothing." But in the next breath he said, "My colleague, whom you have not met, just walked into my office. He worked with that [NCI] program and saw many people helped."

When Ruth quoted Dr. Saia to Frauke a little later, Frauke said, "I don't agree with that at all. I would advise this for my own husband." She spoke of hope and its tremendous importance for healing and health.

Tuesday, December 17.
Dr. John Hill, my doctor in the NCI study program, called. I asked whether he had any report on my hip. He read from what I think was the report on the NCI x-rays something to the effect that the hip is intact and there is no sign of malignancy. I feel so full of gladness and thankfulness.

Wednesday, December 18.

In bed this morning I said to Ruth, "I love to stroke your arms."

Ruth replied, "I love to stroke your hair while you still have it."

We packed up everything for the five-day inpatient hospital stay. Just before we were ready to leave, I thought I'd better check the electric fence, which keeps the three steers in our little pasture. I'd done that two evenings before, got very little light in the tester, but thought maybe this was because of the rain and dampness. But again I got hardly any light in the tester. I started out at the hay bales and made the round of the fence. In the triangle along the road, I discovered that the fence had been knocked down and a post pushed over, maybe by someone turning around. Ruth and I did a quick minimal repair of the fence, and then I plugged in the fence charger and went back out to the cattle gate with the tester. I was fatigued from the haste and stepped into a crack in the concrete cattle gate with my left foot. Fortunately, I didn't lose my balance and was able to pull my foot out. In retrospect, I'm more aware of God's protection than I was at the moment, for I might have fallen and fractured my hip.

Ruth and I drove to the Naval Hospital and went to the hematology/oncology clinic. We waited and waited. Barb Schuler, the research nurse, finally took us into Dr. Hill's office. She said the doctors were still going over the films from Monday. Ruth said, "There's cancer in the hip, isn't there?"

Barb replied, "I'd rather the doctors would tell you. But yes, there is." Ruth and I were taken aback because the word the day before seemed to weigh strongly against that threat.

Dr. Hill came in and put up the one x-ray. He explained that part of the cartilage in the right hip socket seems to be missing. With some weakening of bone, there is an increasing danger of a fracture. I will probably need ten radiation treatments to arrest the cancer in this area. The chemotherapy will need to wait. He says I have a good chance of having no or only very minimal side effects from radiation to this part of the body.

During the first few days after I found out about the cancer, it did not occur to me that my hip problem might be related to it. Daniel was the first to mention this possibility soon after he came from Maine to help us out.

We went through the intake routine at radiation oncology. We drove home at the close of the day. Ruth kept saying how glad she was to have me with her at home. However, because weather reports were calling for a winter storm of from three to six inches of snow, I decided to spend the night at the Westphals' in Bethesda so I will be close to the hospital for treatment tomorrow. Before I left, Ruth said, "Say Bible verses all the way down, and I will sing my hymns."

Friday, December 20.

The radiation treatment today came without delay and seemed surprisingly routine. After maybe ten minutes I was headed home again.

Back home Ruth said, "Your whole life you have stood against nuclear things, and now in this radiation you take it in your own body." This wasn't a criticism or even a questioning of the route I'm taking.

I remember that Yvonne Dilling, while she was staying with us in the aftermath of her chemotherapy for lymphoma, talked about conventional therapies doing violence to the body. That perspective carries some weight with me. Yet few would reject the "violence" of extracting a tooth or amputating a gangrenous leg. An antibiotic does a certain violence to germs in the body, as do white blood cells. We all live as the body defends itself against microscopic enemies. To set things against intruding lower life or a wild multiplying of cells in order to save human life is not wrong in principle.

Jesus used the hyperbolic image of plucking out the eye or cutting off the hand (Matt. 5:29-30) to illustrate literally removing the threatening part to save the human whole.

Walt and Jean Moyer, Brethren Peace Fellowship friends, wrote, calling our attention to Isaiah 26:3. I had not thought of it in relation to our situation, but the verse now echoes within me: "Thou dost keep him in perfect peace, whose mind is stayed on thee, because he trusts in thee."

I have also thought a lot about 1 Thessalonians 4:16-18: "Rejoice always, pray constantly, give thanks in all circumstances; for this is the will of God in Christ Jesus for you."

Saturday, December 21.

Daniel got back around midnight after flying from Maine to BWI Airport. Miriam called from New York early this evening after a safe trip from Moscow. Maren is to arrive at 12:30 in the morning.

Kermit Johnson, retired Army Chief of Chaplains, called. When I commented about the fine doctors in the Naval Hospital, he reminded me, "They are basically doctors. Putting on a uniform does not change that."

Ruth mentioned there are times when she begins to feel so "fransied out," but then a sudden peace comes, and she thinks that someone must be praying for her just then. Kermit says, "That is a miracle. Some people think in terms of a one-track miracle—physical healing. And at times that is given. But miracles from God are given in other dimensions too."

Again and again the thought comes, not that I may have so little time left to live, but rather that so much, so marvelously much, time is being given me. When I look ahead, even having three months left seems like a very considerable period. A further year to live, unlikely as that may be, would come as a lavish abundance of time, almost too much to contemplate.

In the first three weeks through Thanksgiving, there was such a sense of the shortness of time remaining and the preciousness of our closest relationships, as we reckoned with the possibility that I might have very few weeks of relatively enjoyable health left. Though that intensity declined a little, it has returned some in the Christmas season. Ruth said, "One can hardly live this intensely on and on." Yet we should.

In the first weeks after the diagnosis, the assumption that I would be dead within a few months kept coming up in family conversations. Then I began rejecting that line of thought and even challenged it. I could die within a short time, but within the gracious rule of God, I also might be healed or, at least, have considerably more time. I want those closest to me to always keep that possibility in mind rather than resigning themselves to my having very little time left.

Most things in my body are working right—nearly everything. So God has already given me many years of good health.

Sunday, December 22.

Maren got in from the airport very early this morning. At breakfast she told us she dreamed that we were in a family huddle—a tender time—and I said to them, "Grammee is looking forward to seeing me." (My mother died of cancer in 1983.) I remarked that I have thought it would be a beautiful expression of God's love if the most beloved people who have gone before would be the ones to receive us beyond death.

Maren said, "To think of a welcoming committee is certainly more pleasant than to think of going right into judgment." I commented that judgment will come, but later, it seems. My mother brought me into this world. It's possible that she will have a part in my coming forth into that realm beyond. I've thought of meeting my sister Jane, my father, and Ruth's father.

Monday, December 23.

When Maren got up this morning, she announced, "I dreamed about pie."

Daniel drove me down for the radiation treatment and watched the setup. We checked in with a resident, Dr. O'Connell, about the diarrhea that has developed, no doubt from the radiation of my hip. Then we went to see Barb Schuler and Dr. Georgiadis. He put up the early and the later scans. The tumor in the left lung has grown a little.

Maren drove to pick up Miriam and Chuck at the train station. Since Daniel will be leaving later on Christmas Day, we celebrated his December 26 birthday this evening. In the devotional time I felt such an intense inner clarity and catharsis. We sang again *"Denke daran, was der Allmächtige kann* [Ponder anew what the Almighty can do]." I thought of the cancer: God can heal it. I gave Daniel my flask of anointing oil. George Deaton, a very old lay minister in the Eel River Church in Indiana, had given me the flask; at least, I think this is the one he gave me. As Daniel was feeling it inside the wrapping paper, Miriam said, "It doesn't have the feel of an IOU."

Maren said, "Father is going easy on IOUs this year." Daniel wanted to know more about the anointing service. The evening was such a marvelous one for me.

Daniel was lying on the couch. I was sitting in the recliner chair. He said to me, "Father, I love looking at you." So many times the children look at me, as if to cherish the moment for remembering in the future.

Tuesday, December 24, Christmas Eve.

In the morning Chuck and Miriam took me down for radiation. It went fast. Ruth had prepared jars of our honey as gifts for Cindy and Kay (the radiation therapists), for Doctors Georgiadis and Hill, and for Barb Schuler. My hip is bothering me somewhat less. On the way back, Miriam commented about all those dental x-rays we refused to get from our dentist, Dr. Goettee, because of the danger of the radiation to our health.

At lunch Daniel explained what Dr. Georgiadis had said about the culturing of the pleural cells. If cells in extracted pleural fluid are cancerous, they can be cultured rather easily and then used in research. Maren remarked, "In other words Father's cancer cells might outlive Father."

Ruth said, "I hope they don't," as if that would be an affront to me.

We turn to humor and laugh even more, probably, than we did earlier. It's not forced, nor is it analogous to whistling in the dark. It's a way of intimating that death has been defeated.

I looked into the cardboard barrel of letters I had brought from Ohio in 1993 after my father's death. Among Christmas cards I found one that was unused: "To the perfect Dad." When I showed it to Maren, she said, "I'd better seize the opportunity."

We decided to go to Christmas Eve services at the Beaver Dam meetinghouse where Miriam and Chuck were married. It was a simple service, but right and meaningful for me. I was glad for the bread and the cup—receiving Christ's life into this failing body. At the close we stood with lighted candles in a circle around the pews. I was much aware of the blue germ mask I was wearing.

Back home we lit the candles on our Christmas tree, the most beautiful tree we've had in years. We sang many German and English carols. I read from John 1; Philippians 2; and Luke 2. It was hard to sing the verse, "*Ich lag in tiefer Todesnacht* [I lay in the depth of death's night]." Ruth's mother had used that verse in Miriam's birth announcement, as Vater had just died. It was also read at Miriam's wedding service. Now it seems that it was a sort of foreshadowing of the time we are in. This too has been a marvelous evening, full of the gracious presence of God. It was the most beautiful and intense Christmas Eve I can remember.

Wednesday, December 25, Christmas Day.

We had a big array of gifts, which is a problematical aspect of Christmas for me. But the day has been filled with beauty and grace.

I gave the children personal things of mine: Chuck, two old classical atlases; Miriam, my childhood windmill painting and tomatoes I dried in the late summer; Daniel, my Old German Baptist hymnal from childhood and the pocket New Testament Grandpa and Grandma Miller gave me; Maren, the pirate comic strip I drew in grade school and my Scofield Reference Bible, the Authorized Version Bible I had used in my teens and as a college student.

Maren immediately read a bit from the first part of the comic strip. Then she found some treasures in the Bible. Psalm 119:99 reads, "I have more understanding than all my teachers: for thy testimonies are my meditation." I had drawn a little line and written the word *college*. Next to verses in Romans 14 about not giving or taking offense, I had written myself a note: "Sermon beginning with reference to the Roman postal system." I cannot recall what I had in mind. Maren also read from the beginning of Psalm 6, which I had double-marked as memorized. When she paused for me to complete the first verse, I could say, "hot displeasure." Then came the verse: "Have mercy upon me, O Lord; for I am weak: O Lord, heal me, for my bones are vexed." Here I was, getting my right hip radiated. She said, "I just happened to turn to it. You've figured out one way to get your daughter to read the Bible."

Miriam and Chuck gave Daniel and Maren each a framed photo of me. Ruth's frame was empty. Miriam said that it can remain empty "so long as Father is still with you." Ruth replied, "I hope it stays empty for a long time."

Maren said, "We're not going to relegate Father to photographic status just yet."

Ruth gave the children things she had made for me before we were married: for Daniel, the straw manger scene; Miriam and Chuck, the semi-abstract wax portrait of me; and Miriam the little book of Negro spiritual prints.

Thursday, December 26.

This evening I talked with Miriam and Maren about my taking part in the Christian Peacemaker Teams action at the Pentagon on Monday morning. The theme is "Harvest of Violence"—a survey and symbolic representations of the results of U.S. military violence. I would want to bring in something about the cancer dimension. I've been trying to think of the right words for a sign.

Ruth resists my going: "What do you want from it—attention?" I'd thought about that sort of thing as a temptation. She said later, "Pray more about it. Examine yourself."

When Ruth went into the kitchen, Marin said, "Mother can drop a hint like she drops the [outside] cellar door." But it's good she still challenges me in such ways.

Friday, December 27.

Art and Peggy Gish, longtime friends from New Covenant Fellowship in southeastern Ohio, came. They were on their way to the Peacemaker Congress in Washington. I mentioned our big parsnip harvest. In the spring after hearing high praise for parsnips on NPR, I had planted some for the first time in many years. I wanted to think they could be prepared to be tastier than in my recollection. I said, "Parsnips are all right, but when you don't know whether you have much time at all to live , . . ." We laughed, and Art completed the sentence: "you may not want to spend time eating parsnips."

I told them I was trying to decide whether or not I should go to the action at the Pentagon on Monday. Art said, "I can't say whether you should come or not. But if you do come, your struggle with death will add a deeper dimension to the vigil. It's the same struggle."

In his prayer Art said, "Our yearning is that Dale be healed and restored to health. We bring that yearning to you; we pray that your will be done."

Saturday, December 28.
The girls and I finally hit upon a wording for the poster: "For millions, perhaps for me, living with nuclear weapons means dying with cancer." Ruth is hand-printing the words now. We also discussed parking and the problem I'm having with over-active bowels because of the radiation.

Sunday, December 29.
Miriam, Maren, Ruth, and I talked about the witness at the Pentagon. Because of so many bowel movements during the day, I'm more concerned as to whether I can get through the time. Miriam and Maren said they would go into Westminster to get Depends. When they returned, they were singing the German children's song, *"Christkindl, komm in unser Haus, Pack die schönen Sachen aus* [Christ child, come to our house and unpack the lovely things]." Then they said, "We bought an off brand—not Swearing, but Affirm. We knew you'd like that."

I went to bed a little early but lay awake coughing for a rather long while.

Monday, December 30.
Today was the big day. We got up at about 5:30. For the first time in my life I put on an Affirm—in case the urge would come and I'd have nowhere to go. Miriam, Maren, and I met peace activist friend David Braune and photographer Ken Koons at the Brethren Center in New Windsor.

The five of us headed toward the River Entrance of the Pentagon. Ken was already taking photos. The day was so mild. We headed right and found the vigiling group at the columns on the next side. I put on my mask, just in case someone with a cold would give me a hug. I expected to see more people whom I knew. The fact that most of the people did not know me made it easier to be just one of the throng. I was a part of the witness as I had so much hoped I could be.

Then came the action by the Atlantic Life Community. Phil Berrigan led a litany about Pentagon destruction. Blood was thrown on a column and on the steps. I'd never really seen this mode of protest before. The military police were ready with water hoses and bleach, but the chant continued: "Nothing can wash the blood away." I heard there were three arrests.

It did seem a little strange to go from this protest action at the Pentagon to the Naval Hospital for a radiation treatment. But we had witnessed against dealing in death and came for something life-serving.

Tuesday, December 31.

Again for New Year's Eve, we wondered whether this would be our last one together. After the seafood meal, we played the tape that folk singer Steve Kinzie had made for me. The first song was "Happy Land." I could not listen to it without choking up. Ruth came, stood behind my recliner chair, and embraced me. I had Maren read Pascal's *The Mystery of Jesus*, and I read the latter part of Psalm 73. Looking at the candle-lit tree, we sang our German New Year's hymn. Because of my condition, we counted 11:00 as our midnight.

1997

Wednesday, January 1.

So I have lived into this new year. After breakfast I read to the others the fine sermon that theologian George Hunsinger had sent me, "Whether we live, or whether we die." I need to give more attention to that passage in Romans 14:7-9.

Ruth was looking at the live Christmas tree. As she came over to me in the recliner chair, she asked, "What do you want us to do for you? Can we dig you a hole?" She was referring to the tree. We laughed.

Monday, January 6.

Daniel, Maren, and I went for my intake for the first cycle of chemotherapy. Again I packed for the hospital stay. I had the feeling that this time things would work out.

They took blood samples. A little after lunch we saw Dr. Hill, with Barb Schuler and Dr. Georgiadis joining. The blood counts were all right, but they were concerned about my bowels. The taxol is quite toxic, and it seems important that they heal first. We need to wait for the start of the chemo. When they talked about a pain reliever for my hip, I stressed that the pain wasn't really that much of a problem. Dr. Georgiadis said, "You haven't been in the military?"

I answered, "No."

Dr. Georgiadis said, "You bear pain like a Marine." What an odd compliment.

We took Daniel to BWI Airport for his flight back to Maine.

Wednesday, January 8.

I wasn't feeling very well yesterday, but I'm feeling a little better today.

I had an interesting phone call this evening. A few years ago Ruth had left the lights on in the car she drove to school. She called me to come and help. We got the car started and were trying to drive it to our mechanic. But it gave out going up a hill, and a guardrail on the side made it impossible to get the car off the road. There was light rain and much traffic. Fortunately a state trooper came along. He called a nearby garage with a towing service. Very soon J., whom we had turned to for auto repairs before, was there with his tow truck. Ruth said she would take his helper back to the garage, and I could ride with J. in the truck; she would then come to pick me up. J. got in the cab of the truck. I got in on the passenger side. Looking ahead, J. remarked acidly, "That d— Aukerman is a f— radical." Then he looked over and saw me there. He had gotten confused and thought his helper was beside him. I could not think of any good comment to make.

Thinking that I might not have long to live, I decided it would be good to write to J., whom I'd not seen since that memorable ride. So a couple of days ago I took a hand-embroidered angel card and wrote to him, telling him that he had done excellent work for us, that I had advanced lung cancer, and that I wanted him to know I didn't have any bad feelings toward him because of what he had said some years ago.

Early this evening J. called. He had just received my card. He said he had often thought about his remarks. He explained that some other things had been bothering him that day, and he knew he should never have said what he did. He said he was sorry. But then it came out that he too has had cancer. A little more than a year ago, he had to have radiation and chemotherapy for throat cancer, which now seems to be in remission. He told me at length about treatments and about the people who prayed for him. He said, "I'm not very religious." He had been asked, "Why does cancer always hit good people?" and replied, "That's not always the case; it hit me."

J. said he'd be praying for me: "My little prayers don't amount to much, but I'll pray for you." He offered to help if there was anything he could do.

When he referred again to his remark to me, I told him, "That's all forgiven." He gave me two telephone numbers. I can call him any time I want to talk. Through this exchange we discovered a strong bond between us; we both know what it is to struggle with cancer and to seek God's healing.

Saturday, January 11.

This evening I said with emphasis, "The 10th of January."

Maren said, "Actually it's the 11th; but if you want to think of it as the 10th, that's fine."

I replied, "If I'm going to savor the specialness of the day, I want to have the date right."

Sunday, January 12.

Early this evening I worked on autobiographical taping for the first time. I began with boyhood stories about Christian faith, formative dimensions, and the Old German Baptist Church.

Monday, January 13.

I went to the hematology/oncology clinic again. Dr. Georgiadis proposed that I begin chemo today, but he said that Thursday would be all right too. I opted for Thursday so as to give my bowels more time to heal. My hip is doing better. I felt more like myself today.

In my prayer time, I thought of the song I'd learned in worships of the Sojourners Community in Washington, "Here I am, Lord, servant at your feet, ready to do your will." I want to complete the work God has for me, however short or relatively long the time given may be. Paul could write, "I have finished the race" (2 Tim. 4:7). I think of this especially with regard to writing.

Cathy Boshart, a Mennonite friend in Lebanon, Pennsylvania, wrote soon after my diagnosis that I should think about writing another book and that there could be time for this. At first I saw this as a most unlikely possibility. I spent years writing each of my major books; and now I might have only weeks to live. But gradually with God's merciful gift of continuing time, I have begun to think this may be feasible.

Wednesday, January 15.

Maren took me in to have the catheter with the port implanted in my chest. The port is on the right side, about four inches from the point at which the catheter angles into the vein under the collarbone. Everything seemed to go all right.

Ken Koons called. Ruth had asked him if he would be willing to build a wooden box for my burial. We have found out we'll need only that for inside the concrete vault. Ken agreed, and not being one to procrastinate, he already has the yellow and white pine wood for the box. (Ruth is sending him payment for the boards; but making the box is his gift to us.) He plans to go ahead and make it, the idea being that one can never be sure how soon it will be needed. He is drawing on some old designs. He wondered whether we would have a place to store it. Ruth said it could go in the attic of our spring house. I should get to see it. If Ken completes my box and brings it to our spring house, that would be somewhat like the skull in paintings of contemplative saints and hermits—a reminder of one's mortality, though I'm in little need of that.

Thursday, January 16.

We drove down to the Naval Hospital, and I was admitted to the oncology ward. After a month of delays, I have at last received the go-ahead. The first nurse in two tries failed to get the IV needle correctly into the port. That was painful. The port is implanted in my chest a little below the skin. She then called a colleague who succeeded. The taxol began flowing in at 2:40 p.m. The chemotherapy I had been so hesitant about had now started. The poison was coming into my body.

We are very thankful that the door opened for me to be part of the NCI lung cancer research project. I'm receiving the most advanced cutting-edge treatment. For one thing I have a part in research that will benefit many others. The doctors are hoping to demonstrate that extended ninety-six-hour administration of the drug taxol is more effective than what has been the standard large dosage (for each cycle) given during no more than several hours.

Friday, January 17.

Our friend Kim McDowell, visiting me in the hospital, commented: "This is such an interesting time in the lives of your children."

In the hall of the oncology ward, I met a fellow chemotherapy patient, Williams, a retired Navy man. He assured me: "I'm going to beat this. I made up my mind on that right away. I've never lost a battle yet, and I've been through two wars. This is nothing compared to them."

Saturday, January 18.

Ruth and I and the three children were together for much of the day. What a great blessing. Daniel referred to things they as children miss out on that are happening at home when they are away. I said, "Think of how much I may miss out on if I'm no longer with you."

Ruth said, "You will be with us."

I replied, "I don't think I'll know what's happening to you if I'm not with you on earth."

Maren commented, "You will probably be in a better position to know what is happening with us than we will be for what is happening with you."

I finished the faith-motif taping for my childhood into young adulthood.

We ended the evening with a discussion of the steers, the pasture, and the possibility of planting it in trees. We are leaning more and more toward doing that. It's clear that we should give up raising steers, but then we need to do something with the pasture. For the long run, just keeping it mowed seems a waste of effort and energy.

Ruth is hesitant because of the work that will be involved and the uncertainty as to whether I can help even through the first growing season.

I bade goodbye to Maren, who needs to fly back to Phoenix tomorrow. Daniel stayed at the hospital with me overnight.

Sunday, January 19.

In the sermon I gave at Miriam and Chuck's wedding last May, I took as the text Mark 2:18-19 with the wedding feast/bridegroom image and developed the point that we are to live convivially as at a wedding feast with the one who is bridegroom and host. In the time since the diagnosis I've often thought about what I made of that parable. I'm to be glad with Jesus the Bridegroom at the big party of life until I'm the one taken away.

Monday, January 20.

The CT scan of the chest taken to show the state of the disease at the start of chemotherapy indicates that the tumor on the left lung has grown a little since early November. That means for one thing that all the nutritional supplements I've been taking since soon after the diagnosis have not held the cancer in check or turned it back. But we think the supplements have helped me continue to do as well as I have been, in spite of the cancer.

I read the passage in John 15 about the vine and the branches. I want to bear more fruit and bear fruit longer. But as God wills.

As I was walking in the hall, taking my chemotherapy pump on wheels with me, Ensign Barber in her blue uniform said, "Mr. Aukerman, you must be bored."

I said to her, "No, it has been a good time here." Life is too short to get bored. And life is too short to watch the presidential inauguration. I contemplate the one true inauguration—the kingdom breaking in with the ministry of Jesus and Jesus seated at the right hand of the throne of God.

After the taxol I received the dosage of cisplatinum with a lot of IV fluid to flush it through. Ruth and Miriam brought me home late in the evening; we arrived about midnight. The first of the six cycles is behind me, except for the side effects.

Tuesday to Sunday, January 21-26.

Tuesday went fairly well. Wednesday was worse. Thursday and Friday I was terribly weak, with continuing nausea. It was a hassle to try to get fluids down.

I've started what is to be my pattern for the weeks following each cycle of chemotherapy. Twice a week I need to get blood samples drawn at a lab near Westminster to continually check on my neutrophil count and other things in my blood. The reports go to the NCI people.

I thought of Christ's promise to Paul, "my power is made perfect in weakness" (2 Cor. 12:9), but I couldn't discern any fulfilment in the midst of total exhaustion. This has been a time of little spiritual focus, a time for being carried by others praying for me.

Wednesday, January 29.

Monday I still had some loss of appetite, but Tuesday and today I've basically felt rather good.

Tuesday, February 4.

It's been a big day full of visits.

Don and Hedda Durnbaugh came. He is a retired seminary professor of church history and she a hymnologist. I spoke with Don about my idea of sending my biblical and theological books to Prague for the Comenius Faculty library there and for theological students. I have felt a strong tie with Czech Christians since I took part in Prague (East-West) Christian peace conferences in the early sixties. I have not been in Prague since. The contact person I'd been thinking of is Professor Josef Smolik. Don said he is still there, though retired. Don will send me addresses for Smolik and the Comenius Faculty.

Ken Koons came after my nap to continue his photographic record of my struggle with cancer. I hauled a little split wood and carried some in for photo opportunities. Then I sat in the recliner, and he took pictures through the entry window of me reading the Bible. I happened to turn to Psalm 128 and then noticed verse 6 with the blessing, "May you see your children's children!" I told Ken that the fulfillment of this blessing seems rather unlikely for me.

Beth Trickett, the county forester, came for a consultation about tree planting in the pasture. It's clear that with all the needed mowing, it will be a lot of work to take care of the planted trees—much more than just keeping the area mowed down. But Ruth said of the tree project: "It will be such a legacy."

Wednesday, February 5.

Today it is three months since I learned of the tumor. Once or more a day Ruth comments, "How thankful I am that I still have you." My hair is beginning to come out. I almost feel as if it is resting on top of my head and a little pulling would bring nearly all of it out. "But even the hairs of your head are all numbered" (Matt. 10:30). God knows the diminishing number and how many fall out each day.

Friday, February 7.

I've been working away at stacking the wood, bringing it from the piles in the hay patch where friends have sawed and split it. In November I would have seen my time as too precious for work like this. But now it is exhilarating to be able to do it, and the time seems adequate for such work. The big question is whether I will be alive for burning the wood that I am stacking. I look up at geese flying and think that many of them may outlive me.

The packet with the forester's proposal for what trees and how many to plant in the meadow was in our newspaper tube. We are still wondering about the amount of work that will be involved during the first several years. I've been giving much thought and mental energy to the tree-planting possibility.

Saturday, February 8.

Tante Anna called from Germany. She is a friend of Ruth's mother, who has been like another grandmother to our children. She is sending more money for Ruth and me to use in this hard time. We think of her money as underwriting the cost of nutritional supplements for me.

Monday, February 10.

John Witiak, a local friend always so ready to help, took me down for the beginning of the second cycle of chemotherapy. When I finally got to see Dr. Hill, I found out that my neutrophil count is down and I will need to wait at least a week to start.

Sometimes in speaking about the diagnosis I make the comment, "And then everything changed." Yet that is not really the case, though there has been an acute shift in my perspective about how long I might have to live. All that I know about God and Christ has not changed—basically. The love of Ruth, the children, and friends has not changed—except to deepen. My niche in life, though held much more tenuously, has not really changed.

Tuesday, February 11.

This is Miriam's birthday. Presumably, she is in Perm, Russia. Through the Ford Foundation, she is working as a consultant with a grassroots group of Russians there, who are converting a Soviet concentration camp for political prisoners into a memorial site.

I called the county forester today and told her to order the trees we want that are available from the state tree farm. I will also need to order about half of the trees from a commercial tree nursery. So the die is cast for going ahead. I find it a most energizing prospect.

Monday, February 17.

Daniel, who'd arrived home from Maine on Thursday, drove me to the Naval Hospital. My neutrophil count was too low again, so we headed home for another week of waiting. I felt considerably let down. This will make five weeks, instead of three, from one cycle to the beginning of the next.

Wednesday, February 19.

Brethren Peace Fellowship friend Jim Gibbel called me on Saturday to let me know that Gladys Miller, a first cousin of my mother, had died the day before in Lititz, Pennsylvania.

I found out the projected time for the burial and drove over to the Pike Creek Cemetery. This was my first time back in the cemetery since November, when we went to pick out my grave plot. The day was mild, windy—not too cold for a long wait in an unheated car. After about an hour and a half, the procession with hearse and several cars finally arrived. As I came close to the tent, the funeral director greeted me and asked whether I was a minister. I said, "Yes." He asked whether I would have a prayer at the graveside. No pastor from the Lititz congregation had come for this service, and no one had been in touch with me. But there was evidently some expectation that I would be there. I said I would need to go to my car and get my Bible. The funeral director said, "Take your time."

I spent several minutes in the car, turned to the passage in 2 Corinthians 4:16–5:9, and thought of one or two prayer focuses. When I returned, the funeral director was assigning the men (including the excavation worker) places as pallbearers. I stood to the side a little. Then he asked me if I'd be willing to help—and I did. He likely had no idea that here was a person undergoing chemotherapy for advanced lung cancer. I was a little short of breath for the service, but I read the passage and had a prayer. I also talked briefly with the cousins, who were strangers to me and whom I will probably never see again.

Afterward, Ruth saw God's hand in the delay of the chemo so that I could lead in the graveside service for Gladys.

Monday, February 24.
I drove down to the clinic this morning. Ruth questioned my doing so, but when I drive myself, I feel less dependent and more able. My neutrophil count was up, so I could begin the second cycle. I received a portable pump with a line going to the port in my chest. The pump contained the first twenty-four-hour supply of taxol. I need to return each morning through Friday. I feel so thankful and elated.

Sunday to Thursday, March 2-6.
I have been quite exhausted, but the side effects from the chemo seemed a little less than after the first cycle.

Thursday, March 6.
When retired General George Lee Butler, former commander of U.S. nuclear forces, called for the abolition of nuclear weapons, he created a sensation. Kermit Johnson, himself a retired general, gave me Butler's address, and several weeks ago I sent him a copy of *Darkening Valley: A Biblical Perspective on Nuclear War*. Today I received a short letter from General Butler. It was such a good boost.

> Dear Dale,
>
> Marvelous book. I am a Christian and there is a very direct link between my faith, my views on nuclear abolition, and the embedded moral issues. In case you did not see my Jan. 8 speech to the Henry L. Stimson Center, I have enclosed it. You will see therein the depth of my convictions on this score.
>
> Warm regards,
> Lee Butler

Friday and Saturday, March 7-8.
I am back to a better energy level. I trimmed the fruit trees and fruit-bearing bushes and vines.

Tuesday, March 11.

Today is the end of a twenty-two-year era. Our farm neighbors, Steve and Diane and Johnny Arbaugh, came over. They unfastened the barbed wire at the corner of our pasture next to the stile. Our two remaining steers, the middle-sized one and the little one, went through into the Arbaugh meadow. It seems strange not to have the steers in our meadow. I keep thinking I need to go and feed them. The Arbaughs will finish raising the steers, and we will get some of the meat when they are butchered.

Saturday, March 15.

Miriam and I had a splendid day staking off for the tree planting in the meadow. The trees will be twelve feet apart. We used twine to lay out each row and then staggered the stakes so that we don't have straight, symmetrical rows.

Monday, March 17.

I drove down to begin the third cycle of chemo. I had not been in the waiting room long when Barb Schuler came over and said she had results from the CT scan on Thursday. She said, "The doctor wrote of 'regression of the cancer.' We usually speak of decrease in size." There had been some shrinkage: actually 8.5 cm to 6.5 cm, 5.5 cm to 6 cm (slight increase), and 7 cm to 3.5 cm. (When we told Daniel on the phone this evening, he drew the striking conclusion that the decrease in size was about half.) So the cancer is responding really well to the chemo.

My neutrophil count was 1150, however, not up to the new and lower required minimum of 1500, so we need to delay the chemo for at least a week. This means the chemo treatments may run through much of the summer.

I was elated and grateful—eager to share the news with Ruth and the children. Ruth called home from school soon after I returned. Miriam called from work at the Ford Foundation in New York. She was so excited. Daniel called. He had good news too. He has been offered a residency spot in Lancaster (Pennsylvania) General Hospital and will transfer there from Maine. How good that he will be closer.

In bed I read to Ruth from Psalms 116 and 126. The uncertainty about how long I have to live is still very much with us and affects our thinking—but not so acutely when there seem to be some months ahead.

I should be more open in pointing to the prayers of others when I talk with the NCI people about the measure of healing that has come.

Tuesday, March 18.

I wrote an update letter to friends, sharing the splendid news.

Friends,

We want to share with you the latest news here. We are so glad and thankful. On March 13 I had a CT scan. This was to show what was happening with the cancer in comparison to the CT scan taken on January 17. If the cancer was continuing to grow, there would be no point in continuing the chemotherapy. We were hoping that it had stopped growing or even shrunk a little.

I found out the results yesterday. The tumor in my left lung had decreased in size by nearly half. (Even so it is about 2 inches long.) The metastases in that lung and most of those on the liver have disappeared. Very little fluid remains under either lung.

I thought of the verse in 2 Kings 7:9. The Syrian army had been besieging Samaria, and the city was in desperate straits. Four lepers outside a gate of the city decided to cast themselves on the mercy of the Syrians. But when they came at twilight to the camp, the army had fled. God had caused them to hear the commotion of an approaching host. The lepers started to plunder and hide treasures, but then said, "This day is a day of good news. . . . Let us go and tell the king's household." I've taken that text in preaching about the imperative to evangelize.

Monday was a day of great good news for us. Through the chemotherapy and other factors, God is turning back the invasion within my body. In the first weeks after the initial diagnosis, it had seemed quite doubtful whether I would live through the winter. Except for the days of total exhaustion after each cycle of chemotherapy, I've been feeling remarkably well.

I've been reading slowly through the Psalms. It is striking how often mention is made of God's delivering from death. Whether for a longer or a shorter period, God is giving me that deliverance, and we praise him. . . .

We are touched and amazed again and again to hear from still more persons who are praying for us. God hears the prayer of that multitude on our behalf and deals with us so graciously. God's grace to us in this time continues to be so incarnated in

the love, prayers, letters, calls, visits, and help of friends.
Strands beyond numbering are woven into the tent spread
around us. We are deeply grateful to each of you for your part.

We've been sharing the news with friends by phone. Frauke Westphal said this is the first good news that has come in relation to the illness. She emphasized that in November it seemed very doubtful that I would be alive by now and commented, "When one loses one's health, it is astonishing how marvelous a little bit of good news can seem."

The other day I tried to remove an insect that was crawling over the back of my neck. Then it was on the back of my hand, and I flicked it onto the table and crushed it. The body was the size of a small wasp and had yellow and black stripes. Afterward I felt bad that I had not just taken it outside. I am being given an opportunity to live longer, but I had not given that to the insect. Several more of the same unfamiliar species have appeared in the house since then, and I have taken them outside.

Monday, March 24.

Ruth has been gone since last Thursday to celebrate her mother's eightieth birthday in Germany. Maren is here to be my caregiver for the week. Since Maren has been on the edge of a cold, I drove by myself to an 8:30 a.m. NCI appointment to check out whether I can begin the third cycle of chemotherapy. Dr. Georgiadis greeted me in the hallway: "That was a great CT scan," and later he spoke of "the great news." He too figured that the tumor had decreased by half. They want to do another scan about thirty days after this last one. My neutrophil count is not quite high enough, so I need to wait for another week. But this certainly makes things easier for the tree-planting day and for celebrating Easter with the family.

After getting word about the cancer, I've thought rather often of lines from Milton's sonnet:

> Methought I saw my late espoused Saint
> Brought to me like Alcestis from the grave,
> Whom Jove's great Son to her glad Husband gave,
> Rescu'd from death by force though pale and faint.

I think of "Rescu'd from death by force" as applying to myself.

A line from John Donne's "Death be not proud" has also come to mind often: "One short sleepe past, wee wake eternally."

Today is Maren's birthday. She says she can't recall celebrating her birthday before just with her father. In the evening we made a tape of my boyhood farm reminiscences. Then she read her birthday letters—her mother's, her Uncle Gottfried's, and mine. I said, "We can hope that I will be able to write you a letter for your next birthday."

Thursday, March 27.

Maren and I drove to Dulles Airport to pick up Ruth, arriving from Germany. We came close to having a very bad accident on the way back. On a curve as Maren made a little change in direction to avoid another vehicle, our car for some reason started shuddering back and forth. For several seconds the car seemed as if it would go completely out of control. How sobering to think that I've been seeing the lung cancer as the threat to my life, but we could have been killed there on the highway.

Good Friday, March 28.

I read three of the passion narratives and then the story of the woman with the flow of blood, who came to Jesus, touched his garment, and was healed (Mark 5:24-34). Imaging is so widely recommended and practiced; e.g., picturing the cancer disappearing or vanished or imagining some devourer gobbling up the tumor. In contrast I picture the woman (and myself) touching Jesus and having the healing power flow in. Then it's not mind-over-matter self-help. It is the reality of touching Jesus. What is crucial is the sovereign willing of the One beyond. In the story it was the willing of God, if not the conscious willing of Jesus.

When I read the story, I was so moved by Jesus' words to the woman: "Daughter, your faith has made you well; go in peace, and be healed of your disease." The words burned within me and seemed to be words for me personally. I did not seize upon the words; they were given to me. But were they to be heard as God's promise of full healing? I was hoping so. Yet at times I've taken scripture as a sort of literal promise, and things haven't turned out that way. It's all quite simple if we take a common charismatic approach that God always wills healing and we simply need to have enough faith for this to happen. But I believe that God's will, in many circumstances, is not for a miracle of physical healing. How then can we be sure when his will is for healing and then pray with that assurance?

Some of Jesus' teachings about faith and prayer point toward healing, but the extent of one's faith in God and Jesus is being certain that God will heal or act in a specific instance. At the prospect of my own death these past five months, I've received such firm assurance that the gospel is true, that Jesus has overcome the powers of death and meets us, risen from the tomb.

It is crucial to be in touch with Jesus, to have his energizing and healing Spirit flow into me. Jesus says to me, "Go in peace"—into whatever is ahead.

Daniel arrived late this afternoon, and Miriam and Chuck came in this evening. For this third big holiday since November 5 our family is able to be together.

Saturday, March 29.

This has been tree-planting day. For several days Maren and I spent hours putting in the colored flags with the initials of the trees, trying to get a good mix of the big overstory trees like the oaks and the understory trees like the dogwoods. She said it reminds her of making seating charts for her schoolchildren. Miriam had the idea of a master diagram with all the planting locations on it.

Paul Dodd, a Brethren Peace Fellowship friend, came while we were finishing breakfast. He and our family headed to the former pasture. I began unpacking bundles of trees. We had fifteen species: red oaks, pin oaks, white oaks, tulip poplars, white ashes, red maples, European alders, Norway spruces, flowering dogwoods, gray dogwoods, silky dogwoods, redbuds, shadblow serviceberries, arrowwood viburnums, and crabapples. We started with the white oaks. They had little height and long, curving tap roots. We had to shovel holes for them as we did for several other species. For most of the planting, we borrowed digging bars, which make smaller holes. We had 315 trees to plant, plus maybe a few extras.

Jamie Edgerton, our Australian friend, and Jim Wallis, editor of *Sojourners*, arrived at about 9:30 in Jim's pickup. Jim confessed that he had never planted a tree before in his life. I found this quite amazing. We had orientation for the two of them and for the others from the Sojourners circle in Washington as they arrived in succession. Maren served splendidly as work coordinator. I shifted to getting the trees out of the basement and into buckets of water with flags.

Miriam and Chuck were soon planting in the soggy area. They planted more than 100 trees themselves. Some of the planting along the lane, with gravel in the soil, was slow and laborious. Daniel and others did much of that.

Later in the day I planted a European beech and two skyrocket junipers behind the house. This evening Miriam told of "a memorable moment." The tulip poplars were quite small, with short spaghetti-like roots and trunks four to six inches long. Jim Wallis dug a hole with the digging bar and carefully stuck the trunk of a tulip poplar into the ground. As he sized up the roots branching above the grass, he then caught on and reversed the direction.

This has been an unforgettable day, with a beautiful configuration of people coming together to help. Now the trees in their white spiral protectors are spaced across the meadow. Paul Dodd said to Miriam, "It doesn't seem like too much to ask that Dale would live to see the trees grow."

Sunday, March 30, Easter.
Early this morning Ruth and I took our first walk in a while to the end of Stem Road. I read most of the resurrection narratives in the Gospels.

Monday, March 31.
Everything at the NCI clinic went very slowly. But my neutrophil count was up enough—1634, and I could go onto full doses of taxol and cisplatinum for the third cycle.

Friday, April 4.
I had the chemo through the week. This afternoon Ruth ran the Rototiller mainly because of the chickweed and worked up a good part of the garden. I marked off the first two rows for lettuce. Ruth commented, "It's going to be such a huge garden."

I said, "I'm not going to plant a tiny garden."

Maren, standing at a little distance, added, "That is to say, it will be over your dead body that a tiny garden is planted here."

As another aspect of planting for the future, I had ordered a male and a female kiwi, two disease-resistant red currants, two large-fruited gooseberry bushes, and a quince tree. I planted the quince in the upper part of the lawn and set out the other plants inside the north edge of the garden. I wondered whether I would see them through the first growing season.

Monday to Thursday, April 7-10.
I have been exhausted from the effects of the chemotherapy and in bed much of the time. Putting the time to good use seemed too much to pursue.

I am so incapacitated in spirit.

In reading Psalms, I came to Psalm 103. Through the years verse 1 has often come to mind:

> Bless the Lord, O my soul;
> and all that is within me,
> bless his holy name!
> Bless the Lord, O my soul,
> and forget not all his benefits. . . .

I've always regarded "benefits" as general and open-ended. But reading it this time, I noticed that "benefits" is followed by a comma and the words:

> who forgives all your iniquity,
> who heals all your diseases,
> who redeems your life from the Pit,
> who crowns you with steadfast love and mercy,
> who satisfies you with good as long as you live. . . .

So much in that is being fulfilled for me right along. God is the One who can heal every disease in me.

Saturday, April 12.

Rain came today for the little trees. Now I think of rain mainly in relation to them rather than to things in the garden.

Don Murray, a movie actor friend from my time in Brethren Volunteer Service, called, and we talked for quite a long while. He has completed a play about his life, with much attention to his Brethren Service involvements. A New York producer asked Don for an autobiographical play, but Don is not too hopeful that it will be produced in New York.

Monday, April 14.

Today I went down for a CT scan. Before that I visited with my first cousin Glen Miller and his wife, Bernice, in the National Institutes of Health building across the street from the Naval Hospital. Glen was diagnosed with hairy cell leukemia almost thirteen years ago. Strange that two first cousins, who grew up together as Old German Baptist farm boys in southern Ohio, would both be getting experimental treatment for cancer in government facilities a block or so from each other in Bethesda, Maryland. Glen's treatment involves injection of protein molecules that are sticky on one end and have a toxin on the other; they attach themselves to the hairy cells. The treatment has indeed taken the hairy cells down to hardly any. But Glen's bone marrow is producing very few good white cells. At the time of the diagnosis, Glen was only fifty. He says the prospect of dying is easier now; he would rather die in his sixties than become debilitated in more advanced years. He emphasized that what is to come for him is in God's hands and that's enough for him to know.

Monday, April 21.

I went down to NCI, but my neutrophil count was 1400, not up to 1500, so I can't start the next cycle of chemotherapy. Dr. Hill was not able to tell me the results of the CT scan taken a week ago. But he called tonight. The CT scan shows some further shrinkage of the tumor. The lesions in the liver have remained stable. When we called Daniel, he was happy about the news, but he stressed that the tumor may begin to grow again at some point.

Monday, April 28.

My neutrophil count is up to 1500, so I'm starting the fourth cycle.

Friday, May 2.

In the treatment room I talked at length with Dr. Steve Dejter, an internist who is in the same protocol group as I. He is probably about my age and also never a smoker. He regards the program as the best in the world. When I asked why this method of treatment is not more widely used, he said that it is so much more expensive. The pump costs $3,000. I've been carrying around a pump that is worth more than both of our automobiles—maybe worth twice as much as both of them.

Tuesday, May 13.

Barb Schuler, the research nurse, called. The blood work taken yesterday shows for the first time that I'm neutropenic. The neutrophil reading was something like 355. My resistance to infection is now extremely low. When we talked with Frauke Westphal, she said I should have no visitors and make no visits.

Christopher Palsgrove, teenage son of friends of ours, hauled manure from the shed last evening, so I had spent the morning and early afternoon spreading the manure, rototilling it in, and planting late garden—certainly not an approved activity for someone who is neutropenic.

Tuesday, May 20.

Barb Schuler is on vacation. The other research nurse called. My neutrophil count yesterday had gone up to 2869. This was quite amazing—the highest the count has been, I think, since the chemo started. I was so happy and thankful. I've been reading through Isaiah and turned to what came as the next chapter—Isaiah 12—with all its praise. "I will trust, and will not be afraid" (v. 2).

When Ruth came home for lunch, going between her two schools, she was so elated; but she raised the question whether there might have been some mistake. Could this have been the report from someone else? If not, it does seem to be a little miracle, an answer to prayer, and a faith-strengthening gift of God.

In Revelation 5:13, John hears every creature telling forth the praise of God. How can this apply to deadly bacteria and viruses? Will they praise God only in eschatological transposition? Or are they creatures fallen into perversity, out of view for John, and will they lapse into nonbeing at the end?

Tuesday, May 27.

I dropped some things off for the Westphals. Frauke told me that I looked really good. As I was leaving, I said, "Now I will go and fraternize with the Navy."

She said, "I'm sure you do a fine job of it."

Dr. Hill said my neutrophil count is at 1431—just half of the 2869 that had been reported for May 19. We had had some questions about the high count—Ruth especially. But she, more than I, had been telling others that it was an answer to prayer, a miracle. Now it seems that the high count was a mistake, and what we saw as an answer to prayer seems quite obscured. What a disappointment. I need to wait at least another week before getting the next cycle of chemo.

In the treatment room I was reading Jesus' teaching on prayer found in Luke 11. These verses jumped out at me: "Ask, and it will be given you; seek, and you will find; knock, and it will be opened to you. . . . how much more will the heavenly Father give the Holy Spirit to those who ask him!" (vv. 9, 13). Yes, most of all the Spirit—even if healing is not given.

I got x-rays of my chest and lower back, the latter because I had asked about going to my chiropractor for treatment of some back discomfort. Dr. Hill didn't want me to do that before seeing whether my back is in good condition. This evening he called. There seems to be nothing in the lower back except some indication of arthritis. But the radiation doctor thinks I ought to have a bone scan. The chest x-rays show some small decrease in the size of the tumor in the left lung.

Wednesday, May 28.
Paul writes in Philippians 1:24: "But [for me] to remain in the flesh is more necessary on your account." There are times that I keenly feel the need to be here longer for Ruth and the children.

The healing of this cancer, prayed for by so many, would be wonderfully faith-confirming for them and for us. But that has been the case innumerable times when sick people were not healed.

Sunday, June 1.
Jesus healed only a tiny fraction of those who were ill during the time of his ministry on earth. Only those who could come near him (or had advocates who could) were healed. But when faith was present, all were healed. Jesus as risen Lord is not bound by space. It seems that all who turn to him and come close to him in faith should have the same prospect for being healed. But one does not see anything like the sweeping defeat of disease that took place in Galilee. Perhaps the healing ministry of Jesus in Palestine is to stand out as marvel beyond anything that came since then.

After the transfiguration the disciples could not heal the demon-possessed son of the man who came to them. Jesus chided them for their lack of faith (Luke 9:41). The application, seemingly, would be that any disciple should have the faith to heal when asked to do so. Are we simply like those disciples in lack of faith? But to go in that direction would seem to assume that God always wills healing.

Monday, June 2.
Bill Heltzel, our friend and neighbor, is insistent that it's not too early or too much for him to take me down to the hospital. After getting a die injection and waiting a long time, I had a bone scan. While waiting I came upon Matthew 16:25: "For whoever would save his life will lose it." What is the relevance of this to my situation? It seems so clearly right that time and energy be given to struggling against the cancer. Not to do that would be to give up on living. But striving to look to God in faith and trust, seeking to live in and for the kingdom, should loom much larger than struggling to live and not die.

I saw Dr. Hill early this afternoon. The bone scan indicates a questionable place in the middle area of my spine. The doctors want x-rays. Dr. Hill explained that if they determine that the spot on the spine or one elsewhere is a new metastasis, something that has developed since the start of the chemotherapy, this would mean that the chemo I'm getting is failing in this regard. I would need to be taken off it and put on something else—a most unwelcome prospect.

I went for the x-rays. During the long waits, I felt much calm and peace about whatever the findings would be. A number of times I said, "Lord Jesus Christ, Son of God, Savior, have mercy on me a sinner," then the words of the leper to Jesus, "If you will, you can make me clean" (Mark 1:40). Dr. Hill came out of the exam room and reported that the best judgment was that the spot in the middle of my spine is an arthritic lesion. But the other doctor is concerned about my lower back pain and thinks I should have an MRI.

Tuesday, June 3.
Dr. Hill called. I can have an MRI at 2:00 in the morning. Otherwise I would need to wait quite a while for a slot at a more civil time.

Wednesday, June 4.
We left home at 12:30 a.m. for the MRI appointment. Dr. Hill called about 10:45 this morning to say that the MRI was inconclusive and that I needed cross-sectional CT scans for the two suspicious spots in the spine. Coming back to the clinic after these scans, I had such a sense of God's love and peace.

The CT scans were also inconclusive. But an MRI with the injection of a tracer chemical should enable the doctors to make a diagnosis. Dr. Hill went with me to the MRI desk, where the people worked me in for another MRI that took more than an hour, I think.

Scriptures came to me. "This day is a day of good news" (2 Kgs. 7:9). Again and again the words came to mind. But I did not take this as an assurance that the medical report would be good news. In any case the good news of Jesus crucified and risen illuminates this day. "No, in all these things we are more than conquerors through him who loved us" (Rom. 8:37). Nothing can "separate us from the love of God in Christ Jesus our Lord" (Rom. 8:39).

Dr. Hill talked with me shortly after I was dressed again. It seemed fairly certain that one or both spots in the spine are metastatic. The question is,

Were they there before the start of the chemo? That still needs to be pursued by checking earlier bone scans. If it seems that I should be taken off the protocol, he said, "we have other tricks up our sleeve." He also called Ruth to explain things to her. I told him his efforts on my behalf reminded me of a time in my boyhood when I seemed near death, perhaps from poisoning, and Dr. Newbold, a local physician, spent two or three hours with me at our farm house in the middle of the night.

When we talked with Daniel, I said that in the MRI tunnel I had thought of the people he worked with at a clinic in Ulrique, Mexico, and how they did not even have access to x-rays. How much advanced medical technology I can rightly take for myself? As part of a study group, though, there is the prospect that my participation will benefit others. Daniel replied, "All the sophisticated technology and so little return." This evidently sums up much of what he experiences as a young doctor.

When I called Miriam, she took the news quite hard.

Thursday, June 5.
After breakfast I read to Ruth from the latter part of Romans 8. Verses from it had been running through my mind much of the day before. Ruth said, "I wouldn't have missed the last six months for anything. They have been the best time in our marriage." I wouldn't put it quite like that. I would be glad not to have the cancer; but she was thinking of the added time we've been given. There have been other especially wonderful times in our marriage, but this period has been extraordinary in its own way. And we have been closer, more fully in shalom with each other, than perhaps ever before. She says so often to me, "I'm so thankful that I still have you."

We were waiting in suspense for the call from Dr. Hill. He called a little before 11:00 this morning: "I have good news for you." It seems the metastases in the spine were there earlier, so I can come in to begin the chemo. Ruth and I are so happy. How ironical that this report should be such good news.

Ruth drove me to the clinic. We spent most of the afternoon waiting, and I didn't get the portable pump until 4:00. On the way home Ruth was thinking of eating at the Chinese restaurant in Mt. Airy but told me it was my choice. I chose coming on home for a modest meal here. Later she teased me that we needed to come on home so that I could rest—and then we worked in the garden. She did push-plowing and I hoed. How good it was to work together like that in the cool of the evening.

Yesterday after Dr. Hill called Ruth to explain about the MRI, she was very upset and began crying. Just then our friend Janet Heltzel, who works as a teacher's aide, stopped in unannounced to drop off a piece of art belonging to an Elmer Wolfe student. (The art had accidentally ended up in the Taneytown Elementary School.) Janet was able to talk with Ruth and help her through the time. Today when Janet told Larry McKinney, the Taneytown principal, that he had asked her to deliver the piece of art work "at just the right time," he playfully commented, "You mean the Lord used me?"

Saturday, June 7.

I left a little before 11:30 this morning to go to the oncology ward of the hospital—the clinic was closed for the weekend—to get the new supply of taxol. The male nurse on duty was not very familiar with the pump and needed to call in another nurse.

Within ten minutes of arriving home this afternoon, the pump was beeping with the message that the battery was low. Ruth and I got the directions and followed them closely, but the pump would not reset after we put in the new battery. I had Ruth call the nurse who had given me her home number. She had me try various things, but nothing worked. I noticed that blood had worked its way down into the tubing. After much more calling and waiting, we reached another nurse who gave me some instructions, and quickly the pump was running again. But she said that blood might be clotted in the line. If I got a high-pressure beep from the pump, we should go at once to the oncology ward. Maren called and Ruth had just started talking with her when the beeping started.

We fed our dog Shanti and left in a big hurry for the hour-and-a-quarter drive to the hospital. On the way down I was thinking of peace passages. Ruth dropped me off at the side entrance. The male nurse, Fillmore, whom I had had before, greeted me and took me right into an empty room. The most pressing question was whether there'd been clotting in the port. If there was, it could no longer be used. He took the syringe and was able to flush the port. Ruth behind him said, "Praise God!" But there was clotting in the tubing, which he could not flush out. Twice the pharmacy sent him the wrong filter and tubing. Fortunately he was very careful to check everything. Finally he did get the right items.

So much went wrong, but we are thankful that things turned out all right—especially that the port was not ruined and that seemingly no clots were pushed into my blood stream. We arrived home at about 10 p.m.

Sunday, June 8.

In the Pipe Creek service this morning, singing "How Firm a Foundation" with its great promises moved us deeply:

> . . . I'll strengthen thee, help thee, and cause thee to stand,
> upheld by my righteous, omnipotent hand.

> When through the deep waters I call thee to go,
> the rivers of sorrow shall not overflow,
> for I will be with thee, thy troubles to bless,
> and sanctify to thee thy deepest distress.

> The soul that on Jesus still leans for repose,
> I will not, I will not desert to its foes.
> That soul, though all hell should endeavor to shake,
> I'll never, no never, no never forsake!

Monday, June 9.

I talked with Nancy Gossman, the head nurse in the treatment room. She said they think my pump was not set last week as it should have been. She said they will have an in-service consultation about how to keep something like that from happening again.

Sunday, June 15.

I've been having my usual bad days after the chemo. Today I'm still wiped out and quite listless. Ruth seems more bothered than usual by this condition. She keeps trying to find ways to enliven me, but that doesn't help.

Monday, June 16.

This birthday of mine seemed far away after the diagnosis in November. I went for blood work early today. I have been feeling on the upswing. Birthday calls came during the day. So many cards came, especially from people in the Bethany Church in Delaware where I had my last interim pastorate. Ruth was feeling apologetic that she didn't have anything that special for me. But what a treasure her constant, steadfast love is. We had the festive little birthday table for me after our naps.

Miriam wrote me for my birthday.

> Dear Father,
>
> Every milestone this year has been so special, a chance to be grateful for the time we have had together and also a time when

we think with renewed focus about the question of whether we'll be together at this time next year. Your illness has brought so many emotions into the foreground for all of us. And it is a testament to yours and mother's skills as parents that those emotions are ones of overwhelming love and fear of loss. It could have been otherwise. Your presence in my life—the example you have set and the love you have shown—have been among the most formative influences not just of my childhood, but also of my adulthood.

God grant you grace, and if he wills, healing.

Happy Birthday,
Mimi

I also received a birthday letter from Maren.

Happy Birthday, Dear Father,

Nights as a child I was the chronic insomniac, wiggling loose teeth with my tongue, imagining foxes when I heard the crickets, convincing myself that the long strange pain in my leg was cancer. The slanted roof was a small comfort, and the fluorescence squeezing through from the attic room next door in the shape of a house. Best of all was the reliable tap of the Olympia, which was the sound of writing, which was the sound of my father.

You are so much like your father, I hear said. It is inescapable: there are moments when I am.

Like birthdays: born on the decade, we run with the years. It makes our ages easy to remember. We shared this commonality and advantage from way on back.

Of course, I did not hide behind the refrigerator the time Mother and Miriam threw me a surprise birthday party. But then, I was much older, and I wouldn't have fit. The thought did cross my mind, briefly, but all the same. Not comfortable with the crowds around us, not comfortable being the center, being watched. Painfully shy. Loners.

Those attic rooms, like the log house, were a retreat we both needed.

Then I think of this thing that I do, teaching. It is very much my mother's profession, utterly, appallingly social, and I feel her in me strongly every day. At the same time I find in myself as well what I've felt in you over these past twenty-seven years. The two of us writing, rooted in that. ("I thought, she has her father's gift of words," writes Yvonne [Dilling] in response to my Christmas letter.) Yet preaching and teaching are so fundamentally talking work, work that goes beyond what we have time to think and write. Living in the moment with no time to think through a response. Also there's the marked tension: the necessary grounding in solitude, beside the need to be present and working for good among others.

Then, too, there's something unyielding in that Aukerman line, perhaps from Grammee, a stubbornness that both enables and disables us. We do not compromise easily. How can we let go, or give in on what is right? We protest, we challenge, we speak out even though it's not always our gift to. I've found the boundaries and positioned myself there, less by choice than by calling. That is my father.

So there are also those occasional chasms of belief that open between us, where you are that I cannot be, or where I am that you cannot be. What we share also sets us apart from each other sometimes. I'm not walking in your footsteps (if I were, I'd hardly be your daughter): my road is different, just as surely as it is similar. Both of us, though, wanderers and seekers after the grace of the Spirit.

I have a great deal to learn from you yet, and I hope you are around for awhile longer to laugh at my jokes. *Wir zwei sind Kameraden* (We two are comrades). Every moment of that is blessed.

Love,
Maren

Friday, June 20.

We have enjoyed the strawberries so much. Surviving until there would be fresh strawberries again was a pleasant goal. Now I'm wondering if I will live long enough to set out twenty-five strawberry plants of another variety next spring. The Sparkles we have tend to run small after the first picking.

Ken Koons came by to visit. I mentioned that I did not want the burial box Ruth asked him to build for me to be in his way. He said he had worked on it some in the winter. The only pine wood thick enough was stair treads, so he needed to take off the rounded edges, then tongue and groove them with an old set of planes. He has done dovetailing of the corners. I said that the box could be stored in our spring house anytime.

Tuesday, June 24.

Helen Denlinger called about 2:00 this afternoon. Her brother, my cousin Glen Miller, finally succumbed to the hairy cell leukemia at 9:00 this morning. His condition was worsening yesterday. Helen didn't know whether he recognized her last evening when she went there. His wife Bernice repeated to him, as the hospice nurse had advised, "You know, you are dying. And that is all right." He had a restless night. Helen was with him this morning when he died. It was a quick, relatively peaceful death.

Such a bond had developed between Glen and me because of our struggle in faith against cancer. In fact, we had a long telephone talk Friday evening. He said again as so often before, "It's in the Lord's hands." This death touches me the most deeply of any since my father's in 1993. I read in Hebrews: "whoever enters God's rest also ceases from his labors. . . . surrounded by so great a cloud of witnesses" (Heb. 4:10; 12:1). Glen is now part of the cloud.

Maren arrived this evening from Phoenix to spend much of her summer break with us. It's great to have her here.

Monday, June 30.

Ruth and Maren offered to drive me down for the chemo today, but I thought I could make out fine by myself. However, on Interstate 270, a little before the Rockville exit, the left front tire of our 1980 Toyota Corolla gave out. I could have pulled off, but it seemed to be a rather dangerous place for changing a tire, so I tried driving further, hoping I could reach the next exit. But driving on the rim did not go well, so I stopped and waited. An Indian woman in a sari and a younger man, who seemed to be her son, stopped to offer help. She was going to call AAA for me, but just then a Montgomery County policeman pulled up. I told him right away about my condition and where I was headed. He changed the tire and escorted me to the nearest service station to get more air in the mounted spare. I was so thankful to him and to God for this help and for things working out.

I wasn't very late in getting to the clinic. But my neutrophil count was low, so I need to wait before getting the chemo.

Saturday, July 5.

The little trees are holding on remarkably well after more than four weeks with no significant rain. The drought has been weighing down my spirits just a little; but I am more buoyant today.

Sunday, July 6.

The Westphals came for a late lunch. Frauke commented, "Every good week is a gift from upwards."

Monday, July 7.

Ruth wanted to take me down to the clinic, and this seemed a good thing. In the waiting room we talked with fellow patient Dr. Dejter, who has completed his sixth cycle of the same chemotherapy that I am getting. He is planning to go to the fjords of Norway before long. A doctor from Harvard and Johns Hopkins told him that he has a number of non-small-cell lung cancer patients who have been living for years even without therapy.

When Dr. Hill finally came in, he had word that my neutrophil count is down still lower, 900 and something. He and others there have decided it would be better for me to wait a week. Dr. Hill is leaving at the end of the week—a blow for us. I'm to be with Dr. Jawien.

It's now five weeks since we've had any significant rain. I've begun to water the potatoes in the garden. With the Power Wagon, our motorized wheelbarrow, we took five-gallon buckets of water to the expiring gray dogwoods along the lane. Seeing the stunted cornfields makes me sad.

Tuesday, July 8.

Maren and I went over the interplanted rows of extra trees in the meadow to write down the names. She asked, "If I would be doing the transplanting next spring without your close supervision, how big should the clumps be?"

Saturday and Sunday, July 12-13.

Miriam recently returned from a conference in Durban, South Africa, that she had helped organize for the Ford Foundation. She came to Baltimore by train Saturday evening, but Chuck, under thesis deadline pressure, could not come. Daniel arrived Sunday afternoon. How beautiful to have all three children here with us again. Ruth prepared a turkey dinner for us.

Monday, July 14.

Ruth took me down to the clinic. We met Dr. Jawien. My count is 1300, so the doctors have decided to go ahead with the taxol at 60 percent. I assume that this is enough to help some but not like the full dosage. The doctors seem pleased that the cancer has remained stable.

Tuesday, July 15.

Just before Daniel was to take Maren to the airport, I thought about saying the Lord's Prayer together, as has been a tradition in our family when there is a parting. It has occurred to me that living out this tradition might be something to do right at the end of my life or near the end. We three said the Lord's Prayer. I was tearful, not so much because of this parting but because it intimated another parting that may not be very far off. Ruth was at Johns Hopkins Hospital with our friend Marian Witiak, who is having surgery for breast cancer.

Thursday and Friday, July 17-18.

Ruth took me to the clinic—fortunately. I've been having a runny nose and coughing some. It has been enough of a problem that I mentioned it to the nurse. She called Dr. Jawien to ask him. I thought he would check my nose and throat for cold or viral symptoms, but he proposed chest x-rays and blood work.

I got the x-rays, waited an hour for the wet-read report, and took that back to the nurse. A bit later she told us that Dr. Johnson and another doctor had gone down to look at the x-rays. We were pretty sure from this that a major problem had come up. When Dr. Johnson returned, he explained that the catheter from my implanted port runs through the sub-clavian vein (under the collar bone). The catheter had been set to go down somewhat into the vein descending toward the heart. But the farther end had become cocked upward into the jugular vein coming down from the brain. That did indeed sound like a most undesirable twist.

They disconnected the pump right away. Only later did another doctor explain the dangers more specifically: With the catheter cocked up into the jugular vein, any air bubbles happening to come through it might rise into the brain and cause a stroke, or the taxol in high dosage might reach the brain. The part about the stroke was especially sobering. We are thankful they discovered the problem—without at all anticipating it—and so thankful that I did not have a stroke. If there'd been no cold symptoms and thus no x-rays, I would have gone right on into day five, Friday. If the saline

solution and cisplatinum had then been given through the port, air bubbles
would have been feeding through.

Dr. Jawien examined me for admission to the oncology ward. I was in the
next to the last day of my sixth (and last) cycle, and I would receive the rest
of it as an inpatient on a peripheral IV pump.

We got to the oncology ward in time for me to have a late lunch. Ruth
headed home to pick up some things and returned after supper. She wanted
to be there for the operation to remove the port and catheter, whenever that
would come. What a wonderful companion and caregiver she is. Though we
had seen *Driving Miss Daisy* years ago in a movie theater, we watched it on
the very small bedside TV screen. Ruth spoke of the time as a date, and it
was. She slept in the other bed in the room.

In the morning I had the operation for removing the port and catheter.

Saturday and Sunday, July 19-20.
The post-chemo exhaustion has not hit me quite so hard as other times.
Saturday afternoon Ruth went to the spring house and discovered that some
of the little trees in that area were dying. Using a long line of hose from the
faucet outside the house, I would sit in a lawn chair for several minutes
watering one tree, then move on to the next. I am so sorry I did not start
watering the red maple near the concrete cattle gate sooner. Its leaves seem
quite shriveled. Several of the red oaks and two of the gray dogwoods along
the lane have withered.

Wednesday, July 23.
Today a newspaper article on the drought says it could be the worst since
the 1950s. But this afternoon we had a sprinkling rain.

Ruth says to me a number of times a day, "I love you, I love you. I'm so
thankful I still have you." The other day she said, "I love you to death—
literally." And she added, "These months have been the richest of my life."

Thursday, July 24.
This is our thirty-second wedding anniversary.

The remnants of a hurricane passed to the north of us. We received about
half an inch of rain, though the weather forecast was for one to three
inches. The drought weighs on my spirits. It is for me *eine Anfechtung*,
something experienced as an onslaught against faith. Yet God's faithfulness
and goodness come in so many other dimensions. Even the drought has
been moderated some.

Thursday, July 31.

Barb Schuler called to say that the blood counts still look fairly good. She thinks things should be fine for our going to Ohio and Indiana to visit friends and relatives. I am to have monthly checkups in the NCI program.

Monday, August 4.

Wilbur and Sandy Wright, nearby Brethren Peace Fellowship friends, invited us over for the evening. Flora Lynch from Costa Rica, whom Ruth and I have known for a number of years, was there. She spoke an ardent prayer for my healing. She stressed that I must have "100 percent faith" that God will heal me, and then healing will come. After the prayer I said to her, "You were so sick with cancer, but you have lived a number of years longer. Maybe God will give me additional years."

She shot back, "Not 'maybe.' You must have complete faith that God is going to heal you." She spoke about healing being given so that I would then have a witness to share with others. As I see it, I do already have a witness to give about God's working with me whether or not I am given more time.

Thursday, August 7.

Ruth drove me to Bethesda. We were in the waiting room when Dr. Braidnaigh came in and reported on the CT scan. By April the tumor in the left lung had decreased to 39 percent of its original size. Last week's scan showed it down to 23 percent—a further 16 percent decrease. He is very pleased. He said it is rare that such a tumor goes away entirely. The spots on the liver may have been less responsive. He said to try not to focus on the prospect of the cancer growing again but to make the most of this time. We are so thankful that there has been this much further decrease. We had not supposed there would be.

Frauke Westphal called. She was so glad about the CT scan report. She spoke of the findings as a miracle—especially the fact that the fluid buildup under the left lung had gone away and not returned. When she showed the report to Dr. Saia, the pulmonary specialist in her office whom we had turned to earlier, he said, "That is a miracle."

Ruth told Frauke that the love of friends has played such a big part in this healing and that hers and Heiner's love for us has been very significant. But Frauke said, "Your love for each other, the relationship you have, is so crucial." In pointing to the love, prayers, and support of friends, perhaps Ruth and I don't recognize the centrality of our love enough, though we experience it so much.

Friday, August 8.

The day was very full. We have spent months looking for a more dependable car. Our two Toyotas are in marginal condition; each has about 200,000 miles. Today we at last made the decision to buy a 1991 Honda Civic with relatively low mileage.

I told Ruth that a few days ago I read the story of the triumphal entry. Jesus instructed two disciples to spot and untie a donkey and to say to any challengers, "The Lord has need of it" (Luke 19:34). That saying seemed relevant to our car search.

We also had so much else to take care of—picking the blackberries, packing for the nine-day trip to Ohio and Indiana. We got off a little after 6:00 p.m.

We were happy to be heading west. I was driving. I felt a brimming thankfulness, and Ruth said, "I feel like a bride."

I responded, "You look like a bride. You have a bridal glow."

I was thinking that God has been holding back death from me. But that is each living person's situation. It's only more evident for someone like me.

Saturday, August 9.

When we got to the area west of Dayton, Ohio, where I had grown up, we went first to Aunt Betty Miller's. As we arrived, she told us that Aunt Esther Miller had died the evening before. We had planned to visit Aunt Esther on Monday. Instead we would be going to her memorial service.

Larry Fourman, pastor of the Brookville (Ohio) Church of the Brethren, and his wife, Ann, had invited us for supper and for staying overnight. Their daughter Amy and her husband, Jim, came with the firstborn son. So it was that I held a baby for the first time since the diagnosis, I think. It's striking how all our more recent living has its divide—before and after November 5, 1996.

Sunday, August 10.

Ruth drove us to the Aukerman reunion in the pavilion of the Otterbein Home near Lebanon, Ohio. I had a beautiful time being with relatives, many of whom I had not seen since the 1980 reunion. I was very glad that the reunion, held every five years, fell within the time of our trip.

Tuesday, August 12.

We had a good visit with Uncle Harry Miller in the nursing home in New Lebanon. I wanted to read a scripture to him. At first he couldn't think of one he wanted to hear, but then he said that as he was leaving for the Army to fight in World War II, another worker in the factory told him that if he took a copy of Psalm 95 with him all the time he would come through alive. He did that and lived, when nearly all of his buddies were killed in the Battle of the Bulge. Though I couldn't see that as a near-magical promise, it seemed good to read the psalm. I thought Uncle Harry probably meant Psalm 91, but I read most of Psalm 95 before reading Psalm 91, which he recognized as the one: "A thousand may fall at your side, / ten thousand at your right hand; / but it will not come near you" (v. 7). Uncle Harry said he had seen so many dead horses in Germany. The German military relied heavily on horse-drawn vehicles, and "our bombers" would come and destroy them. He said, "War is terrible." As one who turned from the Old German Baptist Church and went off to war, he experienced the horrors of war more fully than anyone else in our family circle.

Wednesday to Friday, August 13-15.
We drove on to North Manchester, Indiana, to visit a cluster of friends there. We went first to see the Kindys. What a marvelously kept truck-farm the Kindys have. They had had five inches of rain in late July. We thought of the drought-stricken crops in Maryland as we feasted our eyes on the thriving corn and grass in Indiana.

Thursday we had an intense evening with a small circle of some of our closest friends. Cliff Kindy asked about spiritual insights that had come through my illness. I spoke of the old question to pacifists about being attacked and its transposition for me in facing cancer, and how I've found that one does not need to fear. Perhaps I should have spoken a little more about deliverance from any domination by fear, for there have been some brief times of apprehension and anxiety, particularly about test results.

Saturday to Monday, August 16-18.
Driving back east across Ohio, we were able to visit my foster brother, Ray Childs, and his wife Micki. We stayed overnight at the home of Howard and Mary Ann Ludwick, who had met in my Brethren Volunteer Service training unit in 1952. Interestingly, Howard told about his mother in Appalachian West Virginia having used slippery elm and burdock root as home remedies when the children were growing up. These are two of the four ingredients in the essiac (anti-cancer) tea that I drink twice a day. All the children disliked the taste of such remedies, and none of them continued that tradition.

As we came closer home, it was sad to see the stricken cornfields again and the brown grass. No significant rain had fallen during the nine days we were away. But the little trees in our meadow do not look much worse, even though there had been a record heat wave the latter part of the week. We had hardly unpacked when a big rainstorm moved in with such dashing rain as we've not had, I think, since last year. I sat on the porch and thankfully took in the sight. More rain the following night brought the total to 2.1 inches, the first big rain here since the beginning of June. The rainfall was a good conclusion for a beautiful trip so full of blessing.

Saturday, August 23.

I was delighted to discover that the red maple on the left near the cattle gate has several tiny new leaves. Weeks ago when Maren was here, the leaves had shriveled. I was not watching it closely enough. I watered it then, and a couple of leaves remained partly green. I kept watering it, but it would have received no water while we were in the Midwest. Now too Maren's locust looks better. I had watered it at times during the drought, not because the locust seemed that valuable in itself, but because Maren had transplanted it from the garden to our lawn on the big tree-planting day.

Sunday, August 24.

In 1974 Larry and Ann Fourman joined Ruth and me for a dedication service in the dining room of this log house, then abandoned, before we started to restore it. We read the passage in Isaiah 61: "They shall build up the ancient ruins, / they shall raise up the former devastations" (v. 4). Today I read in the same passage God's promise to give "the mantle of praise instead of a faint spirit; / that they may be called oaks of righteousness, / the planting of the Lord, that he may be glorified" (v. 3). "Faint spirit" reminds me of the days following chemo. How hard it was to offer praise then. People are to be like sturdy trees as a planting of the Lord. I thought of our little tree lot. All our becoming is to be for praise to God.

Friday to Sunday, September 5-7.

September 5 marked ten months from the diagnosis. During the week I prepared the sermon that I'm to give in the University Park Church of the Brethren service on September 28.

This weekend was the tri-district Brethren Peace Fellowship retreat at the farm home of Jake and Arlene Miller, the first major event for me following our August trip to the Midwest. People greeted me as if they found my presence somewhat amazing.

One Bible study was on the story of Jephtha's daughter (Judg. 11:29-40). Her father vowed that if God would give him victory over the Ammonites, he would offer up as a burnt offering the first person to come out of his house to welcome him back. His daughter was that person. She asked him to allow her to have two months in the wilderness with her companions before she was offered up in sacrifice. Someone pointed that out as an example of community. I remarked that Jesus too was given over to the perversities of the power structures of his time, that the community of faith formed around him, and that we are to stand with those who are victims of perverted power structures. Then our dear friend Wilbur Wright made the currently relevant application that when the life of a friend is spared for a while, others may live out with the person this time before the end.

Eight-year-old Gabriel Dodd came over after the evening session, looked up at me, and asked, "Will this be your last time here?" He had probably heard conversation that put this question in his mind. What beautiful simplicity there was in the question. I said I didn't know—that none of us can know how long we have to live.

Sunday morning Matt Guynn, the retreat leader, came to me and explained that in the closing worship they were planning to have an anointing/commissioning service. Would I be the anointer? I asked for time to think about it. As I mulled it over, the task seemed right.

We sat in lawn chairs in a horseshoe facing the lake. After Matt introduced the anointing, I stood with my back toward the lake with a small bowl of olive oil in my left hand. As people came forward, I rubbed a bit of oil on their forehead with slightly varying charges, such as, "Go forth anointed in the power and peace of Jesus Christ." Even the youngest children came. In the background, they were singing songs like "Take my life." Then at the end Matt anointed me. Many were in tears.

Sunday, September 14.

We had invited a number of local friends for a "thank you evening." Twenty-four adults and seven children came. It was a surprise that our family physician, Dr. Caricofe, and his wife, Betty, came. We formed a circle with lawn chairs under the black walnut trees and began to sing. I commented about the day I got the early call to come into Dr. Caricofe's office and how I happened to find Psalm 116 and meditated upon it before I went in. In the gathering darkness I read the psalm. In the prayer time later, Janet Heltzel mentioned that two doves came and perched over me on a branch as I read the scripture. That was a lovely touch. (I had not been aware of it.) It is remarkable that these birds would come like that where so many people were gathered.

Ruth led in the servant song, "Will you let me be your servant?" I think of the words now so much in relation to her, who she has been for me, especially in this time, and who she may yet need to be for me.

> I will hold the Christ-light for you in the night-time of your fear.
> I will hold my hand out to you, speak the peace you long to hear.

It was a moving and blessed time. The walnut trees spread wide against the moonlit sky. I felt touched by the peace of God.

Saturday, September 20.
We heard from Miriam today that Chuck's defense of his Princeton doctoral thesis on Procopius and Thucydides went well. His doctoral work is now completed.

During my University of Chicago years, I intended to get a Ph.D. Later, various people, and at times even Ruth, urged me to get a doctorate. I believe it was right that I didn't get a doctorate and go in a more academic direction. My gifts are much more for writing, preaching, and pastoring than teaching.

Sunday, September 21.
I read the healing story in John 5 today. Quite a number of sick people were waiting in the porticoes around the pool. Jesus addressed just one of them. We are given no hint as to why he turned to this particular person. The act of healing, it seems, did not depend on the faith of the man or of others (as in certain instances when people brought the sick to Jesus). His response to Jesus' question "Do you want to be healed?" was oriented entirely toward the pool, not toward Jesus. It seems he had no inkling of who Jesus was. Yet Jesus healed him, and that was his introduction to Jesus.

Psalm 30:11: "Thou hast turned for me my mourning into dancing"—for me, though, not quite into dancing.

Tuesday, September 23.
Today I read Hezekiah's prayer in Isaiah 38. Since Christ, we can't make the appeal to God: keep me alive because the dead don't praise you. The dead may praise him far better, even in waiting. I can make the appeal that I may

be of more strategic use for the kingdom here on earth than I would be waiting beyond death.

Wednesday, September 24.

During the greater part of my life I went barefooted much of the warmer half of each year. I have done that too here at this place. When I went to a retreat in the mid-eighties, friends of each person on retreat were to write letters of appreciation and support. Marie Baker wrote of my "green feet." Now with these feet numbed by the chemotherapy, it would be quite dangerous for me to go barefooted. These numb fingers still do reasonably well typing letters into the word processor.

Thursday, September 25.

A curious question: If my father and mother had been staunch Old German Baptists (like their fathers), what would that have led to for me? In my earlier boyhood, I was basically within the Old German Baptist world. But I had such insatiable intellectual interests from about the fifth grade. I think that even with strict, staunch parents I would have "stepped over the traces" (as the Old German Baptist phrase has it), probably not becoming a member of the church.

In faith and spiritual commitments, I have had significant shifts and what I would see as much broadening; but I have not really had breaks, discontinuities, or reversals.

Sunday, September 28.

This has been a milestone day—my first preaching since the diagnosis. Even when Kim McDowell came as pastor and friend before I underwent tests in Suburban Hospital last November, she said that anytime I felt ready to preach they at the University Park congregation would be glad to have me.

I wanted to speak out of my experience with cancer and yet really preach. I did not want to give, in large part, a charismatic-type testimony or narrative. I took "Matters of Life or Death" as a title for the message (this later became "Living with Dying").

So many people told me how good I looked. People who have not seen me since the diagnosis were probably expecting me to look drawn by the cancer and treatments. Though the cancer is still there, I'm certainly in better physical condition than I was last September and October before the diagnosis. Someone even said, "You look robust." People commented on my hair, which has come back grayer than before.

Monday, September 29.
Mark Coates, a fellow art teacher, called this evening to tell Ruth that she has been chosen as Maryland Art Educator of the Year (1998). He is the one who nominated her.

Friday, October 3.
Maren arrived from Phoenix on Wednesday. Today she and I drove to Penn Station to pick up Miriam and Chuck. Daniel is to get in late tonight.

Saturday, October 4.
This was another milestone day. I was being recognized at the On Earth Peace luncheon at the Brethren Service Center in nearby New Windsor. How splendid it was to have the children all there. It was a little hard for me to take in the full content of the citation as Fran Nyce, long-time peace activist friend, read it. I began my response with, "I could say first that I am very glad that this particular recognition does not need to be given posthumously."

The family told me afterward that at the close of the citation for Marie Hamilton, an activist for training in conflict resolution in Pennsylvania prisons, they wished her many more years for such work, but that they wished me "many, many more days." Later I learned the complete wording: "We . . . ask that the healing power of God give you many, many more days to teach and to preach and to write and to share with your family and your brothers and sisters in Christ."

Sunday, October 5.
I spent time preparing for leading the common meal part of love feast at Pipe Creek Church of the Brethren. I was much weaker when Ruth and I went to their love feast on Holy Thursday last March, just after her return from Germany. I mentioned that we often give thanks for food, but hardly ever do we give thanks that we feel like eating. When one has gone through longer periods with little or no appetite, however, one doesn't easily take having an appetite for granted. I pointed out that the disciples spent much of their time with Jesus eating with him.

Miriam, Chuck, and Daniel left in the late afternoon.

Monday, October 6.
This afternoon Maren and I looked carefully at all the newly planted trees to identify the ones that had definitely died. With the terrible drought, only

about 21 of the more than 315 have died. We were especially surprised that only three of the red oaks along the lane have died. Several that I thought were dead had put out a little shoot near the ground. I said, "That is really something, their will to live."

Maren said, "You can identify with that."

Wednesday, October 8.

I don't think I've ever before been so delighted before with the smell of the corn from autumn cornfields. Also, the Canada geese are flying again.

Jeremiah 30:17: "For I will restore health to you." That was the Lord's promise to Israel, but I like to think it is directed to me. Whatever comes, such a good measure of increased wholeness has been given me in this time.

I discovered the remarkable passage in Elihu's speech (Job 33:19-30) that begins by depicting someone in extreme suffering. Then "a mediator, one of the thousand," comes and says,

> Deliver him from going down into the Pit,
> I have found a ransom;
> let his flesh become fresh with youth;
> let him return to the days of his youthful vigor.

This mysterious initiative of the mediator leads into the healing. The afflicted person prays to God, is heard and healed. He proceeds to tell others how God has rescued him from death. Jesus fulfilled this obscure image of the mediator whose initiative led to marvelous change.

Tuesday, October 14.

Dr. Jawien returned my call. Reporting on the chest x-rays taken last week, he said the cancer has remained stable and commented, "That is good." I passed the word on to Ruth and Maren in the kitchen.

"We can live with that—literally," Maren said. I'm still hoping that the tumor will be taken away entirely and that some report will show this. But this gift of life day after day and month after month for however long has been and continues to be a marvel of God's goodness.

Thursday, October 16.

I drove to BWI satellite parking and took a United flight to Chicago for the Christian Peacemaker Teams steering committee meeting. Ben Weese, architect and friend since our time together in Brethren Volunteer Service, met me at the airport gate. We had a splendid time together.

The CPT people all received me with great warmth.

Wednesday, October 22.

The (Baltimore) *Sun* today had a front-page story on the collision of
galaxies. How do I think of heaven in relation to the vastness of the
universe? Sometimes, I suppose, as beyond that expanse. But isn't the
"location" of heaven more like that of C. S. Lewis's Narnia, just behind the
entry through the back of the wardrobe? So near, yet inaccessible except by
transition out of our space and time. The unseen realm of Christ's realized
dominion is that near.

At the close of 2 Peter is the phrase "the day of eternity," which gives
intimation of eternity as quite different from time as we experience it. I
believe, though, that Swiss New Testament scholar Oscar Cullmann was
right in concluding that the Bible does not picture eternity as timelessness.
New Testament images depicting the Beyond speak in terms of
successiveness there. Perhaps there will be successiveness without
separation from what has been.

When Warren Hoover, formerly the director of the National Inter-
Religious Service Board for Conscientious Objectors, called to ask me about
preaching in a Washington City Church of the Brethren service, he
mentioned my determination in my illness. I was struck by the word. I would
not apply it to myself in this connection. I would not even say that I have
been determined to stay alive. That is for God to determine. But I have
sought to be very oriented toward continuing to live.

Sunday, October 26.

I preached in the Good Shepherd service today. I had been wondering what
hymn has the image of leaves falling from a tree; I could not recall the
wording. I received the answer when we sang the opening hymn, "Immortal,
invisible, God only wise":

> We blossom and flourish as leaves on the tree,
> and wither and perish, but naught changeth thee.

Monday, October 27.

Much more than previously in my life I am often amused in my solitary
contemplation of things. I often chuckle to myself. When I chuckle without
obvious reason in Ruth's presence, she asks me to explain why.

Tuesday, October 28.

In rereading the early weeks of this journal, I came upon the statement of Dr. Georgiadis in December that once a tumor of this type starts growing again, there is little chance of stopping it; some people want to try various treatments, but very seldom does anything help. In the consultation at the end of my chemo therapy treatments, Dr. Bruce Johnson did not have such a negative viewpoint. But it's important to keep Dr. Georgiadis's perspective in mind.

I cherish the autumn landscapes that I take in from our place. But beyond death, I would infer, I will not be deprived in this regard. God can provide greater splendors of landscape. But I would think that in the interim, while waiting for the consummation, we will feel deprived of some of those we have most dearly loved.

Thursday, October 30.

Psalm 103:3 calls the self to bless the Lord, "who heals all your diseases." I remarked to God that I would be quite content if he healed just the one disease in me. The others I'll be glad to live with.

Saturday and Sunday, November 1-2.

This was another milestone weekend. On Saturday Miriam brought Jana of Perm, Russia, to Washington for language study and a month's internship at the Holocaust Museum. Jana has been active in the group that is working to make a former Soviet concentration camp into a memorial site. Ruth and I met them at the youth hostel.

After supper Ruth, Miriam, and I found our way to the Edgertons' house in Georgetown. They had invited a number of our Sojourners friends for dessert. Jamie said in his prayer before we ate, "We thank you for Dale, this walking miracle." We stayed with the Edgertons overnight. I preached in the Sunday morning service of the Washington City Church of the Brethren.

Tuesday, November 4.

It was a year ago today that I went to Dr. Caricofe with my nagging cough. So it has been a year since we entered into a very different personal era. When one thinks back, 365 days is an amazing expanse of time.

Thursday, November 6.

At bedtime I read a passage in a psalm about praising God for his mighty acts. I got to thinking: I have been so focused on thanking and praising God for extending my life—trying not to be neglectful of that. But I've been giving too little attention to the incomparably greater action of God in Jesus Christ on our behalf.

Friday, November 7.

We have come to another memorable weekend—a trip to Colorado to visit my sister, Ann, and Mike and their daughters, Hopi and Nicole, with their families. The flight out went well. I wore a mask the whole time except for eating. On the way out I read most of Jennifer Haines' book, *Bread and Water: A Spiritual Journey*. It tells of her four and a half years in federal prisons because of protests at the Rocky Flats Nuclear Plant. Ruth had read it soon after Jennifer sent us a copy and was so stirred by it that she wrote a review. But I was in chemo and had not gotten to it before now.

Saturday, November 8.

Ann and Mike's home is as beautiful as ever. I thought a number of times of how my parents loved to go there.

I was stunned to learn that soon after Mike and Ann had sold the Snugli company, the new owners discontinued making the real Snugli baby carrier (deluxe or standard). Nothing even close to the marvelous earlier Snugli, which my mother and Ann had designed and developed, is on the market in this country. Mike and Ann hope to start making the real thing again, but now they need to find a new name. They have the framework for doing this in their company, Air Lift.

Mike prepared a turkey, and we had a sort of Thanksgiving family gathering. Ann and their daughter Hopi both told me that I looked better than I had at Miriam and Chuck's wedding last year. Ann reminded me that she had said to me then, "You don't look well. Are you feeling all right? Or are you just feeling tired from working so hard?"

Ann proposed a toast. With much emotion Mike made a Thanksgiving statement. He closed by saying to me, "We hope you will be able to visit us ten years from now."

I responded, "Make it two years." Nearly all of us were in tears.

Sunday, November 9.

Late this afternoon, Mike and Ann drove us to meet with Jennifer Haines. She was standing "vigil" on the steps of the Catholic Worker house, waiting for us. She took us to her apartment a couple of houses down the street. Jennifer said she had heated it more than otherwise but was afraid it would not be warm enough for us. She apologized for too many things in her place; but what a simple beauty it has in its bareness. On a wall was a cascade of the thousand paper cranes that she had folded in prison. What is she doing now? "Prayer—and that is hard." She mentioned that she would be praying for us. What a gift to have such a person interceding for me.

Monday, November 10.
As we were leaving for the airport, I said to Ann, "I hope I will see your beautiful home again." At the airport I alluded to a sentence in Jennifer's book and said to Ann and Mike, "We have danced in your love."

As Ann embraced me, she said, "I hope to see you again and again and again."

On the return trip, I completed Jennifer's book and started Norman Cousins' *Anatomy of an Illness*, which I had borrowed from Mike and Ann. Cousins views healing in terms of determination of spirit and alternative know-how.

I read a little in Matthew's Gospel, particularly the Matthew 17 story about the disciples' failure to cast the demon out of the boy. Jesus' rebuke seems to give support to the "100 percent faith" approach. I need to struggle with this problem more. Faith to move a mountain: Is it that we are to have boundless expectancy with regard to what God can and will do—but not tell God what to do?

Tuesday, November 11.
Ruth and I met Dave and Jan Cross for the evening meal at a Chinese restaurant. They, especially Jan, still struggle with having lost two of their three children to cystic fibrosis—at 22 and 23. David had won a national chess championship. Karen had studied in Copenhagen. The two lived with great vigor and spirit. How could a loving, all-powerful God allow them to die? I had sent David and Jan a copy of my sermon. They had given it close attention, and we had a deep-moving talk about the issues. Jan wanted to hear more about my sister Jane's death, and I shared some. Now we are in a far better position to understand their spiritual struggle, for we came to know them only after they had lost the two children.

Thursday, November 13.
I drove to Bethesda for my monthly checkup. I've begun wearing heavy socks and taking off my shoes when I drive. That way I can feel the pedals, even with my numb feet. Things went routinely.

After my nap, I dug a trench in what's to be the new flower bed and planted about sixty daffodil bulbs. In digging I came upon a broken piece of plastic, actually the top part of a thermometer. The first half of the "serenity prayer" was still legible: "GOD grant me the SERENITY to accept the things we cannot change; COURAGE to change the . . . ."

Sunday, November 16.
Ruth drove us to the Bethany meetinghouse in Delaware early this morning. I'd been interim pastor of the congregation for a year and a half into the middle of 1996. I preached the sermon, "Matters of Life or Death." The pews were nearly filled. It was a Spirit-filled time of preaching—the best time I've had giving the sermon. It was important to me that the listeners were so deeply involved.

Tuesday, November 18.
Jesus pointed out that a woman after the travail "no longer remembers the anguish, for joy that a child is born into the world" (John 16:21). I see an odd analogy: When a "new lease on life" comes after chemotherapy, one hardly remembers how bad the chemotherapy was, but is so glad for what it has helped bring. Soon after completing the sixth cycle of chemotherapy in July, I no longer had to cope with the side effects.

Jesus warned: to try to save one's life is to lose it; to lose it is to find it. These reversals can be considered in relation to illness. To cling desperately or with vigorous determination to life is not the right way. But one can continue to receive and cherish life as a precious gift, a gift to be held with open hands and heart *and* a readiness to relinquish this gift in exchange for a far better gift. I want to try to do things that help me live and not die. Not to do that would amount to giving up. But I don't want that effort to dominate my life and thought.

Thursday, November 20.
It seems to me the last Brethren national youth conference had the theme "Come to the Edge," with the image of having faith to soar off the edge (of the cliff). For me, having a residual cancerous tumor two and a half inches across in my left lung is living on the edge. And in many ways that is good. If the cancer is not taken away but remains there, stable but ominously poised, that is all right too. It is a constant stimulus for me to keep turning to God.

Zephaniah 3:17 gives this remarkable picture of God: "He will exult over you with loud singing as on a day of festival." I don't think any other passage pictures God as singing. But how right that the one who is the source of all music and singing does indeed sing for joy in the creation. Music resounds in the heart of the one who puts music into the human heart—a three-part harmony. Is the praise of heavenly hosts somewhat antiphonal, echoing the music that evokes it?

Friday, November 21.

After the risen Jesus intimates to Peter something of the manner of his death, the writer adds: "This he said to show by what death he was to glorify God" (John 21:19). Peter died as a martyr, but the death of any Christian is to bring glory to God. Even when death is not anticipated, a Christian should live life giving glory to God.

Since early adulthood I've thought at times that my death might come in some way because of my peace witness or my "radical" living. (In a number of countries I would have been imprisoned or killed for the type of Christian witness I've sought to give.) Now I assume my death will not likely be tied to that aspect of my witness, though my current situation is a context for glorifying God.

The unfaithful servant said, "Master, I knew you to be a hard man, reaping where you did not sow, and gathering where you did not winnow" (Matt. 25:24). God does not sow illness, accident, and death. But from that adversarial sowing, he also reaps and gathers his own harvest.

Sunday, November 23.

This has been another memorable day—another milestone. We drove to the church house in Bethesda where the German Lutheran Church of Washington meets. Being the last Sunday of the church year—*Totensonntag* (Sunday of the Dead), the pastor lit candles for those from the congregation who had died during the church year. It was so good to be in a German Evangelical service, and, as I expected, the worship was very meaningful to Ruth. The lectionary Psalm was 126, our engagement psalm. One of the hymns was *"Wachet auf* [Awake]." We'd given a recording of that Bach cantata to Vater and Mutter (Ruth's parents) at Christmas 1968 before Vater died in January. Though the service was in German, I preached in English on "Matters of Life or Death."

In the coffee time afterward, Frauke recalled that Ruth and our children had first met their family in Kennedy Airport on a return flight from Germany. Some months later the Westphals were picking cherries in Baugher's orchard near Westminster (over an hour from their home in Bethesda).

Ruth and our children were picking from the cherry tree next to them. Through hearing German spoken, the two families rediscovered each other. Ruth went over and asked, "Haven't I seen you before?" That extremely unlikely encounter was the beginning of our friendship. This made me think: Had it not been for that cherry picking in the mid-seventies, I would not have been preaching in this morning service. Had it not been for the cherry picking, I might not be alive, for Frauke was the one we turned to the same day we got the preliminary diagnosis. Heiner pointed me toward the National Cancer Institute lung cancer protocol group and helped open the way for me to get in. The hand of Providence was so clearly in all this.

Later in the day Ruth and I drove to the Kennedy Center to attend a play by Rita Dove, *The Darker Face of the Earth.* We found a handicapped parking spot that didn't cost anything and, because of my condition, got two half-price tickets in the eighth row. Last Christmas I had given Ruth an IOU that I would take her to a play when I got past the chemotherapy. Assuming I'd live to that point. I said to her, "I do come through on my IOUs." But only by the grace of God.

The play and the production were extraordinary—a South Carolina plantation recasting of the Oedipus story. What tremendous vitality there could be in the lives of slaves! It was amazing to reflect on my being there in the Kennedy Center with Ruth—and this, after preaching in the morning. I didn't even get very tired, in spite of not being able to take a nap. The day has been one of brimming thankfulness.

Monday, November 24.
The Apostle Paul focused on the human inclination to think we're right with God when we're not. In the contemporary world, that inclination is certainly operative. But still more humanly characteristic is the belief that, apart from ultimate things, we are self-sufficient. Thus the vast amount of popular literature on self-realization, self-improvement, and the like.

I read Ruth a letter from Charles Klingler, retired English professor in North Manchester, Indiana. In reflecting about death and his own death, he writes, "And of course I would like to leave Susie with less clutter than now exists here." As I expected, Ruth found this an extremely laudable intention, one very worthy of being imitated.

Tuesday, November 25.
Isaiah 12:2: "for the Lord God is my strength and my song." I think I've always read the latter part of this statement and similar ones in the Bible as

meaning that God is the One the person sings about. But the writer is saying more than that: My strength is imparted to me by God; the singing within me—the impulse, the overflowing, the mode and content—is likewise imparted. When a song sung for others is in this way imparted, there is no performance.

Thursday, November 27, Thanksgiving.
When our children were here for Thanksgiving a year ago, I wrote of the pathos that this would likely be our last Thanksgiving all together." But we have all been granted another Thanksgiving Day, even though we aren't gathering as a family.

I helped Ruth prepare a traditional turkey meal. We invited various people, mainly from the Brethren Service Center in New Windsor.

How thankful I am for the year I've been given, for feeling as well as I do, for the love and support of my family, for the garden and the 300 little trees in the meadow, for having time and renewed energy to bear witness out of what I have been through. If I had died in March or July, the sermon/article "Matters of Life or Death"(or "Living with Dying") would not have been written.

Sunday, November 30.
Ruth read aloud from a piece by Bonhöffer, "*Von der Dankbarkeit des Christen* [Christian Thankfulness]." He makes the point that the way one can truly have one's past is through giving thanks for it—and by looking back with *reue*, contrition.

How marvelously full my life has been. I give thanks for various motifs in my life—all the Christian worships, hymns, and sermons I've experienced (also those of my boyhood); all the devotional times; my parents, parental family, and earlier forebears; the inestimable gift of Ruth as my wife and our children; all friends, spiritual mentors, visits, conversations; all hospitality received; the sunrises, sunsets, cloud formations, storms, memorable trees, vistas; all planting and harvesting, food and drink; every house, room, apartment I have lived in; all nights of sleep, naps, and good dreams; all healthy functioning of this body in its incredible intricacy; all travel in safety; the poetry, novels, theological and other books I have read; the lectures, films, art, architecture, music; all the photographic retrospective glimpses into the life that has been mine; my writing, preaching, leadership tasks; all the help and tempering that have come in the hard times; all reconciliations; all reflective insights. Imperfection has run through most of what has come to me. The taint of wrong has been in all my living of life. Yet God's grace, God's giving, has pervaded, encompassed, and directed all. I can reflect with contrition on the identifiable sins that have simply faded into the awareness of the dark streak in me.

Ruth, Daniel, and I went to the Community Mennonite Church service in Lancaster. In the sharing time, a brother referred to the story of a monk to whom it was revealed that he would die the next day. When he mentioned that the monk proceeded with his usual responsibility of tending the monastery garden, Daniel and Ruth smiled at each other. Gardening is, of course, only one dimension of my response to the imminent threat of death.

Daniel went with us to visit Dale and Lois Brown. Dale, a former professor at Bethany Theological Seminary, has been a close friend through many years. In his meal-time prayer he expressed thanks to God for each of our lives.

I have thought about language in relation to life beyond death. The language we think and live in is so much a part of who we are. Does the particularity of language persist into the beyond, at least for a time? The multiplicity of languages came because of human sin (the Tower of Babel story), but they significantly constitute the marvelous variegatedness of humanity. Surely that variegatedness will transcend into one harmony of communication; but will something of that marvel of variety perhaps be retained?

In my teens and twenties, I had such an insatiable desire to take in great stores of information and wisdom. May some of that desire be fulfilled in the life beyond?

Wednesday, December 3.
I've been having some pain in my lower back. It's probably what I've had for some years, though it does feel somewhat different. The pain was worse again yesterday, and today I called Dr. Jawien and explained my condition. After doing some consulting, he called back. They think I should have an MRI of the spine and a total bone scan. He'll let me know when an MRI can be scheduled. If the problem is a growing metastasis, it will be important to start with radiation sooner rather than later.

Thursday, December 4.
Dr. Jawien called soon after 8:30 this morning to tell me that my MRI was scheduled for 1:15 p.m. There was no mention of a bone scan. I prepared some little Christmas gifts to take along for Dr. Jawien, Barb Schuler, and Dr. Braidnaigh.

The MRI must have lasted more than an hour and a half—the longest yet for me. That makes me wonder whether they found some new problem and were checking it out more fully. I thought of the verse, "Be still, and know that I am God" (Ps. 46:10). How motionless one needs to lie. I also got seven or eight spinal x-rays.

I don't have any resilient confidence that the report will be good, and I'm not trying to have that attitude. Ruth is not uptight. With this uncertainty we rejoice still more in how much we have been given during these months.

I've been pondering the assurance given in 1 Thessalonians 5:24, "He who calls you is faithful, and he will do it"—that is, keep your spirit, soul, and body "sound and blameless at the coming of our Lord Jesus Christ" (v. 23). Not that I have the resources within myself for staying true to the end, but God who calls me continues to recreate me toward wholeness.

Friday, December 5.

Today is thirteen months since the diagnosis. I had to wait till after 1:00 p.m. for the call from Dr. Jawien. The findings are basically "good news": the spinal structures are still intact, and there has been no notable growth of alien tissue. The radiologist, reading the pictures from yesterday, was not able to find the ones taken in the summer, so he could not make a comparison regarding the size of the two metastases in the spine. Dr. Jawien was able to find the earlier x-rays, but he is not a specialist in this. So that determination needs to wait till the radiologist is there again at the beginning of the week.

I am glad for the good news, so far as it goes. No grave development was discovered. But we continue to wait for a definitive word as to whether the metastases have grown.

British New Testament scholar C. E. B. Cranfield wrote me that in my book *Reckoning with Apocalypse* government is seen almost entirely as the beast from the abyss. In that book and in *Darkening Valley*, I am explicit in recognizing that there is the positive side to what government, also the U.S. government, does. I do, though, deal centrally with the beast side of government. It is ironical that I've been in and benefitted so much from a life-serving governmental activity—the lung cancer research protocol of the National Cancer Institute. Participating is a way of affirming that side of government. But it remains that such activities, in part, function as a mask for the beast—and quite specifically in this case for the Navy.

Sunday, December 7.

As a Christmas gift the Westphals invited Ruth and me to go with them to hear Bach's *Christmas Oratorio* by the Washington Bach Chorale. We had heard Bach performances by the Chorale before, but probably because of my illness this concert was the most moving one of my life. They gave the entire six cantatas—3:00 to 7:30 p.m., with an intermission.

"Cantata 4: For the Feast of the Circumcision" has a focus on dying, the fear of death, and victory over these through Jesus. Personal devotion to Jesus, even if expressed too effusively at points in the oratorio, needs to be strengthened in contemporary Christianity and in my own life. As I listened, I thought: What an impoverishment, if one cannot hear all this with faith corresponding to that which inspired it.

Bach recognized the inexpressible greatness and majesty of God, and there is the implication that even the best that humans can offer in praise is completely inadequate. I sat thinking of how even more inadequate are the lesser creations and "achievements" we are inclined to take pride in. How preposterous, in view of the majesty of God, are all our attempts to be highly regarded ("great" or "greatest" in the teaching of Jesus). Yet, the other side is that our feeble offerings can be pleasing to God.

Frauke said to us, "Today is Christmas for me." I felt the same thing.

After returning home Ruth said, "When I hear it later on, I will always remember."

Wednesday, December 10.

In order to make Ruth a scrapbook, I was going over my early letters to her, from the very first one. To get back in touch with what I felt and expressed to her in those years before we married was a delight and a fanning of the flame of my love for her now. Married couples should do more returning to evidence and testimonials of their earlier love. To keep in touch with such fullness of loving relationship can give sustenance through barren stretches.

Saturday, December 13.

This is Ruth's birthday. She has told me a number of times, "You are the biggest gift."

Daniel arrived from Lancaster in time for a late lunch. For the birthday he brought a many-pointed Moravian star, suited for hanging outside under the porch roof. At about the same time, a man and his son came with a backhoe to dig the trench for the garage foundation. That too in a way is a birthday present for Ruth. We have been considering for months if and when to begin such a project. She has wanted a garage, especially with the prospect of being left alone on this place, and it seems good to try to get it built while I'm still alive to supervise.

After my nap the three of us had Ruth's birthday celebration. We had devotions, Ruth opened gifts, and Maren called. I had found a poem "December 13, 1942" (referring to the day Ruth was born), that I had written for Ruth perhaps a year or so after Daniel was born. I read that and the journal entry for this day last year.

A little later as Daniel and I were walking away from the garage trench, Daniel said, "There is always something going on in the Aukerman household."

I said, "I'm not just moping around, waiting to die."

Late in the afternoon Ruth, Daniel, and I walked out the lane to get the mail. A lone, honking goose was flying west toward the sunset. Its solitariness seemed strange. Ruth said, "That's the way I'll be," and we laughed.

In the evening the three of us watched a video that included several segments of the talk that actor Don Murray gave at the Long Beach Annual Conference last July. In one segment Don tells of the project we worked on in 1954–55 when he and I planned to walk across the Soviet Union to Moscow as an effort toward friendship between the two nations. Actually Don had invited me to join him. We had gone to the Soviet Embassy in Vienna but were not able to get any response after that.

Miriam's past human rights assignments in Russia and her decision to start law school this past fall in the hope of continuing in that type of work are a sort of continuation of that long ago project and my efforts through decades to change attitudes toward Russians.

Monday, December 15.

Last evening I read Ruth the meditation for the day from a devotional booklet. The scripture was John 11:1-15. As I was reading it, Ruth pointed to the special relevance of Jesus' comments about the sickness of Lazarus: "This illness is not unto death; it is for the glory of God, so that the Son of God may be glorified by means of it" (v. 4). This morning I was meditating on that verse. It seems this illness has been for the glory of God and Christ. Accident or disease can bring death very abruptly, and the dying may seem to have little within it that would point to the glory of God. In circumstances like mine, what is critically important is not really whether the illness is "unto death" ("terminal" we would say), but whether the life being lived over against the disease points to the grace and goodness of God.

The passage also includes the dimension of Jesus waiting, and his waiting brought greater glory to God. There could be that sort of waiting in relation to healing of the cancer in me. But when a person's health declines significantly, it may mean that God will not restore health to give rescue from death.

My meditation was interrupted by a call from Dr. Jawien. He had tried to reach me on Friday and again yesterday, but without success. Because he had not gotten back to me within a week and a half, I had assumed that no new problem had been found. The radiologist on Friday had given his assessment that the two metastases in the lower spine have increased some in size. This means that I need radiation for those areas. But Dr. Jawien explained that the research doctors there decided this would not be within what is provided by the NCI protocol I am in. So I need to find a "civilian" radiation oncologist.

Suddenly I became a full-fledged patient again and spent much of the rest of the morning and the afternoon in telephone calls, the first being to Frauke Westphal. Frauke recommended that I go with the Georgetown University Radiation Medicine group. They have a center in Frederick. Frauke also suggested that chest x-rays would probably be needed for determining what is happening currently in the lung. Gradually things came into focus. I have an appointment on Wednesday with Dr. K. C. Lee, a radiation oncologist in Frederick.

This bad news brought another sudden reorientation: "time's winged chariot hurrying near." If the cancer in the spine is growing, it may be growing in the lung or elsewhere. But soon I felt a steadying peace about it all: "Thou dost keep him in perfect peace . . ." (Isa. 23:3).

Wednesday, December 17.

I had my appointment with the radiation oncologist. Dr. Lee said that it is not urgent to go ahead right away with the radiation of the lower spine. I can do that, or I can wait until the symptoms get worse. I can hardly see advantages in waiting, but I can see a number of reasons for going ahead; and that is what I asked for. I need to go back on Friday afternoon for the "simulation," that is, getting set up for exactly how the radiation is to be done. I will need ten to fourteen treatments.

I also went to a facility nearby for chest x-rays. The radiologist did the comparison with the November x-rays. I was able to take the x-rays along with me, but the report was not ready, so we do not know what has been happening in the lungs.

When we called Frauke later, she was emphatic that going ahead now rather than later is certainly the thing to do.

Back home here the cement truck pulled in with cement for the footers for the garage. I am so glad I can do this sort of overseeing.

Thursday, December 18.

The January-February issue of *Sojourners* came yesterday. It only occurred to me this morning that my article might be in it. I checked and it was—with the better title, "The Heart of Faith." This was like a Christmas gift—that I could live to see the wider publication of the first article I had written after the diagnosis.

In each of us there is the drive to be seen as the best. We are always making comparisons. But good parents try not to compare their children, and they seek to discourage their children from engaging in such comparisons. Each child is uniquely constituted and gifted; there is so much to esteem and cherish. Should it not be the same for us as children of God?

Saturday, December 20.

A little after 8:00 a.m., I called Dr. Caricofe's office to ask whether they had received the report from Wednesday's chest x-rays. They had, and the receptionist faxed it to me. Ruth pulled it from the machine, and we read, yes, the tumor in the lung has remained stable. To receive this word was a welcome gift for the day. While I was being prepared for the radiation treatments yesterday, I prayed that we would not need to deal right now with growth in the tumor on the lung.

We picked up Maren at the airport. She had a terrible cold and felt still more miserable from a flight that began somewhat after 2:00 a.m. this morning. Since the diagnosis I have been so blessed with protection against respiratory infections, but it's always a strain when a family member in the house carries an infection.

Sunday, December 21.

Ruth woke up with a cold. I felt somewhat down, with the others in the house having colds. In the early part of the Westminster Brethren worship, I didn't feel much like worshiping, but Scott Duffey's preaching gradually drew me in.

Monday, December 22.

The promise that stood out this morning was from John 16:23-24: "Truly, truly, I say to you, if you ask anything of the Father, he will give it to you in my name. . . . ask, and you will receive." I should perhaps be less reserved and more importunate in asking for healing—more like that widow in the parable (Luke 18:1-8). But I want to ask in terms of what is for the glory of God. I don't want to tell God what needs to be done.

I was thinking of the promise in John 16, when I received the first of fourteen radiation treatments this afternoon for the metastases in my lower spine.

Tuesday, December 23.

Last year we bought a balled Norway spruce. Ruth was hesitant about digging it up again this year lest the stress kill it, but late this afternoon Ruth and Maren, with my supervision, dug the four-and-a-half-foot-high tree and wrapped the ball in burlap. The light was fading as we finished. I stood in the dusk, happy that we had been able to accomplish this.

When people drive in here now, they typically comment on the piles of dirt and the trenches for the garage foundation. I usually respond, "Ruth wanted a garage." Maren told me that Ruth in a comparable exchange with our friend Fran Nyce said, "Dale wanted me to have a garage." Maren remarked to me, "The statements are not contradictory. They fit together."

Wednesday, December 24, Christmas Eve.

Miriam and Chuck are with his family on their Minnesota farm. In the early afternoon I went for a radiation treatment. After that I was feeling quite tired and on the edge of being sick. Jefrey Wright, a son of our friends Wilbur and Sandy, came, and he and Daniel brought in the Christmas tree. Maren and Daniel decorated it.

As the four of us sat down for our traditional Christmas Eve seafood meal, I was overcome by emotion—thankful for living to another Christmas, for the beauty of the time, for my family, and yet feeling the pathos that this may be our last Christmas together. I barely brought out the words "Let's sing." Ruth led so rightly in "Joy to the World": "He comes to make his blessings flow / far as the curse is found." The dark curse intrudes into my body, but those blessings encompass it. I was choked up, with tears running down my face. Ruth asked me, "Are you all right? Are you nauseated?" The rest of us burst out laughing. The question brought comic relief.

We went to a beautiful service in the Union Bridge Brethren meetinghouse. As I received the bread-and-cup communion, I thought of God's healing grace in my body. I also thought of how my sister Jane, on the way home from her baptism a few weeks before she died at fourteen, said, "I'm a new me, but I still have my lump."

Back home here we lit the candles on the Christmas tree. The points of candlelight were mirrored in the nearby window. On the porch the Moravian star was shining. I read several scriptures. We sang German and English carols. I was doing pretty well until I read "A Song for Simeon" by T. S. Eliot. I came to the lines:

> Let the Infant, the still unspeaking and unspoken Word,
> Grant Israel's consolation
> To one who has eighty years and no to-morrow.

Thursday, December 25, Christmas Day.
This morning while Ruth and I were still in bed. Ruth said, "Even when I gave you the *Strohkrippe* [triptych manger scene she had made of pressed straw], I prayed that God would give me this man, and now I pray that he will give him to me somewhat longer." That was Christmas 1961. She was not quite nineteen when she sent me this first and quite astounding gift.

We began opening gifts. With a huge expenditure of time and effort, Ruth had undertaken the project of framing pictures of seventeen ancestral couples on both sides of the family—a set for us and a set for each of the children. She had completed only four from each set, but this was her amazing gift. Bill and Janet Heltzel drove in, bringing a gift basket for us. Ruth had asked Bill to make the square frames. They couldn't find suitable strips, but Janet discovered a stack of parquet flooring squares, and Bill disassembled them to make about seventy frames. This was our opportunity to express our heartiest thanks to Bill.

Drawing from old files, I had created for each of the children an album of "ancestral voices"—a variety of written things having to do with my parents, grandparents, and earlier generations. For Ruth I had created an album of selected letters I had sent to her, along with the few poems I had written for her.

Mid-afternoon we celebrated Daniel's birthday—one day early. After supper we lit the Christmas tree and sang. Then Daniel headed back to Lancaster for his work as a medical resident.

Friday, December 26.

Paul Grout called from Vermont. At the close he said, "I always pray for you.
I never forget to pray for you." He said it so simply and tenderly. How can I
thank such an intercessor enough or be thankful enough for such a one?
And there are so many.

Saturday, December 27.

We had lunch at Daniel's apartment before taking Daniel and Maren to the
Philadelphia Airport for their flight to Germany to be part of the eightieth
birthday celebration for Tante Anna, the friend of Ruth's mother, who
became like another grandmother to the children. We also picked up
Miriam, who was flying in from Christmas with the Pazderniks in Minnesota.
When Miriam arrived, it was a glad reunion—the five of us together again.
When we found ourselves alone in an elevator, we gave a triumphant shout.
Then Maren and Daniel headed for their boarding.

   I thought of how my father would say in his decline, "I would not have
missed that for anything," or "I loved every minute of it."

Tuesday, December 30.

Miriam tells me that her American friends often respond that I am
relatively young to be stricken by something like this, but her Russian
friends never have that reaction. The median survival age for Russian males
is so much lower than in this country.

   For a couple of mornings, I have been meditating on the Bartimaeus
story in Mark 10:46-52. Bartimaeus cries out, "Jesus, Son of David, have
mercy on me!"—a good cry to echo. Jesus asks Bartimaeus, "What do you
want me to do for you?" and Bartimaeus replies, "Master, let me receive my
sight" (my words: "Master, let me be healed"). His was not "100 percent
faith" that he would be healed but rather vibrant, abounding expectancy
in looking to Jesus for what Jesus would do. In relation to my illness,
our looking to Jesus has brought marvels of grace. We should be
expectant of further marvels, whether in the form of full healing of the
cancer or otherwise.

   Ruth and Miriam took me to Frederick for the radiation treatment, the
fifth of fourteen. I asked the therapist if they could come in to see the setup.
Miriam found out that the machine that gives the radiation cost nearly
$1,000,000 eight years ago. On an average day, they treat more than thirty
patients with it.

Wednesday, December 31.

Miriam, Ruth, and I were the trio for New Year's Eve. We received a call from Germany just after midnight and talked with Tante Anna and the others still with her on the eightieth birthday celebration. I read a little from my journal entries a year ago and from the album of poems and letters to Ruth. We sang in front of the lighted tree.

1998

Thursday, January 1.

Miriam caught a ride with friends to New York City. Heiner and Frauke Westphal came for the noon meal with us. Just before they left, Frauke found in my big packet a chest x-ray from last January and held it up next to the one taken two weeks ago. She spoke of "the monstrous tumor" earlier and the quite remarkable decrease in size.

Late in the evening Ruth and I sat in front of the tree, with the candles lit for the last time. We did not sing, but simply cherished the time.

Sunday, January 4.

Today marks fourteen months since those momentous chest x-rays, and today I preached in the Westminster Brethren service. When I was told I would need radiation treatments, there was some doubt as to whether I would be able to preach. What a blessing and a gift that I could. Scott Duffey, the pastor at Westminster, introduced the service to the radio audience right at the start. My voice was weak and somewhat hoarse when I began, but it became stronger and held out.

I don't recall ever hearing a sermon by someone whose medical prognosis gave only a short time to live. Ordinarily there is too much of a physical decline for that. Nothing in my experience has been comparable to being enabled to preach in the power of the Spirit, with the authority of the word of God impinging and those listening caught up together in the good news. But all is a gift—to still be alive and able to preach.

Throughout my life I have been too reserved about speaking simply of what God has done for me. Strange that the readiness for doing this should be so strong in this phase of my life.

Monday, January 5.

I pondered the story about Jesus healing the blind man outside Bethsaida (Mark 8:22-26). How beautiful to picture Jesus leading the blind man out of the village. He may have been vibrant with expectancy or just puzzled and

89

compliant, we don't know. That Jesus then spat upon the eyes of the blind man (if we really visualize this) may go a little against our sensibilities. But that, like the resting of Jesus' hands on him, was a physical communication of wholeness. Full healing did not come instantaneously. First the man saw others "like trees, walking." Jesus laid his hands directly on the man's eyes. "He looked intently" and could then see with complete clarity.

Driving back from the radiation treatment, I noticed the message outside a furniture store: "Free interest until 2000." Only then did I realize that the beginning of the year 2000 is less than two years off. Born in 1930, I have, even from boyhood I think, felt a certain personal orientation and expectancy toward the year 2000 and the prospect of living to be seventy (or sixty-nine and a half).

Tuesday, January 6.

As I drove back from the radiation treatment, I was gazing at the bare trees and shrubs near the road and mentally embracing them in their individuality. They each praise God by simply being what they are.

Thursday, January 8.

If I would be given full healing from the cancer, that would clearly be a miracle of God and something very much for the glory of God. But the thought came to me: The sermon—my preaching it, sharing it otherwise, and having it published—is something clearly for the glory of God. And there is the marvel of God acting in all this. The sermon/article and my witness during this time may be of more significance than a full healing would be.

Friday, January 9.

A wooden carving of a seated Kenyan beggar, Daniel's Christmas gift to me, is now on a stool next to the door into the addition room where I have my devotions and write. As I walk past him, I am reminded of my appropriate status before God.

After lunch I was talking with Miriam, who arrived yesterday, and taking my vitamins at the same time. I must have swallowed a long one without any liquid. It became lodged at my windpipe. After coughing quite desperately for maybe thirty seconds, I finally dislodged the tablet. Miriam and I were very aware that people can choke to death. We had each seen charts about what to do, but she couldn't remember anything, and all I could do was cough. She said that when I tried to talk immediately afterward, my voice

sounded more like my father's in the last weeks of his life. The experience
was a sobering reminder of how varied the threats to life are.

Saturday, January 10.
Bill Weishaar, the mason working for us, was able to complete the concrete
block foundation for the garage today.

Ruth suggested driving to Catoctin State Park to hike in the mountains.
Instead, Ruth, Miriam, and I took a walk to the end of Stem Road. When we
turned and headed back, Miriam said, "Catoctin is good; but for us who live
here, Stem Road is good too."

Sunday, January 11.
Scott Duffey announced in worship this morning that the North Manchester
(Indiana) Church of the Brethren meetinghouse had been destroyed by fire.
This evening we called Charles and Susie Klingler and felt more deeply the
pathos of that destruction. In the night a defective gas water heater had
become a huge torch. It made me think of the post-war hulks of bombed out
cathedrals in Germany, especially in Kassel, and the Allies in World War II
who carried out these obliteration bombings. Even the fire destruction of
one well-loved building is such a loss.

Tuesday, January 13.
Today I had the fourteenth and last radiation treatment for the lower spine.
Even though these have not severely affected the way I feel, my queasiness
and fatigue today have been somewhat worse than earlier. It's a relief to
have the treatments behind me.

Wednesday, January 14.
I drove to the clinic in the Naval Hospital for my monthly checkup. After the
routine physical, Dr. Braidnaigh and Barb Schuler came in. Dr. Braidnaigh
told me that because there had been progression of disease, I am no longer
to be in the study. I will need to find a private oncologist to take over
monthly checkups. At whatever point the tumor on the lung starts growing
again, I can check with them about other experimental NCI research
studies that I might possibly enter.

As I was bidding them goodbye, I expressed my thanks and said, "Things
have worked together so that I've had much more time than at first seemed
possible."

Barb Schuler said, "And we hope for much more time for you."

I had a strange feeling as we left the hospital. I had been so uneasy there at first because it was a naval hospital. But the treatments and care I received through the NCI protocol study group are very likely the reason I have lived this long.

Thursday, January 15.
In the afternoon Barb Schuler called with word that yesterday's chest x-rays showed the tumor has remained stable. Ruth came to me from the other phone: "Isn't that wonderful!" She had tears in her eyes. She had been quite worried.

I've been meditating on healing stories in the Book of Acts. Acts 9:33 ff. tells that Peter in Lydda "found a man named Aeneas, who had been bedridden for eight years and was paralyzed. And Peter said to him, 'Aeneas, Jesus Christ heals you; rise and make your bed.' " Peter does not give a command for healing about to happen but describes Jesus' act.

In the "100 percent faith" approach, one seeks total certainty that healing will be given. This is usually based on the assumption that God always wills healing and only human lack of faith stands in the way. Peter, in speaking to Aeneas, had complete faith and certainty; but God gave him that, and he needed only to proceed in it. This possibility also exists in our time, but there is the great danger of human presumption.

Saturday, January 17.
In the evening Ruth lay on the sofa, and I read to her from the album of letters that I'd given her for Christmas. Several of the statements, even before we realized that God had meant us for one another, were like prophecies of what God has done for us through the many years of our marriage.

Sunday, January 18.
I've thought of God's healing power in relation to my radiation treatments. As the radiation was aimed at the invaders in my body, so I pray that God's healing power will work against the bridgeheads of death in my body.

I was stirred by the bread-and-cup communion in the Westminster service this morning. I pray that the elements may be a physical medium for the coming of God's healing.

Monday, January 19.
On our walk this morning Ruth said, "I woke up thinking how rich I am with all those wonderful letters." In the evening she worked on framing more

ancestral photos. She said that when she looks at them, she sometimes thinks of the biblical concept of being gathered to one's fathers. I read to Ruth from things in my journal about several September days in Kassel, Germany, not long after she and I had met in the peace seminar in the summer of 1961. She was 18. We spoke of the Shannon airliner crash. The plane was filled with German agriculturalists, a number of them acquaintances of her father. Ruth said, "How would one feel in that last second? I am afraid I would not think about God."

Ruth had asked me, "*Betest du für deine Todesstunde*? [Do you pray about the hour of your death?]" Her question was an important reminder then; and now when I read it again, it's a helpful prod. I am very aware that my death may be quite near. In the New Testament understanding of the final judgment, I believe that all one's life is weighed and assessed. The time just preceding death can become of overriding importance for someone like the penitent robber on the cross next to Jesus. Or there is the possibility that one's faith may be cast away in that time. But I can't think of indications in the New Testament that Christians should focus on what their concluding thoughts or state of mind might be. What is crucial is to live out of the command of the Risen Christ: "Be faithful unto death" (Rev. 2:10). Perhaps I should say an occasional prayer with regard to how I live the last hour or the last conscious hour. To live prayerfully with the end in view moves one rightly toward it.

I read a letter I sent to Ruth in Kassel, written in Glasgow, Scotland, and dated June 10, 1962—shortly before she was to leave for a year in Brethren Volunteer Service in the United States. The letter speaks to us in our present situation.

Dear Ruth,

I suppose today is your last full Sunday with your family and congregation before you leave.

In any such parting we live through a little eschatology. The last week brings its series of lasts. Then the final day: final awaking, final breakfast with the family, final lunch, final everything. Only in parting can God show us how deeply we are bound to each other.

Each Christian parting echoes the Ascension; each reuniting, His parousia. Each coming together again is a prefiguring of the koinonia at the End. And because He, parted, is with us, we need not be far from any of His.

The year will soon be past—and this life. He has us rehearse
for separation and Reuniting.

Dale

Tuesday, January 20.

I have come across a very relevant verse, Acts 12:5: "While Peter was kept in
prison, the church prayed fervently to God for him." My lexicon gives the
cluster of meanings for the Greek adverb *ektenos*—"eagerly, fervently,
constantly." (Ironically, though, the gathered disciples couldn't believe it
when Peter was miraculously freed from prison.) Luke 22:44 has a
comparative form: "In his anguish [in Gethsemane Jesus] prayed more
earnestly." My intercession should be much more eager, fervent, constant—
not plodding and routine as it typically is. What a gift when intercession for
me is fervent. But right alongside what should be, and easily displacing it, is
religious hype in praying.

Wednesday, January 21.

In the last chapter of Acts, Paul cures the father of Publius on the island
of Malta. "And when this had taken place, the rest of the people on the
island who had diseases also came and were cured" (28:9). The gospels
picture many similar scenes. This near the close of the Book of Acts is the
last New Testament account of such full vanquishing of disease in a
multitude of people.

Some churches teach that God wills the same sweeping defeat of disease
for our time that Jesus and the apostles carried out—if only we have the
faith required. To my knowledge, they have only limited success.

Jesus sent out the twelve apostles with the command: "Heal the sick,
raise the dead, cleanse lepers, cast out demons" (Matt. 10:8). Jesus also told
the disciples of John the Baptist to report to him that "the dead are raised
up" (Matt. 11:5). The groups who give their main attention to healing of the
sick by faith do not, I think, give comparable or indeed any significant
attention to the command "raise the dead." When Jesus was present and
his authority was right there with them, raising the dead was a natural
consequence. However, raising of the dead has not in any distinguishing way
been part of the life and ministry of the post-apostolic church of any period.

Our knowing and our telling of God's truth is "only in part" (1 Cor. 13:9),
and so too, even more obviously is healing through faith. But the completion
of healing, the consummation of what Jesus initiated in the midst of those
multitudes, is soon to come.

Thursday, January 22.

I was thinking about Romans 8:28. Since the diagnosis I have focused on later verses in that chapter but hardly on this one. The Revised Standard Version has: "We know that in everything God works for good with those who love him, who are called according to his purpose." I've preferred that reading to translations along the line that "everything works together for good." Ancient manuscripts have the different readings.

I turned to C. E. B. Cranfield's commentary. He presents a convincing case against the reading "God works." He gives the translation: "And we know that all things prove advantageous for their true good to those who love God, that is, to those who are called according to his purpose." In the subordinate clause of the Greek text "those who love God" is given emphasis by being placed first. For them what is said holds true. Cranfield writes: "The love to God, which is commanded in Scripture, is nothing less than the response of a man in the totality of his being to the prior love of God." That prior love is pointed to in the phrase about their being called. In the wider context Paul is considering "the sufferings of this present time" (v. 18) and things like persecution inflicted by enemies (vv. 35-36). Within the controlling sovereignty of God, such things have their significance for the deepest spiritual good of those who love him.

"All things work together for good" can seem like a bland pious optimism, but that meaning is not in the text. The cancer in me is an insurgent power not put there by God. Yet within God's overruling, the cancer is made to serve the good God intends for me. When I was pushed out of my pastoral work in 1972, that was surely not what God wanted. Yet God used it for our tempering then and for opening the way into the further course of our lives. (One can, though, easily think of various things, such as sexual abuse of children, that are terribly hard to bring within this understanding. Perhaps there is much that would not come within "all things" Paul had in view. Cranfield notes that whether the sins of Christians are within the "all things" has been discussed since the period of the early church fathers.)

Sunday, January 25.

For months a Baltimore friend, Doris Ridenour, has been working to get Charles Marsh and me together. He is a young theology professor at Loyola College in Baltimore, who has published two significant books, *Reclaiming Dietrich Bonhöffer* (Oxford University Press) and *God's Long Summer: Stories of Faith and Civil Rights* (Princeton University Press). When Doris called to tell us that Charles Marsh would be preaching in today's service at Baltimore's Episcopal Cathedral, Ruth and I decided we would go.

The service had a Martin Luther King/civil rights slant. We sang the South African song, "We Are Marching in the Light of God," which was also used as the postlude. In the sermon Charles Marsh told the story of Fannie Lou Hamer, Mississippi sharecropper, who became a civil rights leader. I told Ruth afterward that the service was the most beautiful Episcopal service I could remember. Perhaps because of my condition, I was especially receptive and responsive to the service and to the blessing of the communion. "We Are Marching" keeps echoing in my spirit.

Charles Marsh had a forum discussion afterward and then came to Doris's for lunch with us. As Doris had anticipated, we had so much to talk about, ranging from Marsh's growing up in the South as the son of a progressive Southern Baptist pastor to my experience with Ronnie Dunkins on death row. I also brought a copy of a page of notes I'd taken in August 1960 after a conversation with French theologian Jean Lasserre about his friendship with Dietrich Bonhöffer. Charles asked whether he might submit this to the Bonhöffer Society for putting in the archives. It was a lively and enlivening afternoon.

Monday, February 2.

A few days ago I sent a letter to Gordon and Mary Cosby of the Church of the Savior in Washington, D.C. I had been wanting to express thanks to them for how much their ministry and witness have meant to me. I enclosed a copy of my sermon "Living with Dying." Today a beautiful letter came from Mary: "The sermon which you shared with us has meant more than we can say. Really helpful sermons probably always come out of 'hard times.' . . . We are finding it personally helpful, and also to those in our community who find it 'where they are'. . . .

I am feeling a little better, but am still partly incapacitated by the flu that I picked up from Ruth last week.

Wednesday, February 4.

Paul Grout was here from lunch till after supper. Even though I was quite tired, we had a really good visit. He said, "I wouldn't at all want for you what you have. But God has made such amazing use of it for the good of the church. You are the only one who could write what you did. People have seen you so much as a peace and justice person, and now you are there dealing so clearly with the whole of the faith."

Before he left, I sat in a rocking chair, Paul and Ruth knelt beside me, and Paul laid hands on me and had prayer. As he squeezed his fingers lightly, I thought of myself as clay in the hands of a potter, ready to be molded for use. He prayed for my healing. I sat for a considerable period afterward thinking about the prayer time.

Monday, February 9.

In November I had sent the sermon/article, "Matters of Life or Death," to *Messenger*, the magazine of the Church of the Brethren. Today a letter came from Fletcher Farrar, the new editor, stating that the article will be used in the April issue. I had suggested that timing because of the resurrection focus. I'm very thankful for this development. I see the piece as a legacy, a testament, to share with the church.

Tuesday, February 10.

After school today Ruth hung our set of seventeen ancestral pictures on the northeast corner wall of the dining room, four rows of four and one above. This was my Christmas gift from her. The huge project is complete—also the children's sets.

Friday, February 13.

I turned to Cranfield's translation of Romans 14:8 (in his commentary): "for, if we live, it is to the Lord that we live, and, if we die, it is to the Lord that we die. Whether we live, then, or die, it is to the Lord that we belong." He comments: "all Christians live 'to the Lord,' that is, they live with the object of pleasing Christ, they seek to use their lives in His service, and, when it comes to dying, they glorify Him by committing themselves to His keeping."

Ruth said, "It is so clearly a miracle that I still have you. But for anyone to have any loved person is so much a miracle." For me to have her, for us to have each of the children, is also a marvel of God's grace.

Wednesday, February 18.

I went to Westminster yesterday for chest x-rays. I received each telephone call that came today thinking it might be Dr. Caricofe calling about the report—whether the tumor in the lung has grown or not. I was trying to feel at peace about what might come, but was somewhat uneasy each time I thought I might be at the point of finding out.

In the evening Miriam reported with great excitement that she has been offered a job for the summer. She had been in touch with a woman from the

Lawyers' Committee for Human Rights; she asked Miriam to come by to talk, and then she offered her the job. They are working toward a summer project of assessing the need for human rights work in Belarus and possibly Armenia and Azerbaijan. Miriam would travel to meet with human rights groups in those countries. On the Committee's side, certain things still need to be worked out. For Miriam there is, of course, the big question as to whether my health will remain stable enough for her to feel free to go.

Thursday, February 19.

My sister Jane died of cancer forty-two years ago today.

Still waiting for the x-ray report, I read several New Testament passages and then decided I needed a psalm. I opened my Bible, and Psalm 31 was in front of me as a special gift for the day: "My times are in thy hand. . . . save me in thy steadfast love! . . . Be strong, and let your heart take courage" (vv. 15, 16, 24). When I called Dr. Caricofe's office a little later, they were able to fax the report to me. As I pulled up the page coming out of the fax machine, my eyes fell on the words "mass that has not changed significantly in size." Wonderful news yet again.

It does, though, seem likely that the cancer will start growing and spreading before long. Ruth and I were able to make an appointment with a Johns Hopkins lung oncologist, Dr. Leon Hwang, for next Wednesday afternoon.

Friday, February 20.

This afternoon Ken Koons and Scott Blanchard, the city editor of the *Carroll County Times*, came to talk with me. Ken has taken a great many photographs of me. Scott would like to write a series of accompanying articles. The interview today was primarily a get-acquainted time.

Before they left, Ken asked about handles for my burial box: Should they be iron or rope? I said that iron seems extravagant, and rope would be fine. Ken explained that an old-time method was to drill two holes for each handle, braid strands into a short piece of rope, and insert it. That sounded good to me.

Time is running out for me. (Jesus had a sense that time was running out for him to finish his work on earth.) But strikingly, earthly time is running out for God in relation to me. As with the disciples in his earthly ministry, Jesus still has so much to show us in the little time remaining for each of us. But with the end, God's relation to the creature shifts into transfigured time.

Saturday, February 21.

I told Ruth about the rope coffin handles. She became concerned as to whether there would be enough pallbearers in a graveside service mainly with the family. We talked some about who in the immediate family and otherwise might be pallbearers. I did not feel ready or inclined to deal with that just yet. I commented as I had at times in the first months, "We need to keep in mind that God may still give complete healing."

Ruth replied, "It becomes harder to do that." For me too it has become harder, but the possibility is still there.

I have been assuming that if I start going downhill, there will be time for departure instructions and planning. Yet there is always the possibility that I could die quite suddenly.

Sunday, February 22.

In the worship service today, Luke 6:17-26 was read. I was struck by something I may never have really noticed before. The astounding message about radical discipleship in "the Sermon on the Plain" has an astounding scene of healing: "a great multitude of people . . . came to hear him and to be healed of their diseases; and those who were troubled with unclean spirits were cured. And all the crowd sought to touch him, for power came forth from him and healed them all."

Ash Wednesday, February 25.

This afternoon Ruth and I drove to a Johns Hopkins satellite oncology center at the north edge of Baltimore for an appointment with Dr. Leon Hwang. We laid out our situation. He sought to be nondirective. He said that much depends on the personality type. His mother does not like to go to a doctor or be stuck with a needle; she takes what comes. Others are very aggressive and quite determined to do what can be done to hit the cancer. We said that I'm in between.

He made it clear that several months' extension of life would be about as much as could be expected in a good response from any second-line chemotherapy. He said I could enter one of Johns Hopkins' many Phase 1 studies, all very experimental. Of standard therapies he pointed to gemcitabine. It would be given by infusion once a week and does not ordinarily cause much in the way of side effects. It stops the advance of the cancer in 10-15 percent of cases.

The consultation helped us think about options.

When we reported to Daniel this evening, he responded, "God really is the One who gives longer life. More chemotherapy would work against the cancer. But your body is working against the cancer. Your spirit and your faith are working against the cancer."

Thursday, February 26.

I slept very well, better than for several nights. Ruth did too. We feel so much peace about what seems to be emerging. I can continue my present routine and hope the cancer remains stable for quite a while. We rejoice in each good day that God gives. We might turn to the gemcitabine treatment or conceivably some Phase 1 study later on.

In the middle of the evening, Ruth made some soup. She told me left-over things she had put into it, then added, "And my love is in it." But at exactly the same time I chimed in with, "All your love is in it." A couple of days ago when we reflected on a dessert she had concocted, we said simultaneously, "That was sort of Frenchy." We are given these casual intimations of how deeply joined our minds are.

Friday, February 27.

Ruth and I saw the first robins this morning.

We all crave human approval. But a high approval rate is insignificant compared to our worth to God: What we are and do has significance for God in working out his eternal purposes; God values each of us and our contributions. Thus, in the teaching of the New Testament, we are to seek to please God. There is that amazing possibility, compared to which human acclaim is nothing.

I read several poems by the seventeenth-century poet Henry Vaughan. From "The dawning," I had taken as epigraph for *Reckoning with Apocalypse*:

> Or will thy all-surprising light
> Break at midnight?

In "Ascension hymn" Vaughan points to what will be:

> He [Christ] alone,
> And none else, can
> Bring bone to bone
> and rebuild man,
> And by his all-subduing might,
> Make clay ascend more quick than light.

Saturday, February 28.

This evening we talked with my second cousin, David Miller, who is an oncologist in New Jersey. When cancer seems to be stable in his patients, he recommends that they wait—just as we have decided to do. He said that the side effects of gemcitabine are usually mild. He mentioned that he prays for me daily. His counsel was a helpful confirmation of the direction we have chosen.

Sunday, March 1.

I was thinking about the glorious appearing of Christ. If we take Jesus' command seriously to always be watching for this, we know that it could come at any time. But the present is not a period of obvious worldwide upheaval and cataclysm, which is foretold in scripture as prelude. However, "the day of the Lord will come like a thief in the night. When people say, 'There is peace and security,' then sudden destruction will come upon them as travail comes upon a woman with child" (1 Thess. 5:2-3). But it is extremely unlikely that the End will come before my end.

Thursday, March 5.

Today is sixteen months since the diagnosis. Ruth pointed out that this is four times as long as the median survival expectancy I learned about in the early weeks. Though we hope and pray for a continuation of what I am being given, the cancer might start growing again at any time, and the survival expectancy could abruptly become shorter than it had been in the initial period.

Saturday, March 7.

The penitent robber on the cross says to the surly one, "for we are receiving the due reward of our deeds; but this man has done nothing wrong" (Luke 23:41). We should also recognize that in our dying it is our sin that has brought this that comes upon us. God in Jesus Christ graciously overcomes one's sin and death. The way out is brought by the death of the One who did no wrong. The penitent robber experienced that. "For the wages of sin is death, but the free gift of God is eternal life in Christ Jesus our Lord" (Rom. 6:23).

Sunday, March 8.

Another letter has come from a friend in my Brethren Volunteer Service training unit in 1952. He also has cancer. He was a peace activist type, who several years ago became a zealous fundamentalist. He is very concerned that I am not saved and that he will not see me "on the other side." I appreciate the love behind his concern. I had sent him a couple of pieces of mine in which I express my faith; but it seems I'm not within his guidelines. In writing him today I again made the point that right-wing churches typically deny much of what Christ has revealed to us. I pointed to the parable of the Unforgiving Servant (Matt. 18:23-35) as having implications for political attitudes. Perhaps I should try to write an article along that line.

Saturday, March 14.

Ruth and I drove to the Baltimore Travel Plaza to pick up Miriam, arriving from New York for the first part of her spring break. All the way down Ruth was singing old German hymns. These were a comfort for me too.

Hebrews 11 speaks of those who are "strangers and exiles on the earth. . . . they desire a better country, that is, a heavenly one. Therefore God is not ashamed to be called their God, for he has prepared for them a city" (vv. 13,16)—not rural spaces with considerable distance between people, not suburban separateness of dwelling and grounds, but people close, their lives flowing together. I recall little cities on the Greek islands I passed when I went by boat to Mykonos. In the evening it seemed that everyone came into the street for shared life.

All God's people together in the consummation are pictured simply as city. In Revelation 21 the new Jerusalem is envisioned as "the Bride, the wife of the Lamb" (v. 9). Any earthly metropolis seems so contrary to or remote from that image—more like Rome as the great harlot (Rev. 17).

Or to take another image: "In my Father's house there are many dwelling places" (John 14:2). As humans we each need our own place and space, but we also need to move out of that into shared life with others. In the life beyond, these needs will be met.

Sunday, March 15.

Ruth, Miriam, and I drove to Lancaster to visit Daniel.

Before the three of us headed home, Ruth suggested that we sing "*Lobe den Herren* [Praise to the Lord]," for we had not been able to sing it with Miriam on her birthday. Ruth also sang the German hymn "Spread Wide Both Your Wings" with the closing "*Will Satan Dich verschlingen, / So lass die Englein singen: / Dies Kind soll unverletzet sein* [Should Satan want to devour you, / then let the angels sing: / 'This child shall not be harmed']." She said she sings it again and again as a prayer for the children. As something comparable she mentioned that when I cough in the night and she reaches over to put her hand on my arm, she takes that time to pray for me.

Friday, March 20.
Dr. Caricofe thought I should see my dermatologist about the place on my right temple. So this morning I went for an appointment with Dr. Patricia Brown. She removed the spot, which she thinks is very likely a basal cell skin cancer.

Miriam had very good news this evening. Chuck has received a Mellon fellowship for research and teaching in Roman law at Emory University in Atlanta. That would be for just one or two years. They seem to be leaning toward his taking this. Miriam has two more years of law school.

Sunday, March 22.
Daniel brought Mennonite friends Rob and Wendy Shelley here to spend the night. They had flown back from medical work in El Salvador because Rob's father died. Ruth and I met them this morning. For nearly a year and a half, we have been dealing with the prospect of my imminent death, whereas Rob's father was taken suddenly with a heart attack.

Wednesday, March 25.
This afternoon we had the second appointment with Dr. Leon Hwang at the Johns Hopkins Oncology Center. I am thankful for the way things went. He is willing to take me on as a regular patient, and I will go to him for monthly checkups. Now I have an oncologist whom I can turn to at any time. He thinks that I should have a bone scan and a CT scan (particularly of the liver).

Saturday, March 28.
Philippians 1:20: "It is my eager expectation and hope that I will not be put to shame in any way, but that by my speaking with all boldness, Christ will be exalted now as always in my body, whether by life or by death." The root of "exalted" is *megalo*—that Christ will be seen as great. The translation gives an interpretation to the Greek *parresia*, which means openness, confidence, boldness. I too want to be confident and bold in pointing to Christ, whether I have more time for living, or whether I die before long. Strikingly Paul points to a dark alternative—being put to shame. I would want to be delivered from doing something or becoming something that would be the opposite of magnifying Christ. I am reminded of Cardinal

Bernardin of Chicago who faced charges of sexual abuse (later retracted) while he was struggling with the pancreatic cancer that took his life.

The news media spoke of Bernardin as having chosen to be very public in his dying. I think of myself in relation to that. I would not say I chose such a direction; things have unfolded that way. Maybe this is what happened for him.

Friday, April 3.
I had the bone scan yesterday and the CT scan today. I didn't feel well for awhile after drinking the large amount of barium solution. I was told that I should be able to pick up all the film and the radiologist's report on Tuesday. So that may be the day when we find out whether or not anything bad has been happening.

Joshua Blistein, nineteen-year-old son of a college roommate of mine, came this morning to visit us and help around the place. I had ordered ten red oaks, mainly to replace several that had died in the line along the lane. The tap roots were long enough that we needed to use a posthole digger. I planted two this morning and helped Joshua plant the rest.

Saturday, April 4.
I was not too tired and was delighted with the jobs accomplished.

Monday, April 6.
Maren is here for her spring break. She and I planted twenty-six Cavendish strawberry plants, and then broccoli, red cabbage, and cauliflower.

After four years of teaching in a bilingual classroom in Phoenix, Maren has decided to go to graduate school. She's done the applications and visited the schools.

Mutter, Ruth's mother, arrived from Germany. What a great blessing to see her face to face again. Soon after the diagnosis this had seemed unlikely. She brought us telephone greetings, cards, and letters from relatives and friends in Germany.

Wednesday, April 8.
I met Ruth at school and we drove to pick up the radiologist's report and the films. She brought them to the car. Together we read what we had been afraid of finding in reports over the last months. The tumor in the left lung has increased some in size. There are now nodules up to 1 centimeter spread in the left lung and in the upper and middle portions of the right

lung. There are more lesions in the liver. Otherwise, no metastases in new parts of the body were discovered; but the metastasis in the middle of my spine may be growing.

Ruth and I were thankful we had some time to think about this development as we drove to the appointment. Dr. Hwang said before that if we wanted to try more chemotherapy, gemcitabine seems to be the best possibility. For treatment of lung cancer, it has a 10-20 percent response rate. Ruth and I had talked things through on the way down and agreed to start with the first of the weekly infusions next Wednesday.

It's not that we are grasping desperately for something that will give longer life. But I want to continue to resist this agent of death as long as doing so seems to make sense. My oncologist cousin, David Miller, had advised us that Canadian studies have shown that later-stage chemotherapy tends to bring better quality of life for the time remaining in comparison to supportive care by itself.

As I gazed at the blooming trees and shrubs, I thought that it seems unlikely that I will see another spring or plant another early garden. Yet I'm not resigned to dying soon. It's possible that God will continue to hold back death, but it seems that if God were going to give full healing from the cancer, this would have come by now. We can still be aware of the possibility of healing, but there doesn't have to be healing. My family and I have been given seventeen months filled with marvels of grace. If there are only a few months remaining, that is all right. For that, too, one can give the Hebrew assessment, "*Shalom* [It is well]."

Now I'm back into that earlier post-diagnosis sense of trying to be selective in what I find important enough to devote time to.

This evening we watched two long reels of family movies made when the children were very little. What splendid reminders of how blessed and full my life has been. I relish seeing Ruth as a mother in her latter twenties, even more than viewing the children.

Thursday, April 9.

The April issue of *Messenger* with my article arrived today. I was hoping it would come about now as a sort of counterweight to the scan reports. Fletcher Farrar, the new editor, did splendid work on the piece and came up with a new title that I like quite well— "Living with Dying."

This evening Ruth and I attended the evening love feast at Westminster Church of the Brethren. In this reenactment of the upper room drama, men and women have traditionally sat at separate tables, particularly because of the feetwashing. Ruth and I arrived just as the service was about to start. Most of the tables had mixed seating. Ruth and I went to a vacant table. Fran Nyce and Dottie Gosnell came to join us. I think Ruth and I had never sat together in a love feast before; being able to do this was a special gift. When we came to the feetwashing, Ruth washed my feet. She leaned her head against my knee. She was very moved as I was.

On our wedding night soon after we were alone together, we washed each other's feet. There had been a love feast type meal and the bread and cup in the part of the celebration held in her parents' apartment that afternoon. Her washing my feet again at this time was such an intense expression of her giving of herself for me and of the mutual servanthood we have sought to live out toward each other.

When we arrived back home, Miriam and Chuck were here. Maren had met them at the bus station in Baltimore. Daniel arrived from Lancaster a little later.

Good Friday, April 10.

Maren needs to fly back to Phoenix tomorrow, so this was our day together— a time more precious and intense again because of the heightened threat to my life.

We went to the community Good Friday service held in the Westminster Brethren meetinghouse. In the organ prelude sequence, I was stirred by the Taizé melody for the words, "Jesus, remember me when you come into your Kingdom" (Luke 23:42). Maybe that will be sung to me at the close of my life.

The tulips and primroses around the house are in their full glory. The daffodils are still blooming.

Good Friday is the only day that Kenny Keefer could come to pour our garage floor. Miriam asked me whether we were going to write something in the concrete. That brought back a reminiscence from my boyhood. On the family farm in Ohio, my father had welded big metal pipes together for a swing set for my younger sister, Jane. We poured concrete footers around the bottoms of the pipes. At the time I was immersed in Latin and classical history. I figured out what the date was as calculated from the founding of Rome and marked it in AUC (*ab urbe condita*). As we thought about an inscription for the garage floor, doing something similar seemed a nice whimsical touch. Chuck came up with the inscription and scratched it out with a nail: DHA.RMA FECERUNT MMDCCLI AUC. (Ruth and I built this, 2751 years after the founding of Rome.)

Saturday, April 11.

On the Saturday before Easter last year we planted more than three hundred trees in the meadow. Today we had another family work day, and I supervised. I figured out which trees to move to replace trees that had died, and Miriam led in the big effort. Transplanting even a little tree with a ball is a much bigger effort than planting a small bare-rooted tree. I then mowed around some of the trees. I was delighted with and thankful for how much we got done.

Miriam agreed with me that the time has come when I should be writing instructions regarding things around the place and other matters.

Sunday, April 12, Easter.

The verse that came to me early this morning includes the words of the Emmaus pair, "Did not our hearts burn within us while he talked to us on the road, while he opened to us the scriptures?" (Luke 24:32). That has been my experience again and again since the diagnosis. I need the Lord to go with me for what is ahead.

I've been pondering the hope expressed by Paul that "now as always Christ will be honored in my body, whether by life or by death" (Phil. 1:20). Whether it be life or death is not really what matters but rather that Christ is exalted in whatever unfolds.

Stan Holcombe, whose wife has been losing out to cancer, called this afternoon. Unfortunately he and their children don't feel they can talk with her about the possible imminence of her death. Talking together about the possible nearness of my death, even as we hope for more time, has been so important and freeing for our family.

I hope that I will be given enough time to do certain things, especially completing this journal manuscript. As in the early weeks following the diagnosis, I don't feel rushed or constricted, but I am more selective about what I give time to. Seeing that things are in good order around the place and mowing the yard and around the little trees seem like fitting priorities.

God can use the new chemotherapy, if I'm able to take it, to turn back death for another period of time. But if the cancer continues to advance, I feel peaceful about that too. There is acute sadness in parting; but also here on this earth God wipes away some tears from our eyes and gives the buoyancy of joy.

Wednesday, April 15.

Ruth, who is on spring break till tomorrow, drove me down for the first infusion of gemcitabine. Mutter (Ruth's mother) went with us. I asked the nurse, Keith, about the dosage. Apparently one gram per square meter of body surface is standard. I was surprised to learn that I have an estimated two square meters of body surface area. I get two grams per treatment.

As I was having the infusion, I turned to Mark 5, which I have often read for the story of the woman who touched Jesus' garment. But today Jesus' words to Jairus stood out: "Do not fear, only believe" (Mark 5:36). Jairus had just learned that his daughter had died. What he was fearing most had come, it seemed, with all finality. The command "only believe" is somewhat strange. But he was to believe, having faith to the exclusion of fear. For me there may be no rescue from death, as for Jairus's daughter. But I can take Jesus' command for myself. Faith in this Master should shape and fill my days, whatever comes, to the exclusion of fear. But such faith is God's gift.

I came home, changed clothes, and spent perhaps an hour and a half mowing around the trees in the meadow. They are such a delight to see as they put out their leaves. If I don't live to see any of them become old enough to bloom, I have at least had this second spring with them. Each species has its own special spring beauty, even without blooms.

Thursday, April 16.

Paul Grout came for breakfast with us and was here for most of the morning. He was on his way to speak at the Youth Roundtable in Bridgewater, Virginia. As always, his presence with us was like an infusion of love, peace, and faith.

I've been a little more tired and last evening began to feel increased numbness and tingling in my feet and hands. But so far I've not been hit by severe side effects. In the afternoon I was able to finish mowing around the trees.

Saturday, April 18.

I've felt quite exhausted for the past two days. But the exhaustion from the chemo has not brought the sort of laming of the will that came each bad week after the taxol and cisplatinum.

Sunday, April 19.

Ruth, Mutter, and I drove to Lancaster and had several hours with Daniel. I am feeling some better.

In a phone call this evening, pastor friend Larry Fourman made the point, "You should distinguish between what comes to your body from the chemotherapy, and the presence of God." I was for a moment puzzled by the remark, but I think he meant: Don't let the side effects of the chemo lead you to suppose that God's presence has been withdrawn; that presence is with you in spite of the side effects of the chemo.

Monday, April 20.
After four years of teaching in a bilingual classroom, Maren has decided to go to graduate school in education and has been exploring the various possibilities. She called today from Phoenix after visiting the program at Berkeley, which she liked very much. Maren is strongly inclined toward going there for a master's degree; we are excited with and for her.

Wednesday, April 22.
This afternoon Ruth drove me down for the chemo. I got into the elevator with a robust-looking man perhaps in his late thirties. I looked at him from the side and thought to myself: "Be glad you don't have advanced lung cancer." But when I entered the waiting room of the Johns Hopkins Oncology Center, he was sitting there. And later, when I walked into the treatment room, he was in a big chair getting his infusion. He may not have lung cancer, but how wrong my perception had been!

Dr. Hwang came by and said they may need to decrease the dosage if my blood counts go down much more. I told him about the times when I've felt increased numbness in my feet and hands. He said to keep watch on my buttoning buttons and walking; if these become really affected, "we would need to stop."

In a call this evening, Frauke Westphal pointed to how remarkable my extension of life has been and how remarkable my attitude. I felt she gave me too much credit. My attitude, my prayer life, has left much to be desired. The prayers and support of so many have been of great importance. And all the good has been through God's grace.

Friday, April 24.
Yesterday and today my breathing has become more constricted. I am coughing a lot more, and I'm really dragging.

Late this afternoon I took my temperature and was astonished to read 101.4 degrees. It had been a little under 100 degrees in the morning. Keith, the oncology nurse, told me to take my temperature regularly and call if it reaches 100.5 degrees or more. It was a bit too late in the day to reach anyone at the John Hopkins Oncology Center in Green Spring, so we used an after-hours number. The oncologist on call said I should go to an emergency room for chest x-rays and blood work. We could have gone to Frederick Hospital, which is closer, but it seemed wise to keep things under the Johns Hopkins umbrella. Ruth left a message on Daniel's answering machine and then drove me down. The emergency room was crowded. The chest x-rays showed pneumonia. It was a boost when Daniel arrived and could serve as my advocate. He and Ruth tell me I am poor at being my own advocate. The oncology ward was full, so I got a room on the neural ward. It was well past midnight before the oncologist on call got to me and put me on intravenous antibiotics.

Saturday, April 25.
I slept well. By morning my breathing and cough were considerably better. When the team made their rounds, they said I can probably leave tomorrow. This afternoon I thought about how much needs to be done at home. I asked Daniel, "How little should I work—or how much should I work—when I get home?" He and Ruth broke out laughing. He took a cautionary tack.

Sunday, April 26.
The oncology team came by and gave the okay for me to go home. When I asked about physical activity, Dr. Tsieh said that what I felt able to do would be all right. Daniel interjected, "He works like a farmer." Then the doctor expressed some caution.

We can be thankful that I responded to treatment for the pneumonia so well and so quickly.

I had hoped to take part in the rally this afternoon in Lafayette Park (across from the White House) for closing the School of the Americas.

Monday, April 27.
Mutter left this afternoon to return to Kassel, Germany. It has been such a good three weeks together. No doubt both of us (she is eighty-one) thought about whether we will see one another again. God only knows.

After sunset I checked the three rows of Sparkle strawberries in the garden. They have a good many blooms, so I covered them with the straw that was between the rows. I should let a few berries develop on the newly planted Cavendish strawberries—rather than plucking off all the blooms— to get some idea as to whether the claims about their extraordinary taste are justified.

1998

Saturday, May 2.

These past three days since the chemotherapy I've felt exhausted and listless, drained mentally and spiritually. This evening Ruth asked me, "Do you feel ready to die?"

I said I hope that when death closes in, it comes fairly quickly. I added, "I haven't felt like praying. I try to get back to scriptures I've leaned on earlier—but nothing new. It makes me wonder whether having entered into this new chemotherapy is worth it."

Ruth commented to Miriam on the phone that if I'd been like I am now when she first knew me, she would hardly have fallen in love with me. That scenario would not have occurred to me, but it was her way of saying that under chemo I am only a shadow of the person she fell in love with and married.

Miriam observed, " 'For better or for worse.' "

For a few days I've been having some discomfort in the middle part of my spine. There's the metastasis in the T-8 vertebra, but that may not be the cause.

Sunday, May 3.

As we took our morning walk, Ruth observed that I have become "rather high profile" in moving toward death.

I said to her, "That puts me on the spot." In writing about facing death, I haven't assumed I would be able to continue in such faith. That has been a gift and endures only as gift day by day—even when obscured by the side effects of the chemotherapy.

Ruth said, "I hope you don't become violent or abusive." She was thinking in terms of medication, I in terms of a brain tumor. Lung cancer tends to travel to the bone, the liver, and the brain. May God spare me the last.

This morning Ruth was at the table finishing a letter. As I leaned toward her, she looked up and said with strong emotion, "It came to me that faith is believing in spite of death."

I had been scheduled to preach today at the Green Hill (Maryland) service about four hours drive from here. But when the pneumonia hit, we needed to cancel.

This afternoon Ruth and I talked of driving to Catoctin State Park in the Blue Ridge Mountains for a spring walk. Instead we worked with the little trees on the spring house side of the woodlot. She mulched with grass clippings, and I put shields on the smallest ones. The trees are such a delight as they leaf out more and more. We were like Adam and Eve tending trees in the garden. I had no sense of breaking the sabbath.

Last summer the leaves of the red maple nearest the cattle gate shriveled from the drought. I kept watering it, and two tiny new leaves appeared. This spring I could not detect any sign of life in the tree. But today when I took the spiral shield off and checked down to the base, there was one small, frail shoot. I have felt a bond with that little tree in its seeking, against the odds, to live.

When we talked with Miriam this evening, I told her, "An idea came to me today. I've always wanted to go to Armenia. I thought Mother and I could fly over while you are there in June. But we wouldn't want to impose on your time." I was caught up in the whimsicalness of the idea.

Miriam replied judiciously, "That would be quite a trip."

Monday, May 4.

This evening was the teachers' awards banquet organized by the local Chamber of Commerce. I didn't go because I would have needed to pay $25 for my ticket and would have been exposed (with low blood counts) to infections in a big crowd. Ruth had been nominated for one of the eight outstanding teacher awards. Though she was sure that she would not get an award, she came back an award winner. This award, I think, came mainly because she had received the recognition as Maryland Art Educator of the Year. Our children were so elated for her.

Tuesday, May 5.

Today is exactly a year and a half since we found out about the tumor on my left lung. As we learned more about the prognosis, even a year seemed like an amazing expanse of time.

Even a year and a half, as precious and savored as day after day has been, recedes into what the psalmist wrote about the years of our lives: "they are soon gone, and we fly away" (Ps. 90:10). Our spirits are constituted for more than this fleeting span of time.

Wednesday, May 6.

Today I had an appointment with Dr. Hwang and also the fourth chemotherapy treatment. Unfortunately he is moving on from Johns Hopkins, so we will be losing him as my oncologist. My blood counts have dropped still further, so he reduced the dosage by 25 percent. Hopefully this dosage, if continued, will let the counts come back up and the side effects lessen, especially the fatigue.

Daniel had sent Dr. Hwang some information on thalidomide as a drug against cancer, which he had received from the Westphals. Dr. Hwang told us that the benefits demonstrated by that drug for some types of cancer were not that impressive.

In the evening Frauke Westphal called and told us more about thalidomide. She said she disagreed completely with Dr. Hwang. At a dinner party, she and Heiner talked with Dr. Steven Hirschfield of the Division of Oncology Drug Products of the Food and Drug Administration. Dr. Hirschfield strongly advocated thalidomide. Though the agents that work against blood vessel formation for tumors have been in the news more recently, they seem to be many months away from experimental use on human beings. But thalidomide is comparable and is being tested with some types of cancer, though not with lung cancer. Frauke expressed such a strong sense of God's providence in her sitting beside this man at the party.

Regarding the thalidomide tragedy in Germany and elsewhere, Frauke explained that when pregnant mothers used the drug as a sleeping tablet, it suppressed the blood vessel formation for the unborn child's newly developing hands and feet. But against cancer such suppression may bring significant help.

Frauke has a sheaf of articles about thalidomide that she will copy and send to us. If the gemcitabine is helping, then so far, so good. But if there is progression of the disease—I'm to have a CT scan on May 28—she thinks I should by all means go on thalidomide.

Dr. Hwang is transferring me to Dr. David Ettinger, the renowned John Hopkins lung oncologist, whom I would have seen in December 1996 if we had not entered the NCI research study. We have no idea how Dr. Ettinger will feel about thalidomide.

There is a temptation to set one's hope on new treatment possibilities, and Frauke's call was certainly heartening and encouraging. But we want to set our hope on God and his gracious will for us. Turning to this or that medical treatment, however, fits in as a corollary aspect of looking to God for longer life.

I often think of myself in relation to King Hezekiah. Isaiah told him, "Thus says the Lord: Set your house in order; for you shall die" (Isa. 38:1). God is the One who then, in response to Hezekiah's plea, gave him fifteen more years of life. But the healing was not simply by divine fiat. "Now Isaiah had said, 'Let them take a cake of figs, and apply it to the boil, that he may recover' " (Isa. 38:21). The fig poultice, within God's gracious determination for Hezekiah, had its very real role. So too all my "fig poultices." But the central direction of Hezekiah's hoping and trust was not toward that lump of figs. Behind all good that comes is God's prevenient grace.

Thursday, May 7.

Today I went to Frederick for x-rays of my spine, because of the pain I've been having. When he had asked me to rate the pain in the middle of my spine on a scale of one to ten, I said, "At its worst, perhaps five." I find such a pain-rating question difficult.

I still read very little in the newspaper, but, since childhood, articles on astronomical immensities always evoke my interest. Today's (Baltimore) *Sun* had an article with the heading, "Second biggest 'bang' is detected." Intense gamma rays from a blast twelve billion light years ago reached earth on December 14. One scientist estimated, "For about one or two seconds, this burst was as luminous as all the rest of the entire universe"—thus as bright as all else that came from the big bang perhaps two billion years earlier. Twelve billion years ago did God contemplate that burst in relation to confounding its human detectors in 1997?

Friday, May 8.

The radiologist's report on the spinal x-rays came this afternoon from Dr. Caricofe's office. So far as we can figure out, my back pain is probably not cancer-related.

Saturday, May 9.

A pair of purple finches have built a nest in the center of the basket of New Guinea impatiens hanging on the front porch.

We've had two weeks of rainy, drizzly weather probably from El Niño. We haven't been able to plant the late vegetable plants we bought or to cultivate and hoe the early garden. But the little trees are growing splendidly—in contrast to last year with the drought.

Since the treatment on Wednesday, I've had hardly any side effects—in contrast especially to last week. My feeling much better is presumably the result of the reduced dosage. Being nearly free from side effects is a blessing and a welcome change in the usual pattern of chemotherapy weeks.

Sunday, May 10.

It's been a memorable Mother's Day. I was able to preach in the Glade Valley Brethren service—a twenty-five minute drive from here. They had asked me to preach the "Living with Dying" sermon, even though some in the congregation had read it in *Messenger*. A sixty-three-year-old man named Wayne Frederick was there. His heart is functioning at 15 percent, and he is waiting without insurance for a heart transplant. He said to me with deep feeling, "You must have known I would be here."

I said, "God knew."

After supper Ruth and I went through our wedding album. Ruth read the wedding sermon preached by her cousin, Gustav Hamann. We had not gone back to it for many years. We had asked him to take as the text Revelation 19:6-7 with "the voice of a great multitude. . . crying,

> 'Hallelujah! For the Lord our God the Almighty reigns.
> Let us rejoice and exult and give him the glory,
> for the marriage of the Lamb has come,
> and his Bride has made herself ready.' "

Gustav had begun by commenting that he'd at first found the text a very odd one for a wedding. After all these years the text strikes me as a little strange; but it ties into the eschatological aspects of what our life and witness have been. I no doubt selected the text. Ruth reflected that she was so much in love she went along with it. Amazingly Gustav, who was relatively young when he died of cancer, brought in Luther's saying, "If I knew today that the world would end tomorrow, I would still today plant my little apple tree and pay my debts." (The part about debts, it seems, has generally been dropped and forgotten.) Several people quoted this saying in relation to our big tree planting.

Monday, May 11.

Prompted by the Revelation 19 text, I turned to my beloved passage in Isaiah 25. "And he will destroy on this mountain the covering that is cast over all peoples, the veil that is spread over all nations" (v. 7). Yes, on the central mountain, through the death and rising of Jesus, God has accomplished the ultimate destruction of death's ever-descending shroud (or mourning veil). Begun on that mountain, the great feast celebrating this triumph reaches out to embrace all the nations (v. 6). The Lord of hosts "will swallow up death for ever" (v. 8)—a strange image. The all-devouring infernal power is swallowed up by the One incomparably greater. In Jesus God took death to himself, enveloped and, within that totally decisive encounter, did away with it.

Tuesday, May 12.

I continue with the important tasks. But I'm not driving myself to do all I can. I'm working at a relaxed pace. Sometimes I compare my situation to the child who is to put away all the toys before being taken to bed. The child works at the task—but slowly, lest bedtime come still sooner. It might not be good for me to complete the tasks.

Thursday, May 14.

Again yesterday I received the reduced dosage of gemcitabine, and, as was the case last week, I haven't been hit by fatigue and exhaustion. I was able to mow the lawn after the long rainy spell.

A letter came from Fletcher Farrar, editor of *Messenger*, saying he wants to use my article "The Problem with Pluralism." It was a boost to know that God still has assignments for me. I put a copy on a disk and got it ready to send.

Sunday, May 17.

Ruth discovered that there are five eggs in the purple finch nest in the hanging flower basket on the front porch.

As we were looking over the little trees late this afternoon, I noticed an arrowwood viburnum with several heads of unopened blossoms. Then I spotted another viburnum that has a couple of heads of blossoms. I was delighted. On the big tree planting day more than a year ago Paul Dodd made the comment, "It doesn't seem like too much to ask that Dale would live to see the trees grow." My own prayer was that I would live to see some of the trees blossom. This prayer has been answered—almost too soon in a way. But for me to live more than a year to see so much growth this spring in the trees and now these blooms is a wonderful gift.

Tuesday, May 19.

Dot Holcombe died yesterday afternoon. Ruth and I and she and Stan have had so much in common as we faced the imminence of death by cancer. She lived for three years after the diagnosis in May of 1995.

Ruth and I have been having a sharp disagreement over mowing around the little trees. She thinks that if we don't mow many of them will die. I think that all but a few of them are big enough to survive and grow surrounded by taller grass. I don't feel I should put in all that work mowing or that we should spend a large amount of money to hire it done.

But this morning Bill Heltzel came over and mowed around all the trees.

This afternoon he and Janet called. They said that, as a gift to Ruth, he would be doing the mowing for the rest of this growing season. How beautiful of him to do this—and it will certainly help the trees some.

Yesterday I was able to plant the tomatoes, peppers, and eggplants that I couldn't get into the ground during the rainy weather. Today I finished planting the late garden with beans, zucchinis, melons, cucumbers, corn, squash, and sunflowers.

Monday, May 25.
Two years ago today Miriam and Chuck were married. I was ill with the cancer then but didn't know it.

As I was showing them around the place, I discovered that a gray dogwood not far from the spring house has a single head of tiny blooms. So I have lived to see this kind of dogwood bloom—again sooner than I had expected.

Tuesday, May 26.
Two or three tiny purple finches have hatched out in the nest in the hanging basket on the front porch.

As I worked this evening in the woodlot, a mockingbird on the electric wire overhead went through its repertoire. During my years in Maryland I've thought of mockingbirds as a superlatively imaginative creation of God.

Our strawberries are finally ripening. These Sparkle berries tend to run small, but they are delicious. So I've lived into another strawberry season.

Wednesday, May 27.
Last evening as Ruth was cutting my hair, she said that when she cut my hair a little while after the diagnosis she supposed that would be the last time. But we've been given more time.

Ruth suggested that for another sermon I might focus more on the issue of salvation. Several friends have been concerned that I might not be in the right spiritual state for dying. This morning I began thinking of a message along that line. When Paul Grout was here last, we talked about his standing invitation to come to Vermont and I would preach in a service of the Genesis Church. Ruth thinks we should plan on it, but I am more hesitant about whether I will be up to that big an undertaking. If a message comes together, at least that part would be ready.

I had my seventh week of chemotherapy this afternoon. Dr. Hwang spoke with us briefly. He is hopeful that the CT scan will show "stabilized disease."

If it does, I will continue on gemcitabine, with a CT scan every two months to monitor what is happening.

Ruth thinks I look so much better than a few weeks ago. Even if we get a bad report from the scan, these relatively good weeks since the reduction in dosage have been another wonderful gift from God. I'm always mindful that in relation to the cancer God "is able to do exceeding abundantly above all that we ask or think" (Eph. 3:20 AV).

Thursday, May 28.

This morning I went to Frederick for the CT scan. It was a considerable ordeal, because injection of the contrast causes nausea and vomiting. But that passed rather quickly.

What I really want is that even a bad report will not bring a negative shift in how I see what is ahead for me, that whatever unfolds will be full of the marvels of God's grace. In faith there is an abundance of reasons to be hopeful, no matter what.

I was reading in Colossians 2:15: "[God] disarmed the principalities and powers and made a public example of them, triumphing over them in him." Victors in war had their triumphal processions. Jesus' persecution is vaguely comparable. He carried the cross in a processional. His sentencing and execution were made into a spectacle, manifesting the triumph of his enemies. Yet that is precisely what brought exposure and defeat to his enemies. Because of this vanquishing of the powers, we can look toward the completion of that triumph over every inhumanity brought about by those powers.

Saturday, May 30.

Chuck's mother and sister Lisa flew into BWI this afternoon. Chuck and Miriam met them, and the four came out here. The little tour of our place took us to the new garage, which looks so good now with all the oak siding on it. We showed Ellen and Lisa the Latin inscription on the right front corner of the floor, that begins with our initials, DHA.RMA . . . . Chuck's mother thought of a TV show that I had never heard of, *Dharma and Greg*, and asked about the Dharma in the inscription. None of the rest of us had noticed it before. We could not remember the meaning and consulted the dictionary. In a phone call this evening, Maren defined it as "the way to live." She explained that the word, with its origins in Hinduism, is not confined to religious usage. There can be a dharma of gardening, a dharma of marriage.

Monday, June 1.

During the night a thunderstorm passed through. I was delighted to find nearly .7 of an inch in the rain gage this morning, enough to help the garden, the little trees, and the nearby farm crops.

Miriam and Chuck and Ellen and Lisa headed on to Princeton for the graduation ceremony tomorrow in which Chuck is to formally receive his Ph.D. in classics.

Tuesday, June 2.

The report on last Thursday's CT scan was slow in coming. This afternoon I called Dr. Caricofe's office and asked them to request it. We got the good news we were hoping for. The main tumor and the metastases in the lungs seem to be stabilized—no further growth. There has been some decrease in size of the metastases in the liver. This presumably means that I will continue on the gemcitabine. By the grace of God, I'm in the 10-20 percent who are helped by gemcitabine as a second-line chemotherapy. We give thanks for the good news.

Wednesday, June 3.

Ed Yohn came to put a brick surface on the ramp to the west door of the garage. He told me in the early afternoon: "I didn't feel good at all when I came here. I got up early and was very tired. Now I feel great. I feel the presence of God. The presence of God is in the breeze here." He was so surprised and glad that I seem to be doing as well as I am. I brought him the bricks by wheelbarrow from behind our shed.

Thursday, June 4.

This morning we had an appointment with my new oncologist, Dr. David Ettinger. He is a witty, ebullient man, perhaps in his late fifties. He summarized the CT scan report for us and commented that there was no way of being sure that this result came from the gemcitabine: "It could come from the nature of the disease." He was soon asking me whether I was taking vitamins, coffee enemas, and shark cartilage. He seemed to imply the viewpoint that there is always the possibility that such things may help. He said that a colleague of his is doing a study on the possible effectiveness of green tea extract.

Dr. Ettinger recommends that I continue with the gemcitabine with three weekly infusions, then a week off, for about a twelve-week period. Then I'm to have another CT scan. If the cancer remains stable, I may be taken off the gemcitabine and simply be monitored. He said patients often think that continuing to get some chemotherapy decreases the likelihood of new progression in the disease. But studies show patients doing just as well with the chemotherapy put on hold.

Ruth and I came away from the appointment so thankful for the consultation with Dr. Ettinger and for the confirmation that time is being given us.

What a blessing it is to be able to breathe without difficulty. How good to breathe air in and out normally.

Friday, June 5.
Today is nineteen months since the diagnosis. I contemplate the prayers of so many on my behalf and believe they are more determinative than the chemotherapy.

Ruth discovered a tiny white oak coming up near the end of our two rows of peas. I transplanted it near the beginning of our lane. Also, down the lane there is a tree we planted from the shipment of red oaks I had ordered to replace trees that had died. But this "red oak" has small, soft needles. It may be a bald cypress, since it is a deciduous tree. A bald cypress has a conical shape, so we will probably do well to transplant it away from its spot near the edge of the lane.

Sunday, June 7.
My sister, Ann, and her husband, Mike, arrived yesterday afternoon and were with us till a little past noon today. They had been at a hospice convention in Washington to exhibit products of their company, Air Lift.

Tuesday, June 9.
Three Nicaraguan Christians from a Pentecostal church in Managua are being hosted by the Westminster Church of the Brethren. There has been a sister-church relationship for a number of years with delegations going both directions. We hosted Candida, Daniela, and Rolando this evening. Fortunately our friends Wilbur and Sandy Wright with their children could come to speak with them in Spanish. Just before the three visitors left, they asked to pray with me for healing. Candida told a story of a younger man in their church who had been healed of a life-threatening lung infection. Daniela spoke in full voice in the prayer with intense importunity (so far as I could follow), pleading for a miracle of healing. The other two prayed along with her in low voices.

When Ruth asked about the economic picture for the church, they spoke of 70 percent unemployment. These three had come to us out of that poverty. Like Peter and John coming to the lame man at the gate of the temple, they had no monetary resources, but they gave to us out of their wealth of faith "in the name of Jesus Christ of Nazareth" (Acts 3:6).

Friday, June 12.

Our cousin Heidi Campbell, now living again in Germany, came Wednesday evening. She had colon cancer several years ago, but it has been in remission. She seems to be doing well and at seventy is still her amazingly active self.

This morning Heidi expressed interest in going to the Holocaust Museum in Washington. She had never been there, nor had I. Usually one needs to work further in advance to get tickets, but Ruth got on the telephone and was soon telling about her husband with advanced lung cancer and a visiting relative, a cousin of André Trocmé, who is featured in the museum. (Ruth had about the same relationship to André; he and her father were first cousins.) She was promised tickets. We picked strawberries and than headed to Washington.

Some of the most haunting scenes for me were the newsreel segments of tens of thousands of Germans marching in formation or shouting "Sieg, Heil!" On the way home Heidi mentioned that she thought the mentality of the American populace in the Persian Gulf War was similar. The subservience of that populace to the official propaganda and psychological manipulation was closely analogous, though quite different in its manifestations.

Ruth spoke of this displaying of evil as problematical. How distressing it is to survey such a colossal outbreak of demonic powers. Yet the immense evil perpetrated during those years provides easy justification for museum visitors, whose morality seems so remote from the immorality of the perpetrators. In the chapter "Hitler and the Woman Caught in Adultery," in *Darkening Valley: A Biblical Perspective on Nuclear War*, I sought to diminish that sort of remoteness. Today we have nuclear arsenals that are ready to annihilate far more people than the Nazis did. The Israelis perpetrate their totalitarian inhumanities against the Palestinians, who are seen as an inferior race. During World War II, the Nazis had millions of "slave" laborers. But in our world organized by the dictates of Western capitalism, many hundreds of millions of exploited, impoverished workers do the bidding of those who are the masters of the earth.

The museum has a panel about the rescue efforts of the villagers of Le Chambon, and there is a picture of André and Magda Trocmé and the four children. Heidi spent a year in the Trocmé household there at the end of the forties. She said that to hear André in the pulpit was like listening to an Old Testament prophet. "He was also speaking to himself. That all those villagers worked together as they did in hiding Jews must have taken its impetus from André's preaching."

Saturday, June 13.
The purple finch nest in the hanging flower basket on the front porch is empty today. The four fledglings were still in it yesterday.

Sunday, June 14.
Daniel returned from his vacation week in New Mexico this afternoon, and we picked him up at the airport. Afterward he was with us for a little celebration of my birthday (two days early) with *"Lobe den Herren* [Praise to the Lord]," the last part of Psalm 73, prayers, and the opening of gifts. Daniel gave me some splendid Australian sheepskin slippers. For months Miriam has been knitting me a sweater, but it's not quite finished. There's a good prospect now that I will live long enough to wear it.

After Daniel left, Ruth and I walked a good way up the hill behind our house. On the walk with Mike and Ann a week ago, Ruth had spotted a very small white oak out in the corn rows near the woods. We found it again, and I dug it out and transplanted it along the lane.

Tuesday, June 16.
Today is my second birthday since the diagnosis. This second is a more remarkable blessing than the first.

My birth too was a deliverance from death. It was a very difficult home delivery in the farmhouse of my early childhood. My head was too big—it's always been rather big. For a number of weeks afterward, my mother was extremely ill with child bed fever (I think it was) and could have died.

Ruth decided to have a carry-in supper this evening for friends and neighbors who have given us so much help. She prepared a large turkey, a big tossed salad, drinks, and four flat German cakes with our fresh raspberries and strawberries for toppings.

We were going to eat on the front lawn, but a severe storm broke just as people were arriving. Limbs came down. A big bushy limb from the ailing maple tree along our lane toppled over and was dangling over the lane.

Stan Holcombe took two saws out and cut off the lowest branches so that people could drive through. The Arbaugh clan was quite late because the calf hutches had blown over and they needed to chase calves.

After the storm there was, a short, stubby rainbow east of our house, especially for me, Ruth said. I don't recall a rainbow on my birthday before. Ruth brought in the four cakes, each one with a letter, D-A-L-E, and candles. Her love and that of the others infused the evening. I read the passage from Job 33 about the sick person being delivered from death. I also brought in Malachi 4:2: "You shall go forth leaping like calves from the stall." As people were leaving, several said they hoped to celebrate my next birthday with me. It was a lovely evening with these friends.

Thursday, June 18.
When Ruth brought in the mail, a birthday package from Maren had arrived. Her letter read:

Dear Father,

Often when I think of you I think of a particular visit to Baugher's market and how old brother Baugher recognized you and came over to say hello. With a hearty handshake he noted, "You've still got a working man's hands."

Now, more than a year and a half after the cancer diagnosis, with a tumor in your lung, metastases in your bones and liver, after chemo and countless IVs, you still have those hands, weathered and lined. In spite of hospitalizations and pneumonia and fatigue, you've had plenty of chances to roughen them on the handle of a hoe. This is not any remarkable heroism so much as it is grace, and you count it as blessing.

You've historically worked hard, probably too hard. Still, it's a lesson I learn from you, over and over, about living meaningfully, about making every moment count. You get that from your mother, maybe. If it isn't weeding or canning, it is shelling hickory nuts or writing a sermon on your obsolete Mac. Garden (and non-garden) variety stewardship.

You've learned a bit more about pacing yourself over these months, learned to listen to your body, to conserve your physical and mental energy. You've found the inner strength, even, to delegate the push-plowing and plant less potatoes. You've learned that goes with stewardship, too. It may be that you will need to find further ways to step back from physical labor, and the grace for that.

But even if your palms should come to lose their calloused feel, even if they turn as soft as your daughter's puffy city hands, you will show other ways of living meaningfully, of setting about for life to matter. As for me, I am thankful we are given time, yet, to plant trees and ideas within view of each other. You still have a working man's hands, and I've still got time to toughen mine up a little.

Happy birthday. I love you.

Love,
Maren

Friday, June 19.
One of the European alders in the woodlot is now a few inches taller than I am.

Sunday, June 21.
Last evening we drove to Mary Catherine Fifer's home in Delaware. Her husband, Fred, drowned three years ago in the lake next to their house. She mentioned as she had before that it bothers her to think that she will not be married to him in heaven. I replied, "I like to think that in the life beyond my relationship with Ruth will be fuller and more complete that it is here on earth."

She said, "You 'like to think,' but we don't know." I believe, however, that such a conclusion is more than speculation. It is a well-based inference from what we know of God in the biblical revelation. God joins a man and a woman in marriage and shapes their life together as they seek this from him. In the life beyond, God brings completion and consummation to all that has been good here on earth. There will not then be the marriage bond in its uniqueness among so many other relationships. But surely that relationship, rather than being suspended or diminished, will be brought to new fullness within a marvelous intermeshing of glorious relationships. In that marvel the uniqueness of the one relationship will have faded away.

Tuesday, June 23.
Yesterday we drove to the home of Kermit and Lynn Johnson near Rehoboth Beach. On their coffee table was *The Good Book: Reading the Bible with Heart and Mind* by Peter J. Gomes. I'd seen a number of references to the

book, so I picked it up. When I opened it, the first words I read were these: "Second, evil has a brain. Someone has said that cancer is not simply a medical condition that results in death but a disease with a brain and a strategy of death. It works to wear down the body, to outwit the physicians, outmaneuver the therapies, strategies, and potients. It almost seems as if it has a will of its own, and it can never be underestimated. Evil is like cancer; it has a brain and a strategy, and millenia of experience" (p. 263). There seems to be much in the book that I would question, but this passage is extraordinary. Cancer has often been used to refer to a specific evil: for example, this or that is like a cancer in the society. But Gomes takes it as quintessential image for evil as such. And to recognize that evil "has a brain" brings out a central part of the biblical understanding of evil.

Wednesday, June 24.
Miriam's birthday gift arrived. She had finished and sent it just before leaving for Belarus. Even with all her law school studies and other involvements, she finished knitting the light gray sweater, the most beautiful one I have ever had; and it fits me perfectly. She wrote:

> Dearest Father,
>
> Although this reaches you belatedly, I hope you know with how much love it comes to you. We have all wondered, as I knit this, whether you would live to wear it, and we can be so grateful to God that you have. Life now seems so full of milestones, and your birthday is yet another one. We pray that you will reach many more of the milestones ahead. And we all love you so.
>
> Happy birthday,
> Miriam and Chuck

Friday, June 26.
This afternoon Ken Koons brought the pine box. His editor, Scott Blanchard, was with him to help carry it. The box was on his pickup—it was just a little longer than the six-foot bed. Both Ruth and I were surprised at the size. Ken has created a beautiful box—dovetailed sides of yellow pine; a white pine top with some beading and screws for holding the lid down; white rope handles, three on each side and one at each end. The exterior has a light oil finish, with no finish on the inside. (Perhaps we should unscrew the lid before there is a need to do that. I would like to have a look on the inside.) I had thought initially of boards simply nailed together. But Ken acted for the

family in all the skill and love that has gone into this creation. It is so right for me in contrast to a $3000 or $4000 funeral-package casket.

At the time Ruth asked Ken to construct the box, it seemed the box might be needed soon. As I continued to live month after month, however, Ken became hesitant to finish the box, even though it was somewhat of an obstruction in his basement workshop. He thought that completing the box meant it would be used soon. But not so long ago Ruth assured him that we would feel all right about having it finished and stored at our place. We had the men put it in the attic of the garage.

The box makes me think of pictures of the resurrected Jesus in which there is a rectangular coffin with the lid pushed to the side. Ruth has such a coffin in her painting of Jesus and Mary Magdalene, which hangs in our dining room.

Our friend Dot Holcombe asked that her body be cremated. Stan intends that for himself as well. He spoke of all the land that is being used for burying people. Cremation has other practical points in its favor, such as costing less than a conventional burial. Cremation is not a big problem for God in terms of the resurrection. In the life beyond, we will not be disembodied spirits. Each person is to receive "a spiritual body" (1 Cor. 15:44) that will have some continuity with the earthly body, but that continuity may not involve the atoms and molecules of this present age at all.

Personally, I believe that burial of the body better intimates and correlates with the resurrection hope of Christians. Jesus' crucified body was raised from death—transformed into a glorified body. We await, through the resurrection, the resplendent completion of what the body has been in this life.

Saturday, June 27.
I have been thinking of the line from Psalm 23, "Surely goodness and mercy shall follow me all the days of my life" (v. 6). The natural extension of that under God is "and I shall dwell in the house of the Lord for ever."

Monday, June 29, to Monday, July 6.
Maren is spending several weeks with us. She and Ruth and I drove to Putney, Vermont, for a week's vacation. The Honsakers, members of the Genesis Church there, were visiting relatives and gave us use of their beautiful home with a view of the valley and mountains.

We made day trips, mostly to state parks, and nearly every day came to a lake where Ruth and Maren would swim. On Wednesday we climbed the relatively easy ascent to the top of Mt. Olga in Molly Stark State Park. On Saturday we climbed Bald Mountain in Townshend State Park. With my slow pace, the climb and the return took about three and one-half hours, but we were elated afterward when Maren checked a book giving fifty hikes in Vermont and found that the one up Bald Mountain was listed as "moderate to strenuous."

On the way back, we picked several quarts of strawberries. As we were leaving the strawberry farm, Maren said, "Mother got to eat out fancy, and Father got to pick strawberries. The vacation has been a roaring success."

We also spent the evening with Paul and Dorothy Grout in their home. Paul was amazed that I had gone up Bald Mountain: "Thank God!"

We told them about my burial box. Paul said he would also like to have a burial box made so that they would be prepared. He added, "I want to stand ours on end and use it as a bookcase. I would want it to be fully functional." We were laughing together about the boxes. Somehow it was a blessed merriment. I left their home with a glad sense of having been touched by the Spirit.

The next day I was thinking: The Grout box would be for whoever dies first. Then a thought came that had not occurred to me before. It is extremely likely that the box built for me will indeed be mine. But the uncertainties of life are such that it could be needed first for Ruth or one of our children.

We went to Putney because of Paul's longstanding invitation to preach in a Genesis church service if I would be up to it. I wanted to speak on something that could come out of my dealing with cancer. Several weeks ago Ruth suggested that I deal with salvation. I took the theme "The Day of Christ," the last judgment.

How good it was to be in the service. Paul used the phrase "live with abandon." He had a laying on of hands for Ruth, Maren, and me. I had been given time and a sufficient measure of health for both vacation and preaching. On Thursday I am to resume chemotherapy.

Thursday, July 9.
The July *Messenger* arrived with my article, "The Problem with Pluralism." This too I have lived long enough to see.

Saturday, July 11.
Miriam came from New York yesterday after having returned from Belarus on Wednesday. Maren, Miriam, and I walked through the woodlot. We

spotted a mockingbird nest with one egg in the little spruce transplanted from the garden. This is the first bird nest in the woodlot. Even some of the redbuds are as tall as we are.

Thursday, July 16.
After chemotherapy Ruth dropped Maren and me off at Border's Bookstore in Towson. I spent the time going over the section on death and dying. On the five or so shelves of books, there was hardly anything from a Christian perspective. I was drawn to Henri Nouwen's slender volume *Our Greatest Gift: A Meditation on Dying and Caring*, and Maren offered to buy it for me as a late birthday gift. I began reading it this evening. A key concept for Nouwen is that of befriending death. I'll need to see more what he makes of this. I don't think death is viewed as friend (or the equivalent) anywhere in the New Testament. "The last enemy to be destroyed is death" (1 Cor. 15:26). God can, though, make death an inimical power subservient to his purposes within the fallen world.

Nouwen believes that one's dying should be one's "greatest gift" to others, that which has deepest and fullest significance. I think this can be the case, but would question the generalization. Within the providence of God, various things a person has done or shared may have more significance for others than the person's death. Nouwen's sudden and unexpected death from a heart attack had impact on a great many people only because of what they had received from him otherwise. If I had been killed in 1990 by the steer that attacked me and gored my leg, my death would not have had much to offer to others.

Monday, July 20.
In a telephone conversation, Ruth's mother said to us, *"Ihr lebt von Wunder zu Wunder* [You live from miracle to miracle]."

Friday, July 24.
Two tiny mockingbirds have replaced the eggs in the nest in the woodlot.

Today is our thirty-third wedding anniversary. Still another year has been given to us.

Monday to Friday, July 27-31.
Ruth and I drove to Ohio on Monday. I did most of the driving. Helen (my first cousin) and Eldon Denlinger had us for the evening meal, along with Bernice Miller, my cousin Glen's widow, and several others. We looked at old photos. It was a lovely evening.

Before Bernice left, I told her that I often recall what I heard Glen say again and again, "It's in the Lord's hands," meaning what was coming yet for him and how long he would live. Bernice replied, "But God gave us the will to live." In other words, Glen's statement was not to be taken as passive resignation. God has breathed the breath of life into each of us and given us the will to live. When our will is subordinate to the will of God, that is good. To continue to live as a human being on earth before God is good, but then God transposes that good into something higher. (The powers of disintegration can, however, become so dominant in a person that the goodness of living becomes questionable.)

We learned from Helen that Aunt Eileen has been receiving treatment for lung cancer. We'd known nothing about this. Tuesday morning we visited her and then Uncle Harry in the nearby nursing home.

Wednesday we visited Don and Phyllis Miller in Richmond, Indiana, and then drove north to Don and Olive Colliers' near Sunfield, Michigan, where I had been pastor in the early seventies. Don and Olive had organized a carry-in meal. There were almost twenty of us—a memorable time. Some who came had been "on the other side" when I was asked to leave because of my radical peace activism and work with the poor; but that conflict has faded into the past. We went to Michigan partly with the thought of again meeting people with whom we had been in conflict.

The next morning Don and Olive took us to visit an elderly member of the church, who is living in a senior apartment in Lansing. Because she had been very much on the other side in what happened in 1972, we felt it would be especially important to visit her. During the visit no one mentioned those earlier troubles. We simply had some time with her and sought to show her that we love her.

We visited Harold and Edith Benedict. Edith has been ill with cancer. We had the evening with Irene Trowbridge, who hosted us for overnight. Irene Trowbridge is into her eighties and suffers a lot from emphysema. She recalled that as her pastor I had encouraged her to stop smoking.

I was struck by a photo of her and Wayne as a young married couple. She was quite beautiful and he handsome. I thought of Arnold Bennett's *Old Wives' Tale*. Early in the novel the teenage sisters, Constance and Sophia, are amused to observe certain decrepit old women. But by the end they have become the decrepit old women whom girls are tittering about. Bennett so tellingly depicts the pathos and starkness of the transition into physical and mental decline, which time brings. But he grasps only that. An aged person need not be "a paltry thing," except for afflictions such as advanced Alzheimer's or totally incapacitating strokes that bring an effacing of personality.

Miriam and Chuck had given me cassette tapes of *The New Testament as Told by Max McLean.* I'd met him when he came to present Mark's Gospel at the Furman University Pastors' School in 1992. Ruth and I listened to most of Luke, Acts, and Romans as we drove. The text is somewhat abridged, but one hardly notices. McLean communicates the word of God with extraordinary clarity and power. The listener is taken from a saccharine Jesus to the Christ who turned the world upside down. If I become hardly able to read on my own, I hope to hear scripture from these tapes.

A verse that especially struck me was Acts 20:24. Paul told the Ephesian elders: "But I reckon my own life to be worth nothing to me; I only want to complete my mission and finish the work that the Lord Jesus gave me to do, which is to declare the Good News about the grace of God." Paul was not clinging to his life for any autonomous, intrinsic value to himself; his life continued to have significance only in its relation to God and God's purposes for his living.

Paul could tell the Ephesian elders that they would not see him again. "They were all crying as they hugged him and kissed him good-bye" (Acts 20:37). Especially with people in Michigan, the thought came to me that I might not see any of them again. (But I had thought the same thing when we visited relatives and friends in Ohio and Indiana a year ago.) We can hardly know for sure what will be our final time together, and even if finality is virtually certain (say, the cancer is spreading badly in my body), one can hardly experience parting moments with the full depth and intensity that would be right. Grace for that can come in actual dying.

Saturday, August 1.

On the way back, Ruth and I stayed overnight near Deep Creek Lake in western Maryland and hiked this morning in the state park. The trees "clap their hands" (Isa. 55:12) in praise to God. But dead trees still lift gaunt arms in adoration. Fallen trunks and leaves nestling into decay, residual bits of God's organic creation, continue a muted praise. Each human body, living and dead, has its part in praising the Creator. We don't usually think of a corpse as expressing praise. The one who may have done the praising has moved on. But each dead body is like the corpse of Jesus, testifying to God's victory over death.

Here is a letter from Stanley Hauerwas, a professor at Duke Divinity School:

Dear Dale,

Thank you so much for sending me the letter and letting me
know how you are. I remember to pray for you from time to
time, and am glad to know that God wants you to live a while
longer. That's very good.

Peace,
Stanley

His conclusion "that God wants you to live a while longer" is a splendid
way of summing up what has come to me.

Tuesday, August 4.

Disease can be a reaping of what one has sowed. It can be judgment from
God, but it need not be that at all. Jesus said about the man blind from
birth, "It was not that this man sinned, or his parents, but that the works of
God might be made manifest in him" (John 9:3).

A German friend, who in deep concern has been in touch with us since
my diagnosis, has informed us that he too has just received a cancer
diagnosis. He has told very few people; this is to remain a secret. A little
younger than Ruth, he is a very successful and prominent person. He
expresses an approach very different from mine: "The good thing is I am not
feeling bad or sick at all and there is a good chance to get cured. And since
I am a strong person, I have made the decision to survive my cancer. It
helps to . . . know all the 'tricks.' " I ask God's merciful blessing for him
in that stance.

Thursday, August 6, Hiroshima Day.

I had called the forester about the disease affecting the twenty-five
flowering dogwoods in the woodlot. She came this afternoon while I away
for the chemotherapy, but she left a letter. The dogwoods have the worst of
the possible diseases—the fungus Discula anthracnose. She wrote,
"Everything else looks fabulous! You had an excellent planting crew."

We need to try to remove and destroy all the dropped leaves in the fall
and start a spray schedule in the spring to "control" the disease. I think we
will give up on these dogwoods, remove them very soon, and maybe plant
redbuds in the spring.

Friday, August 7.

Miriam came from New York. As we were driving in the lane, she and I got out to check the mockingbird nest in the biggest Norway spruce in the woodlot, but the fledglings were gone.

She and Ruth and I were talking about what we had been through with the lung cancer. I made the comment, "The hardest part is still ahead."

Miriam replied, "The hardest part may be behind us." She explained that, though she was much younger then, learning that Grammee (my mother) had cancer and would very likely die before long was harder for her than actually losing her grandmother later on. She thinks that the family and I may already have gone through the most difficult phase of facing my death.

Perhaps only later will the family or I be able to say what period has been the hardest.

Saturday, August 8.

Miriam discovered that the one lawyer in the trio that went to Belarus in July also had a father with cancer. A few days ago she learned that his father had died, and she wrote him a sympathy note. He wrote back: His father had been given the good prognosis that the pancreatic cancer was in remission, and he was very hopeful; but he, a World War II veteran, had gone to see the movie *Saving Private Ryan* and had died of a heart attack while watching it. Miriam had seen the film and spoke of it as terribly graphic and gruesome. How devious and unpredictable are death's stratagems!

I have received a notice that I am to be on call for jury duty. I intend to ask for exemption because of the cancer. Miriam said, "I can't imagine your ever being selected for a jury in any case." Several times through the years when I have received such a notice, I've written a statement about how I question the entire criminal "justice" and penal system in this country. Never did I hear anything further. On the other hand, by going onto a jury, one could try to exert some countervailing influence within what one sees as a perverted system.

Sunday, August 9.

I went through books and all sorts of odds and ends that were on the long, floor-level shelf behind the table in what had been the computer room. Among various treasures I found a hardback folder that held early letters I had sent to Ruth, one being something I had written as a present for Ruth on her twenty-fourth birthday in 1966, a couple of weeks before Daniel's birth—an account of the pregnancy as we had experienced it together.

Neither of us could recall reading it since that birthday. We had a beautiful, reminiscent time this evening as I read her the five pages and a poem I had written for her.

> You daughter of Elisabeth, who great
> With child discern an as yet hidden One
> Greater unspeakably
> Than your near mystery,
> With awed exulting you commemorate
> The Birth through which your bearing was begun.
> Sprightly the baby leaps and you know why.
>
> My Moabite Maria of almost
> Accomplished days, frail lower maid by much,
> Mary's delivery once
> Has brought deliverance:
> Your labors borne and coming are not lost;
> Her child has burst the binding graveclothes' clutch;
> He frees through us a third, to magnify.

Thursday, August 13.

Miriam and Chuck were here at our place when I returned from chemotherapy. They were on their way to Atlanta in a long van. Chuck will be teaching and doing research at Emory University on a Mellon fellowship, and Miriam will be back in New York for her second year of law school. I was happy to have Chuck pick out a boxful of my books on Greek and Roman topics.

Tuesday, August 18.

I had the sad task today of digging out the twenty-five flowering dogwoods. In Gospel parables and images, plants that are at fault through not producing are done away with. The dogwoods were not discernibly at fault but were victims of a wretched fungus that is so widely destroying what may be the most beautiful native flowering tree in this part of the world.

Wednesday, August 19.

Ruth came back today from moving art things into the new school building: "It is so good to come home. Home is the place, but home is mainly you." She wonders what it will be like to return to this place without my presence.

Thursday, August 20.

Clyde Carter called this morning. A pastor and peacemaker, he's been so good staying in touch with me since the diagnosis. As we were closing the conversation, I thanked him for his prayers. Then he told me something he had told to only a few others. Over some period of time, when he lifts me "up in prayer," he has felt very weak; his hands go limp. He said that he must be careful not to pray for me when he is driving a car or mowing lawn. He needs to be sitting, relaxed, and not holding anything. He has never experienced anything like this before, though he has had it in a more limited way when praying for a couple of other people.

He said, "I don't know what that means. If I get to the end of the day and have not had that experience, it's a reminder that I still need to pray for you."

I thought of the verse, "Bear one another's burdens, and so fulfil the law of Christ" (Gal. 6:2). It seems that my debilitation is visited on Clyde—greater weakness really than I currently have to cope with. I am very touched by his vicarious solidarity with me.

I drove down for the chemotherapy treatment. There was a poster on a stand in the waiting room that almost seemed like something out of the peace movement. There were graphs and summaries: Some 496,000 Americans have died in five wars fought in this century. Cancer claims the lives of 550,000 in the U.S. each year. The government spent $61 billion on the Gulf War but spends $2.3 billion (National Cancer Institute) a year on cancer research—thus, 26 times as much for that war. The poster was a call to participation in The March on Washington (for increased government commitment to cancer research) on September 26.

Friday, August 21.

I drove to Frederick for a CT scan. When we were most of the way through the scanning, the technician told me, "I know I am not supposed to say anything, but I've looked at the pictures of the liver. I've not looked at the pictures of the chest. But in the liver I see a big difference—an improvement." I'd brought in the scans from late May. I think he was so happy for me that he was compelled to share this.

On the way home I stopped by Ruth's school and went to the art room. I wanted to tell her the news as soon as I could. We don't know if the overall report will be as good. The improvement the technician told me about is in itself a reason to be thankful. "Praise the Lord. I will give thanks to the Lord with my whole heart" (Ps. 111:1).

Saturday, August 22.

When doing remarkably well, it's easy to slip into a hubris, or at least an exultation apart from God. I've been thinking of the verse: "You are not your own; you were bought with a price. So glorify God in your body" (1 Cor. 6:19-20). I've had a sort of secondary and correlative redemption from dying soon. Even more than before, the days are not my own but are assigned for giving glory.

When we called Maren in the evening, Ruth told her than Daniel is thinking of going for part of each year to Ecuador to practice medicine after he has finished his Lancaster residency in a year and a half. I commented that earlier it had seemed unlikely that I would live till Daniel completed his residency. If I do, that might create a problem with regard to where he locates.

Maren replied, "We are very glad for you to be creating problems as long as possible."

Sunday, August 23.

The Bowermans, an Old German Baptist tenant farm family with eight children, lost ten high-producing dairy cows when lightning struck a tree during the last severe storm. When we got in touch with them, Margaret mentioned to Ruth that it seemed like something God had done. Imagining that they were struggling with the meaning of this "act of God," I wrote them a note in which I mentioned that just as diseases are to be seen as rebel powers within God's creation, so also are the rampaging and destructive forces of nature.

A few days ago I came across a sentence I had copied many years ago stating that lightning takes large quantities of nitrogen out of the air to make it available as a nutrient for the ground. As psalmists recognized, lightning intimates God's glory. But lightning that destroys and kills is a creature veering out of bounds, showing the distortedness of creation. Rampages of nature can be judgment of God. Some are traceable to human degradation of the environment. But God "sends rain [and the awesome, erratic might of lightning] on the just and on the unjust" (Matt. 5:45). Jesus calmed the storm that could have sunk the boat, killing all of them in it (Matt. 8:26). Comparable deliverance is still given but, as with healing of deadly disease, only from time to time.

Monday, August 24.

This was Ruth's first day teaching again. Maren had her first class in her graduate work at Berkeley.

Friday's CT scan report came by fax, confirming what the technician had told me. The lesions in the liver have shrunk or gone away by about one third. Also, the main tumor in the lung is somewhat smaller.

I was thankful for the report—such good news. At the same time, I felt a little disappointed for I'd hoped there might be an even greater decrease. It's right that I remain hopeful for a greater measure of healing, but it's crucial that I rejoice in what is given rather than be disappointed in what is not given. Otherwise, I'm like the child at Christmas surrounded by many gifts but unhappy that the one desired gift is not there.

Thursday, August 27.
This morning I had a second appointment with my oncologist, Dr. Ettinger. He hadn't received a copy of the radiologist's report, but he read the copy I brought along with the pictures and exclaimed, "Fantastic! This is great!" After looking at the pictures and examining me, he said, "You are doing tremendous."

He recommends that I continue on the gemcitabine for three three-week sessions with a week off after each session and then have another CT scan. His elation about the report was good therapy for me.

Friday to Sunday, September 4-6.
The fall gathering of Brethren Peace Fellowship was held in the Genesis meetinghouse in Putney, Vermont. It was a good weekend for me. Jim Gibbel had asked me to give some reflections Saturday evening. I did that, commenting especially on 2 Corinthians 12:1-10 about the thorn in the flesh and power in weakness. The Sunday worship service renewed me. Just as I was ready to take the communion cup, we were led in the South African song that has the refrain, "Hallelujah! We sing your praises, all our hearts are filled with gladness."

Tuesday, September 8.
This afternoon a light shower moved through, followed by a double rainbow. I stood gazing at it for quite a long while. In spite of the splendor, we usually have only a short attention span for rainbows.

Saturday, September 12.
During my nap time, Ruth, Daniel, and Miriam were discussing Mutter's inquiry about Christmas wishes. When I came upon the conversation, we all

agreed that my nap had been well timed. I commented, "My being with you for Christmas, that will be my gift to each of you."

Daniel said, "If you don't come through on that, Father, we will really be bummed."

Sunday, September 13.
Last Monday they asked me to preach today in the Pipe Creek service. I spent much of the latter part of the week preparing a sermon based on the passage in 2 Corinthians 11:30–12:10, "Power in Weakness." I thanked the Pipe Creek folk for their prayers on my behalf.

Friday, September 25.
Ruth took a "dependent care" day, and we left very early for a lung cancer symposium in Arlington, Virginia, sponsored by ALCASE (Alliance for Lung Cancer, Advocacy, Support and Education). It has been a most stimulating day. Some of the lectures were more for medical professionals, but we could follow most of it. We were already aware of much that was presented.

"Lung cancer is by far the most lethal of all malignancies. Among cancers it is the leading killer in the U.S. and globally. In the U.S., 180,000 new cases are diagnosed each year."

With lung cancer "the vast majority of those not cured die within two years of diagnosis." Cures are pretty much confined to Stage I and Stage II operable cases.

Several times a graph on the mortality from lung cancer was projected on the screen. With keen interest I studied the line for stage IV. At two years it looked like about 6 percent survival, but then it went plunging right on down to near zero.

A lawyer in the struggle against tobacco presented the case to show how for years the tobacco companies have done everything they could to make cigarettes more addictive. Their business is selling nicotine, and they need to get people hooked. The tobacco industry is so clearly a demonic principality.

Randomized studies have shown that supportive care without chemo is more costly to HMOs on an average than is treatment by chemo—this because of the costs of hospitalization, radiation, etc., that are needed. I found some reassurance in that information, because I have been uneasy about having so much money spent on my chemotherapy.

Friday to Monday, October 2-5.

This has been a remarkably full and extraordinarily rich weekend, celebrating the fiftieth anniversary of Brethren Volunteer Service, a very important part of my life. My energy level held up, though I took three or four rest times each day. A key verse for me was, "They who wait upon the Lord shall renew their strength" (Isa. 40:31).

Over the years there have been more than 5,200 BVSers. That means millions of lives have been touched directly by these volunteers.

Don Murray stayed with us for the weekend. He had just come from playing a part in a TV episode shot in Montreal.

I had also encouraged Don Miller, my closest boyhood friend and now retired general secretary of the Church of the Brethren, to come to the celebration. Ruth had prepared a lot of food ahead, and Saturday evening we hosted a reunion for seventeen people, most of them (counting wives) from the training unit of the two Dons. Another former BVSer, Donna Gochenour Haldeman from Ruth's unit, has been struggling with ovarian cancer. Like me she had been treated with taxol and cisplatinum, but she nearly died from the treatment. Before people left, they formed a prayer circle with Don Miller taking the lead. Donna and I sat on the couch and we all joined hands as the group prayed for our healing. This too was a very meaningful highlight of the weekend. I told someone, "It is a miracle that I am alive, and we live in that miracle as long as it is given."

I'd been asked to give the invocation for the Saturday evening service. I sought to exalt God's grace behind it all. Don Murray was the keynote speaker for Saturday evening, replacing Charles Boyer, former BVSer and Brethren leader, who is recovering from chemotherapy for leukemia.

Don quipped that he knew he had been given this assignment because he was "the one man there who had kissed Marilyn Monroe—presumably." He also mentioned an incident at a Brethren Annual Conference, when he gave a presentation on nonviolence to a Brethren Service luncheon. In the time for questions, someone asked him, "What does it feel like to kiss Marilyn Monroe?" and he had replied, "That is just what we have been talking about. It's a matter of nonviolent resistance." Don then went on in our service to read parts of his autobiographical play—how he had become a conscientious objector and had achieved some success in his Sardinia refugee resettlement project.

Monday morning Don and I talked. It reminded me of the long conversations we had during our time together in BVS. He said that even as a child, whenever he saw a movie in which an Indian "extra" would be shot and fall dead to the ground, he would begin to wonder about the Indian and his life, distracting him from following the story. Much of Don's life reflects his concern for those who are regarded as counting for nothing. Every Christian should have such an eye.

I asked Don about life after death, and we talked for a while on that theme. Later Don said, "I wonder if we need to try to figure out what life after death will be like. What God gives will be wonderful—and a great surprise." There is much truth in that, and I agreed there is a danger of wanting to know too much and becoming speculative. But I would say that we should not take a strongly agnostic position either. In the New Testament we are given intimations about the life beyond, presumably because God wants us to have some inkling, even some very limited view, of what we are headed into. We should not want to know more or less than these intimations reveal.

Friday, October 9.
Though the weather was very cool and sporadically drizzly all day, the current BVS unit based in New Windsor came to our place for a foil dinner and campfire. Before the group left, they sang for Ruth and me the South African song "Freedom is coming, this I know. . . . Jesus is coming, this I know." As Christians we know the former because we know the latter.

Saturday, October 10.
I had chemotherapy again on Thursday after two weeks off. This evening I am terribly fatigued and have no will to do anything. I feel discouraged and uneasy about the various things coming up—the two preaching engagements, a weekend with death penalty opponent SueZann Bosler, a trip to California to see Maren. This weakness looms large over against such plans.

Sunday, October 11.
The night of rest helped a lot. The events ahead seem doable again.

Monday, October 12.
I was thinking of what we can know about life beyond death, and this verse came to mind: "Beloved, we are God's children now; it does not yet appear what we shall be, but we know that when he appears we shall be like him, for we shall see him as he is" (1 John 3:2). What we shall be, then, is hidden from us, but we know that we shall see Jesus face to face ("as he is"), and

we shall become much more like him than is possible on earth now. But this will be no solitary beatific vision. Jesus lived in fellowship with others. Part of being like him will be the reveling with earlier loved ones and new loved ones.

Then will come the culmination of the earthly process pictured in 2 Corinthians 3:18: "And we all, with unveiled face, beholding the glory of the Lord, are being changed into his likeness from one degree of glory to another."

Saturday and Sunday, October 17-18.

I had a preaching engagement with the Green Hill Church south of Salisbury, Maryland, nearly four hours drive from here. Originally, I was to preach on the first Sunday in May, but that was when I had pneumonia. Ruth drove me over later on Saturday. It was a beautiful day; we were delighted to be able to do this together.

In the morning service, I preached on "The Day of Christ"—being ready for the exit from this life and facing Christ in the last judgment. Ruth still has difficulty with this sermon, even after the revision. It's hard for her to think that departed loved ones are with Christ more fully than they were here on earth and yet they still have the final judgment ahead of them when Jesus Christ appears. The implied interim and the sequence seem clear to me from the New Testament.

Tuesday, October 20.

Merle Crouse, a friend since we were in BVS together, came by to see me. As he was leaving, Merle, a lifelong bird-watcher, mentioned that a Carolina wren had just flown onto our front porch. I was jarred by this identification. Soon after we moved to this place, I had identified these wrens as Bewick wrens and through all the years had happily used the wrong identification. I checked in my bird book and confirmed my error. So, this late in my life a mistaken opinion, held firm through a quarter of a century, was corrected.

Friday to Monday, October 23-26.

As I looked ahead to it, this seemed like a daunting weekend, especially at times when I felt very fatigued. But the weekend was filled with life and blessing. I had invited SueZann Bosler to come from Florida to give her testimony in several settings on the death penalty, and we hosted her on Saturday.

When Ernie Rice introduced SueZann to the combined Westminster Sunday school class, he said, "We have two walking miracles with us here this morning." He meant SueZann and me. I was struck by the pairing. God had saved her from death and given her this ministry. God has given me unexpectedly longer life and further ministry to live out.

She began by saying, "I am a victim," and proceeded to give content to that. She told us about December 22, 1986. People were often coming to the door of the Brethren parsonage in Miami, Florida, asking for help. Bill Bosler, her pastor father, always had something for them. But that day a man (probably on drugs) began stabbing her father with a knife at the parsonage door. Hearing his cries, SueZann went to intervene and was herself attacked—taking knife wounds in her back and into the side of her head. Her father died of twenty-two stab wounds.

The most moving moment for me in the testimony was not in her account of the attack, but her retelling of the third trial of James Bernard Campbell on June 13, 1997. There in the courtroom SueZann was given the grace to move beyond what she had felt previously. She looked at Campbell and said to him, "I forgive you." This was her "closure." She felt a newly given peace sweep over her. In that trial, through her efforts, his death sentence was changed to life imprisonment without parole.

Tuesday, October 27.

Yesterday morning it was mild outside. I wanted to air out the addition room where my word processor is. The southeast window is a little hard to raise. I got it up, but I felt a little pain in the middle of my back immediately afterward. This morning after Ruth left for school, the pain became really bad. I could not do much more than try to cope with it. I was able to get an afternoon appointment with Dr. Caricofe. He ruled out kidney stones. The pain is around the T-8 vertebra where there has been a metastasis. He sent me on to Frederick for new x-rays.

Wednesday, October 28.

Dr. Caricofe called and reported that the x-rays show no change in the metastatic areas from the previous time. This is very good news, but I'm to check with Dr. Ettinger to see if I should have an MRI as well. Dr. Caricofe also said quite strongly that he didn't think it would be wise to go to Oakland on the weekend to see Maren. "You might end up in a hospital out there, and that would be very complicated." This corroborated my own thoughts, as I have intense pain when I get up from lying down. Daniel can still fly out and have the time with Maren.

Because of the pain, I decided to make an appointment with my chiropractor in Gettysburg. I had not gone to him since the diagnosis because of the metastases in the spine. He said it would be safe to do a gentle manipulation of the T-8 vertebra, where the problem is. He also said that the x-rays from Tuesday were from the lumbar area and did not show T-8.

After the treatment I was very fatigued and dejected. The adjustment did not bring any dramatic change. This much back pain, even if unrelated to the cancer, was just another complication. And then I wonder if I would have gotten into all this if I had not raised the difficult window.

Thursday, October 29.

After school Ruth drove me to Frederick again to get x-rays that would show the T-8 vertebra. She told me that one of her "art helpers," a child, came and asked, "Is your husband going to die?"

Ruth replied, "Yes, but not right away." That seemed a safe enough answer.

I had extreme pain getting off the x-ray table.

Friday, October 30.

My back has given me less pain today. That helped out a lot. I went over my latest article, " 'Hands Off That Other Throat': Political Implications of the Parable of the Unforgiving Servant." I printed it out and got it ready to send to *Messenger*. This too I want to share with the church. It challenges certain attitudes that are dominant in society as a whole but are especially strong in the religious right.

Some weeks ago I decided not to risk the trip to Chicago for the late October meeting of the Christian Peacemaker Teams steering committee. This evening Paul Dodd, who went in my place, called from the meeting. Over a speaker phone, the nineteen of them in the group sang two songs for me. I was touched. The one was "They that wait upon the Lord shall renew their strength." I'd had that scripture in mind a lot in these past days. The other song was a spiritual unfamiliar to me, "Lord, keep my feet, while I run this race."

Tuesday, November 3.

Yesterday afternoon I was having some piercing pain again. I called my chiropractor, Dr. Atkins, and went over things with him. He thought I should come in for another adjustment. Ruth drove me to Gettysburg after her school day. Dr. Atkins said that the contorted muscles had pulled the T-8 vertebra back out of alignment again. He gave me an adjustment to bring it into alignment. Since then I've not had any further sharp pain, and that is a great relief.

Thursday, November 5.
Today marks two years since the day of the initial diagnosis. Though healing has not been given, twenty-four months filled with blessing upon blessing have been granted us.

Dr. Ettinger thinks I should have an MRI of the spine. One is now scheduled for next Tuesday.

Friday, November 6.
This afternoon Miriam, who is here for two days, and I spent some time in the woodlot. She had last year's diagram of the tree layout. I gave instructions for replacing the diseased dogwoods and others that have died. We have some volunteer trees around the house yard, and we will order some redbuds. If I am not alive in the spring, Miriam will have the instructions recorded.

Sunday, November 8.
Today has been another big day. We left early for the Conestoga meetinghouse near Lancaster. This is the third oldest Church of the Brethren congregation in the United States. I'd been asked to preach a peace sermon—the first such sermon that I have preached since a little before the diagnosis. I spoke from the first verses of John 10: the voice of Jesus the Good Shepherd and the alien voices all around us calling us into commitments to the ways of violence. I continue to see an urgent need for such preaching and teaching.

I used the comment, as I occasionally do, that the way each German lived during the Nazi period made it either a little easier or a little harder for the Nazis to do what they did. So too the way each of us lives makes it a little easier or a little harder for this society to go with its immense commitments to violence. There is, I think, only a limited minority, a remnant, who makes it harder.

Monday, November 9—the fourth day of my third year.

I read the account in Luke 20 about the Sadducees questioning Jesus on the resurrection from the dead. Jesus was certain that there is such resurrection ahead. (We can ground our confidence in his certainty.) We are to be like angels. The shadow of mortality will no longer rest upon us. We cannot really envision human life without that shadow. The God of Abraham, Isaac, and Jacob "is not God of the dead, but of the living; for all live to him" (v. 38). To the extent that we truly live, we live toward and in God. But that is also the case for God's people who have departed this life. They continue to live toward and in God. The consummation ushered in by the appearing of Jesus will bring glorious fulfilment to that. In this life even those who most resist living toward God have him as the source of their existence.

Fletcher Farrar, editor of *Messenger*, called. He likes the article, " 'Hands Off That Other Throat': Political Implications of the Parable of the Unforgiving Servant," and wants to publish it. He thinks it will generate as much discussion as the "pluralism" article did, and he welcomes that.

In the evening I read to Ruth some journal pages covering a time after the turning in our relationship in the park in South Bend, Indiana, when our friendship turned into a life commitment. I noted her comment about the unfolding of our friendship, "We had the spiritual attunement and the other came."

Tuesday, November 10.

After school Ruth drove me to Frederick, and I got an MRI of the middle and lower spine. Getting up from the MRI table brought severe back pain, and I've had more pain in my back since then.

My morning meditation was on 1 Corinthians 3:21-23: "For all things are yours, whether Paul or Apollos or Cephas or the world or life or death or the present or the future, all are yours; and you are Christ's; and Christ is God's." I had quoted it in German in a letter I sent to Ruth as she was sailing back to Germany after the turning.

So much is given us as Christians—abundance beyond imagining. Paul can speak of "all things." We are given the Gospel and the word of God. We are given spiritual life grounded in the One who is Life of the universe. We are given loved ones, brothers and sisters in the faith, Christian leaders in their witness; and these represent for us the totality of God's people, the communion of the saints. We are given a tiny representative view of God's earthly creation receding into the whole; and we are given the unfathomable immensity of heaven above us. What we need for our physical living is supplied.

All things are given to us, but as part of the same movement, we are given to Christ, we are Christ's. The movement culminates in God where it began.

Paul includes "life or death" in his listing. Death has the appearance of the event of total deprivation. The person who has just died has nothing; the future is lost. But such is the dynamism of God's giving that death itself is caught up into it. What seems the ultimate deprivation is gateway into greater receiving and into being "Christ's" in a fuller way.

Paul writes in Romans 8:32: "He who did not spare his own Son but gave him up for us all, will he not also give us all things with him?" Giving the Son was so overwhelmingly central and marvelous that "all things" go with it as natural accompaniment. To be given the Son brings with it all that belongs to the Son.

Wednesday, November 11.

This afternoon Dr. Caricofe's office faxed me the report from the MRI. It is bad news. There is now metastatic growth in the thoracic vertebrae from 6 to 12, with T-8, where the pain is concentrated, being particularly affected. After school Ruth drove me to Frederick to pick up the MRI pictures. Ruth asked to speak with the radiologist. He put several of the pictures onto the view box. One could see that T-8 was all gray and somewhat enlarged from the cancer. The neighboring vertebrae all had some darker metastatic areas.

Dr. Caricofe called early this evening. He thinks it is important to get lined up for radiation treatments as soon as possible. These would be for managing the pain and for preventing my spine from collapsing and paralyzing the lower half of my body.

Frauke Westphal told us by phone, "This is not a new disaster. It is the old disaster coming in this way."

With this report the possible nearness and actuality of my dying looms large again for Ruth and me. We spoke and prayed through tears. Ruth said, "The devil wants us to stare at death, but we are to gaze at Christ." I felt God's peace in coping with this development. I hope there can be treatment that will keep my spine from giving out before other vital parts of my body.

All along I have sought miraculous healing, even though there is no hope of a cure medically. The MRI shows that God does not have such healing in mind for me. My physical decline is not that far along, but the cancer demonstrates its stalking dominance. Yet even as I see such indications, I keep the possibility of healing in view.

Ruth said, hugging me, "We will need to give each other lots more hugs again. They will need to last me my lifetime."

Thursday, November 12.
Ruth took off the day of school, and we worked on getting radiation treatments set up. The various things we needed to work on fell into place. I was to have had chemotherapy this afternoon, but an oncologist filling in for Dr. Ettinger, who is out of town, took me off the chemo. In the middle of the day, I was able to see Dr. Lee, the radiation oncologist in Frederick, whom I had nearly a year ago for radiation of the lumbar spine. He says that he will try to radiate nearly all the affected thoracic vertebrae. We were encouraged to find out that this will be possible. There are to be ten treatments, beginning next Tuesday. Yesterday we were reeling some under the onslaught. Today we have been working on countermeasures and don't feel quite so vulnerable. Miriam told us that she and Maren had talked long into the night about the grim news. They reminded each other that there were other times when the prospects seemed very bad.

In retrospect the injury to my weakened spine from raising the window was probably a blessing in disguise. Without it the condition of my spine might have become still worse before it would have come to our attention. So my error in judgment that resulted in all that pain really did work for my good and now makes more sense to me than before.

Friday, November 13.
After school as Ruth and I were returning from a walk along Stem Road, she said, "I hope it will come for you that you will feel you want to go home. You will not want to leave us, but you will feel right about going home."

Saturday, November 14.
Charles and Susie Klingler, friends from North Manchester, Indiana, have been on a circuit in the East and spent several hours with us.

Charles had written that he would gladly give me his remaining time on earth. When I mentioned this, he replied, "That is easily said because it cannot be done."

I said, "When my sister, Jane, was dying of cancer, my father would say, 'If I could only die instead of her.' But that is not the way life works."

Charles answered, "But that is the way love works."
As they were leaving, he embraced me and said, "If not here, there."

Monday, November 16.

Ruth told me, "I'm trying to cherish each day as it is given and not to look on ahead." She meant looking ahead to the suffering that may be coming for me and to what life without me will be like.

Tuesday, November 17.

I've been meditating on Philippians 1:19-26, one of the most significant passages about death in the New Testament. "For to me to live is Christ, and to die is gain. . . . My desire is to depart and be with Christ, for that is far better" (vv. 21, 23). I believe that a better state for me is ahead beyond death, but I do not yet prefer to depart and enter it. I would much rather "remain in the flesh" and be with my loved ones here.

This afternoon I had the first of ten radiation treatments for the thoracic vertebrae. Once again I lay listening to the hum of the machine sending those rays into my body, killing cancer cells and working for healing.

Scott Blanchard and Ken Koons, who are working on the series for the *Carroll County Times*, took me down for treatment. Back home as we were talking, I said something like, "If all this about God and Jesus is true, then indeed a better life awaits us beyond death." Ken pointed to my "if" and asked, "Do you have doubts?"

I replied that the possibility that the Christian faith is an illusion can never be fully eliminated; it is there. But I don't find myself pulled back and forth between faith and doubt. I am so sure that the Gospel is true, that Jesus is the One who has come from God, that he died for us, that he rose from the dead. Trust that he did indeed rise is the cornerstone of my faith. There are all the intellectual considerations that come together to point to the truth of the faith, but also I find it so surely true because I have lived my life with this One who was raised from the dead. This faith is what bears me up as I approach the end of my life.

I can't project what will be ahead for me spiritually. I hope my faith holds firm and steady, but I could be given over to *Anfechtungen*, spiritual attacks. May God deliver me from those.

Wednesday, November 18.

Since soon after the back pain began, I've been sleeping downstairs in the addition. The bed here where I have the word processor is from my father.

One can raise the head of the bed, and that helps me in getting from a horizontal to a vertical position with less pain. Ruth wanted to move another single bed in for her; but there is hardly space for one, and I said I hope the radiation treatments bring enough improvement that I can return to sleeping upstairs again.

Janet Heltzel suggested a baby monitor. Ruth had her get one for us, and she set it up. This morning Ruth was so elated, "I can hear you breathing and when you rouse. It is just like having you sleeping beside me."

Thursday, November 19.

Doug Hess, the Old German Baptist physician who also has stage IV lung cancer, called this morning. He mentioned that when the radiation is going into him, he prays that the beams will hit the bad cells and the good cells will be spared. My prayers during radiation have not been focused in quite that way. I find it good to pray that the healthy cells will not be damaged.

Friday, November 20.

Dale Brown, retired Bethany Seminary professor, was here for a little more than an hour this morning. He made the comment, "Your legacy will be what you have written. That's the legacy that will continue." He said that nuclear issues are coming into the public consciousness again and will only increase with future developments. I thought of Stanley Hauerwas's observation in a piece he sent me, "We want to be remembered." But what is crucial is the cry, "Jesus, remember me . . ." (Luke 23:42).

Cathy Boshart wrote me, "Keep on ministering as long as you have breath." Ministering and breath may come much harder later on.

Sunday, November 22.

Today I preached the "Power in Weakness" sermon in the service of the German Lutheran Church in Washington. After the onset of the worst back pain, I had strongly considered canceling this engagement. But I was feeling up to the assignment, and the time went well. A year ago on the same Sunday, the close of the church year, I preached there on "Matters of Life or Death (Living with Dying)."

Tuesday, November 24.

This morning Ruth and I went to Johns Hopkins Hospital for a consultation with Dr. Ettinger about further treatment. For some months the Westphals have been suggesting that I try thalidomide as the next step, based mainly on their conversation with Dr. Steven Hirschfield, of the Division of Oncology Drug Products of the Food and Drug Administration. We were uneasy going into the consultation, because we thought Dr. Ettinger might be very negative about thalidomide.

He commented that we had gotten "a lot of mileage" out of the gemcitabine, which I have been on since the middle of April. He pointed us to navelbine by weekly infusion as third-line chemotherapy. He advised us that at best there would be a 10 to 20 percent chance that it would help. (We had been told of the same prospect for gemcitabine.) When we brought up thalidomide, he was totally against it. He said, "If you want that, you will need to find another oncologist." I expressed our high regard for him as my oncologist and asked about our going with the navelbine and staying with him, but getting the thalidomide through another physician. He was willing to go along with that.

Here at home I talked with Dr. Caricofe, my primary care physician. He agreed to prescribe thalidomide. Both he and the pharmacy need to get special clearances. Miriam said that she had read about an active movement protesting any revival of the use of thalidomide, because it caused severe birth defects in thousands of babies in the 1960s.

In the evening we called my oncologist cousin, David Miller. He thinks our two-track combination is a good one. He has two patients who are doing well on thalidomide. He mentioned that he often prays with his patients—those who feel comfortable with this. I don't think I have ever had a doctor pray *with* me, but I know that a number of my doctors have prayed *for* me.

Judy Cumbee, an anti-death penalty and peace activist, called and reported on the action last weekend to close the School of the Americas. If I had continued in good health, I might have gone. In the service, names of Latin American resisters who had "disappeared" (been killed by School of the Americas graduates) were sung. Crosses with the names were lifted into the air, and there was the cry, "Presente!" They too were recognized as part of the protest.

The thought came to me: When I, in what will likely be a more normal way, have disappeared, there can still be the sense, "Presente!" Not that I would be a ghostlike spirit hovering. But to live with Christ beyond death is not to be far from dear ones alive in Christ before death. That bond into the unseen may be felt especially on celebrative or momentous occasions.

Thursday, November 26, Thanksgiving.

This is my third Thanksgiving since the diagnosis—a day to give thanks for. I turned to 1 Corinthians 15:57 as a central expression of thanks: "But thanks be to God, who gives us the victory through our Lord Jesus Christ."

Ruth and I drove to Lancaster and had a beautiful time with Daniel. With his assistance she was occupied with meal preparation and washing windows. But for me simply being there with Daniel was a gift to be treasured.

I noticed Psalm 115:17: "The dead do not praise the Lord, / nor do any that go down into silence." In this Hebraic perspective, the most notable aspect of going "down into silence" was the cessation of praise to God. But with the New Testament, we move beyond that apparent state of things. Those who are beyond death live toward God (Luke 20:38) and praise him. I can make the appeal that I may be a more strategic use for the kingdom here on earth than I would be waiting beyond death.

Monday, November 30.

I had a CT scan this morning and then a radiation treatment. Later in the day, Doug Hess, the Old German Baptist physician with advanced lung cancer, came with his wife Suzanne. He said someone had asked him, "Does ever a day go by that you do not think about your cancer?" I was intrigued by the perspective implied in the question. It would not have occurred to me that there could possibly be a day without some thought of the cancer threat; that shadow lies over every day. Doug said too that he thinks it is quite impossible to live a day without thinking about it.

Tuesday, December 1.

The report from yesterday's CT scan came. It is very good news: The cancer in the lungs and liver has remained unchanged since August. So the spread of the disease in the spine is not paralleled by spread in these areas. This report is encouraging and makes me think I may have somewhat more time left than I thought a few days ago.

I had the last of the ten radiation treatments. The pain in my back does not bother me as much.

Thursday, December 3.

Dr. Caricofe called and told us that Aetna Insurance will not cover the thalidomide treatment. The tablets are terribly expensive. The cost for a year could be $30,000. As a drug for lung cancer, thalidomide is very experimental, unproven, and not approved. We don't plan to try to pay for it ourselves. It would be too costly and might not help at all.

Saturday, December 5.

Mutter, in a call from Germany, commented that if God intends to give me considerably more time, he can do that without thalidomide.

The union of a man and a woman in marriage was part of God's original plan for humanity. But the shadow of death looms over every marriage and is recognized in the traditional marriage ceremony: "till death do us part." However, death does not annul the extraordinary blessing and wonder that God gives in marriage. For the surviving spouse, the marriage should still be seen as a central part of the fullness of one's life and given thanks for. What God has granted in marriage is drawn up into the consummated lives of those who have lived life together on earth.

Romans 6:9-10: "For we know that Christ being raised from the dead will never die again; death no longer has dominion over him. The death he died he died to sin, once for all, but the life he lives he lives to God." Jesus on earth came under the dominion of death, and at the end he yielded to it. He died because of human sin, but in that ultimate encounter with sin he shattered its death-dealing grip on himself and on humanity.

A Christian (like anyone) dies because of sin. But that encounter with death is drawn into Christ's dying. One is given over into what sin has brought, but is then finished with sin and death. We are taken beyond the snares of sinning, and death's dominion over us is ended. We cannot in this present really fathom what that unshadowed life will be.

Sunday, December 6.

My back has improved enough that last night I was able to sleep upstairs again with Ruth—a most welcome change. No more baby monitor, at least for a while.

Thursday, December 10.

This afternoon I received the first infusion of the third-line chemotherapy, navelbine. I haven't felt much in the way of side effects, and that is a big help. I'm to have ten-minute infusions weekly for a few weeks and then see Dr. Ettinger again.

Sunday, December 13.

Today is Ruth's birthday. Remarkably, this is the third birthday we have had together since the diagnosis. We had a little celebration yesterday before Daniel returned to Lancaster. Maren arrived from Oakland last evening, and we had another celebration with her today. Viewing of Paul Grout's video, *Stations of the Resurrection*, was a high point of the day. It is a powerful, quite extraordinary presentation of the biblical message as depicted in his art, all centered on Christ.

Saturday, December 19.

Today was another memorable day. The first of a seven-part series on my life and struggle with cancer appeared in the *Carroll County Times* today. They are using the title "Living with Dying." On tree-planting day last year, Ken Koons took an exceptionally fine picture of me holding a spade at a hole I'd just started to dig. My face shows exhilaration, but I also look like a stricken person. Scott Blanchard's article was very well done. Ken said that to his knowledge the *Times* has never before done anything comparable to this. He sees it as the biggest single project he has ever been involved in. He has asked whether he can continue with the photographing after the series, and I said, "Certainly."

It's strange that a maverick peacemaker, so out of step with dominant political sentiment in this county, would be featured in this way. In the article Scott emphasizes my peacemaking.

He said to me, "You are probably inherently uncomfortable with being the focus of a lot of attention." Though I did not initiate the series, I see it as a way of sharing with others what we have tried to stand for in our lives. Without the cancer there would not have been this series. Or if I had died before last spring, the series would not have developed in this form.

Monday, December 21.

Mutter and Ruth's brother Gottfried arrived from Germany late this afternoon. Daniel came from Lancaster at the end of the evening. Ruth is teaching through Wednesday.

Ruth and I have a new early morning pattern. We go out to the end of our lane and get the newspapers. The carrier who delivers the *Carroll County Times* has been doing us the favor of leaving two copies. We are thankful that Scott Blanchard emphasizes the faith dimension.

Wednesday, December 23.

This morning Maren drove me to Green Spring for chemotherapy. We then drove to Penn Station and picked up Miriam and Chuck. The family circle here is complete.

In the afternoon Miriam, Chuck, Daniel, and I dug up the Norway spruce that has been our Christmas tree for 1996 and 1997. Last year Ruth was hesitant about digging it out again, fearing that it would die. But by this year it has become for her our post-diagnosis Christmas tree, and she wants to have it inside the house again. Ken Koons came to photograph the digging.

Thursday, December 24.

In today's article Scott quotes something that Brethren elder Reuel Pritchett told me when I was interviewing him for the book *On the Ground Floor of Heaven*: "I'm not afraid to die, but I sure hate to leave."

We went as a family to the Union Bridge Church of the Brethren Christmas Eve service. Back home here I read scriptures, and we sang carols in front of the candle-lit Christmas tree. I felt less emotional than in the two previous years about the possibility that this would be my last Christmas with the family. I could focus more on the depth and wonder of what we were singing about.

Friday, December 25.

I've been given this third Christmas since the diagnosis.

Saturday, December 26.

This is Daniel's birthday. Yesterday I found a little time to write him a letter for his special day. In our birthday devotions, I read Psalm 121.

The headline in the *Times* article today quotes Daniel regarding his experience of this Christmas. He spoke of "the grace of God, or the grace of life," as the reason I am still alive.

There is also a splendid photo of Ruth looking down at the blooms of the Christmas rose in the snow in the flower bed outside our kitchen. In the caption under it, Scott used something I had mentioned to him: "In 1953, children at a refugee camp where Dale was working put on a play about the Christmas rose and people who didn't believe Christ had been born. 'They saw the rose blooming in the snow,' Dale said. 'They said, "Well, if there can be the miracle of the Christ rose blooming in snow, there can be the miracle of the Christ child coming." ' "

Tuesday, December 29.

We've spent several evenings looking at old family movies and slides. How marvelously much goes into the shared living of two people in a marriage.

Thursday, December 31.

Maren took me down for chemo. But my neutrophil count was so low (650) that I was given no chemo. Instead I was put on antibiotics to help ward off infections.

Miriam and Chuck returned to Brooklyn yesterday to celebrate the new year on their own. Daniel came in the middle of the evening from Lancaster. Iris Bazing, a German-American physician at Johns Hopkins, joined us for the evening and overnight. Maren, Gottfried, and Mutter are still here.

Approaching midnight, Ruth lit the candles on the tree, and we sang the many verses of the traditional German New Year's hymn. Just at midnight I was reading from Isaiah 40: "The grass withers, the flower fades; but the word of our God will stand for ever" (v. 8). The winsomeness of childhood and youth fades; our aging bodies decline; the close of life comes so quickly. The grave jeopardy I live in is just one more among innumerable illustrations of how ephemeral human life is. But God's word remains; it rises in impregnable sovereignty over all that vanishes. God's promises impinge to lift what has vanished into participation in that "for ever."

1999

Sunday, January 3.
This afternoon Ruth, Mutter, Maren, and I drove to the Catoctin area in the Blue Ridge Mountains. I'd never before seen Cunningham Falls surrounded by snow. We hiked a little but not too much because the snow was melting some and we did not have boots to stay dry. Once again I could take in the marvel of the forest trees in the snow landscape.

On the bridge at the foot of Cunningham Falls, a short, attractive woman perhaps in her late thirties, asked Ruth whether she was Ruth Aukerman. She recognized us from the newspaper series. We also met her husband, whose mother has lung cancer.

I think of the villagers of Le Chambon, who worked with the Trocmés in sheltering Jews in occupied France. When praised for their extraordinary courage, they answered that they had done nothing remarkable, they had simply done what was needed. That is the way I see my coping with the cancer. I've been featured in the newspaper series, but what I have lived out is not extraordinary. It is remarkable, a miracle of God's grace, that I have lived as long as I have. But others, also in this area, who struggle with cancer or comparable diseases have no doubt come through as well or better than I have. Others have faced their affliction with deeper trust than mine. Yet I was the one singled out for sharing my story. I've been held up as a model of faith and courage when others around are very likely better models, but perhaps something of what faith should be has been communicated.

Thursday, January 7.
Bill Heltzel took me for chemo. My neutrophil count, though still low, is up enough that I received the full dosage of navelbine. I am scheduled for weekly infusions through the remainder of January.

Friday, January 8.

Heiner Westphal called to give us the number of Mary Jane Walling at the Food and Drug Administration; we talked with her and she will try to arrange for me to get thalidomide.

Mutter was telling me again in our tea time about Ruth's accident as a child. She was eight years old and imitating other children by sliding down a banister in the old mansion where a number of families were crowded together. She lost her balance and fell about one story down through the open space onto stone steps. Her shoulder hit one of the steps and she had a broken collar bone; if her shoulder had not hit first, she would very likely have been killed. She had a brain concussion and a buildup of blood on the brain, the seriousness of which became evident only after two or three days. She was taken to the surgery ward of the main hospital in Kassel. Mutter stayed with her for nearly a week. Fortunately, the pressure decreased without surgery. When Ruth had improved some, she went through the ward playing her flute and singing for the patients. When she was to leave, the head nurse said they didn't want to give her up, for she was the only child there and had been such a sunbeam for the others.

Later Ruth was sent far away to a home for children in Berchtesgaden where she could receive physical therapy. The weeks there away from her family were hard for her. She got a tiny allowance, and when she returned, she had spent all of it on gifts for her parents and brother. Ruth was left with slowed motor coordination, and this made her less athletic than the children around her.

I cherish these early childhood glimpses of the woman I have shared my life with and whom God's providential hand kept from being killed.

Saturday, January 9.

Miriam and Chuck are here again. Chuck has more job interviews in Washington over the weekend. Daniel is coming this evening. He is to fly to El Salvador tomorrow where he will work for four weeks in a medical clinic with his friends Rob and Wendy Shelley.

Wednesday, January 13.

Mutter called from Kassel, Germany, early this morning. Ruth and I were relieved that she had arrived home safely. On Saturday evening Daniel had been trying out a blood pressure monitoring device that he had given Ruth for Christmas. When he measured Mutter's blood pressure, the upper figure was over 200, and the lower was over 100. Suddenly she became the sick person in most immediate jeopardy. Even though her blood pressure remained high, the medical advice was that she could fly on Tuesday as scheduled. A close friend came from Kassel to meet her at the Frankfurt airport.

Monday I received more information about getting thalidomide and called the company that manufactures the drug. Today a case worker contacted me. Then he called the insurance company that handles our prescriptions. Evidently he was able to show that thalidomide is now an approved drug. He called back to inform me that the insurance company would cover the cost except for the co-pay. I was quite amazed. Right now it seems to make sense to wait to see what the CT scan in February shows. Maybe the navelbine is keeping the cancer in check.

Sunday, January 17.
We called my oncologist cousin, David Miller. He said that on December 15 thalidomide was shifted from experimental to approved status. This is probably the reason we will be able to get the insurance coverage.

Saturday, January 23.
Jamie and Julie Edgerton called. Their daughter Natasha has been accepted to her first-choice university in Australia, and everything is working out just right. They are planning to return to Australia for several weeks to help Natasha, but Julie has been having stomach pain and nausea. Tests have shown a big area in her stomach that may be an ulcer, but the doctors are not sure what it is. Julie will get the results of the biopsy on Wednesday. So they are in the intense time of waiting and wondering. Julie has been a champion swimmer and a model of robust health.

Wednesday, January 27.
Jamie called this evening. The place in Julie's stomach is cancer. She will need to have her stomach removed and learn to live without a stomach. There is no indication that the cancer has spread. So they do have the prospect that the cancer can be completely removed from her body. They plan to leave for Australia on Sunday and have the operation done in Melbourne later in the week.

They have poured themselves out for us in so many ways during our hard time, and now these very close friends of ours are hit. We feel so deeply with them.

Friday, January 29.

Paul Grout was with us for several hours before going on to speak at a winter youth retreat not far from here. I showed him the burial box in the attic of our garage. He said again that he wants to have one that he would use as a bookcase until it's needed. In Vermont last summer I thought he was joking about the bookcase, but now I realize that he does intend to do this.

Tuesday, February 2.

This morning I had a CT scan and also x-rays of my right hip.

Dr. Ettinger thought I ought to have my hip x-rayed because I have been having some discomfort. With my condition any ache or pain raises the question as to whether it might be cancer-related. Actually, for several days now my hip has not been bothering me. But I've had some pain again in the middle part of my spine—around the T-8 vertebra. Maybe the cancer is reasserting itself after the radiation. Whenever I've had radiation, I've been told that the same area—at least bone area—cannot be radiated again.

It's easy to be apprehensive and anticipate the worst when there is some pain. But I need to be on guard against thinking negatively. I give thanks for each day that I'm still able to walk and for each day that is relatively pain-free.

Thursday, February 4.

Today at a memorial service for Howard Gosnell, a Westminster church friend, I was struck as never before by the promise of Jesus in John 14:3: "And when I go and prepare a place for you, I will come again and will take you to myself, that where I am you may be also." It seems that at least part of the meaning of this coming again has to do with Jesus himself coming to receive dying followers into his presence. What more resplendent welcome beyond death could there be than this? At the end one can echo the prayer of Stephen: "Lord Jesus, receive my spirit" (Acts 7:59).

Friday, February 5.

Today is two years and three months since the diagnosis. This afternoon I finally got the report from Tuesday's CT scan and x-rays. It is basically good news. The main mass and the other lesions in my lungs and liver have remained stable in size. But there are a few new "small patchy areas" in the left lung that could be "inflammation or further metastatic disease." And there is now a tiny amount of fluid under the left lung. There does not seem to be metastatic growth in the right hip, though x-rays for this are not very reliable. God be praised for the good news.

Last evening Jamie Edgerton called from Australia. Julie's operation had gone well. The surgeon could leave a tenth of her stomach, and that will enlarge a little. No signs of metastatic spread were found.

Saturday, February 6.

This morning Miriam had an interview with Circuit Court Judge Pierre Leval in New York for a year's clerkship after she graduates from law school. This was her first choice among the positions she was applying for. He offered her the position, and a few minutes later she accepted it. So that stressful uncertainty is resolved.

Daniel returned from working four weeks at the clinic in El Salvador. While driving us home from Dulles Airport, he said, "Now that I am back safely, I can tell you that El Salvador is the most violent country in the western hemisphere."

Monday, February 8.

Late this afternoon I had an appointment with Dr. Caricofe. It seems that everything is coming together for me to get thalidomide. People taking thalidomide are to be closely monitored, because of the danger that the drug may somehow cause birth defects. There is a lot of paperwork to be done. I took the prescription and a copy of the consent form to the pharmacy. The thalidomide may come within several days.

Wednesday, February 10.

Larry Fourman has been in the area, and we have had long talks. I half playfully shared a concern with Larry. I've met with all sorts of opposition in my life. I like to think that I've encountered some of it as I have sought to be faithful to the gospel. Jesus warns, "Woe to you, when all men speak well of you" (Luke 6:26). The positive appraisal I've received from the *Carroll County Times* series is not typical for me and makes me feel uncomfortable.

Thursday, February 11.

This afternoon Ruth and I had an appointment with Dr. Ettinger. He believes the small patchy areas are spread of disease, but he is not too concerned about them. He sees the disease as basically stable, but he doesn't think the navelbine is playing a decisive role. He is taking me off of it. He asked how things stand for the thalidomide. His position seems to have changed and he almost welcomes the fact that I'm ready to go on thalidomide. He said, "You may make a believer out of me yet." He didn't even mention other options except very experimental Phase I studies through Johns Hopkins. I'm to be on thalidomide for two months, then get another CT scan, and see him again. Ruth and I were happy about the way the consultation went.

Saturday, February 13.
We were saddened this evening when Wilbur Wright told us of the death quite a while ago of Rolando Serrano, who was in our home in June as part of the visiting delegation from a church in Managua, Nicaragua. After Hurricane Mitch he drank some bad water, became very ill, and died. Rolando was part of the group's fervent prayer for my healing.

Tuesday, February 16.
I've been pondering the eschatological passage in 1 Thessalonians 4:13-18. Paul states that his intention in writing these words is so "that you may not grieve as others do who have no hope." Each of the first three sentences points to "those who are asleep" or "those who have fallen asleep." This seems to have been a common way of referring to those who have died, but to me the phrasing implies a quiescence. Paul does not suggest that there is life beyond death. He does not suppose that those who have died have already entered into the completion of what is to be hoped for after death. His focus is on the glorious coming of Jesus and the consummation. "Jesus died and rose again" (v. 14), and at that coming, God will bring with the risen Lord those who are asleep into the fullness of resurrection life. "The dead in Christ" will be drawn completely into the movement he made into that life.

"For the Lord himself will descend from heaven with a cry of command." The one whose non-domineering witness to God was so widely rejected, with that pattern continuing through the centuries, will speak the ultimate word that will finally silence all contrary words. Those who are Christ's will "meet the Lord in the air." What will then be finds description enough in the words, "and so we shall always be with the Lord."

Paul makes no mention of the last judgment. This may be an aspect of meeting the Lord. For those who are Christ's, judgment will be swallowed up in the victory of his resurrection life revealed.

In 1 Thessalonians 5:9-10, the assurance is given: "our Lord Jesus Christ . . . died for us so that whether we wake or sleep we might live with him." When we "sleep" in death, that state is determined and shaped by what Christ has done for us. We are to live with him then as we live with him on earth, awaiting the consummation.

The Union Bridge Pharmacy today finally received the initial shipment of thalidomide for me. At bedtime I will start with a dosage of 100 mg. Maybe this fourth-line chemotherapy will help; maybe it won't. But having the insurance coverage and other things work out for trying it seems a marvel of God's grace. It is also significant that I am a guinea pig in checking out this still experimental drug.

Saturday, February 20.
Miriam and Daniel are here. This afternoon we transplanted trees to fill the strip behind the spring house and some other empty areas. We got a lot done. I mostly supervised but was very tired after we had finished.

Tuesday, February 23.
This morning I finished pulling together the pieces for the journal. I went to Westminster and had three copies made. Then I sent the original copy to Julie Garber, book editor of Brethren Press. For the first time, she'll have the full proposed manuscript to consider. I wrote Julie that if my health seems to be stable, it may make sense to go ahead and publish the "uncompleted" journal. Ruth pointed out that readers who are dealing with end-of-life issues would be in the midst of a process as I still would be.

Not long after the diagnosis, when Cathy Boshart encouraged me to think about writing another book, the prospect seemed unlikely. But I have been given time.

Friday, February 26.
Ruth said this morning, "Wouldn't it be wonderful if it is shown in your body that thalidomide can help against lung cancer." I have lived to see crocuses blooming again.

Saturday, February 27.
Late this afternoon Ruth and I started out the lane to get the mail. On ahead of us a pair of black animals crossed the lane and the stream and ran gracefully across the meadow to the other channel. They were of considerable size, low to the ground, maybe two and a half feet long plus the tail. We called Ken Koons this evening and described what we had seen. He was quite certain they were two fishers. I don't think I even knew there

were mammals called fishers (because they eat fish). Ken said that fishers have been re-introduced into western Maryland, but he was not aware of their being in this county. It's amazing that I saw two such unusual animals in this phase of my life.

Tuesday, March 2.

A letter has come from a woman in New Market who is dealing with ovarian cancer. I met her last November when we were both getting treatments. Led by God, I gave her a copy of the article "Living with Dying." A day or so after that we were together again in the waiting room and had a chance to talk. Then several weeks ago I sent her a copy of the newspaper series.

She writes that our encounter became a spiritual turning point for her. She had been so afraid. Since then she has come into a journey of new spiritual discoveries. We had talked about the importance of being in a Christian fellowship. She was welcomed back into the Presbyterian church in Emmitsburg where she had been an inactive member. Now she is very happy there. I have generally not been quick enough to take the initiative to witness to strangers. But that time I caught on to God's prompting, and he was able to use me.

Sunday, March 7.

This has been a big day. Ruth and I drove to the University Park meetinghouse near Washington. I shared with a Sunday school class what reading the Bible has meant to me, especially since the diagnosis. Then I preached on the theme "Why I Believe." I don't think I have ever before drawn together in a sermon or article the main reasons for my faith. Almost a year and a half ago I preached there on "Matters of Life or Death" ("Living with Dying").

As I was preaching, I felt rather weak and a little light-headed (this can be a side effect of thalidomide). It even occurred to me that I might not get through the sermon. Ruth said later that she had never seen me so tired in preaching. But I think, through God, I experienced power-in-weakness.

Tonight I was worship leader for the area Brethren Lenten service held at the Pipe Creek meetinghouse. As the call to worship, I took the verses from 1 Corinthians 15, which begins, "O death, where is your victory?"

At the close of the service, I took the arm of Walt Wiltschek, who had preached. I did not trust that I would be steady enough to walk down the two steps from the pulpit level.

Wednesday, March 10.

When Ruth returned home with the mail, there were two envelopes from Brethren Press. The one envelope was reassuringly thick. I opened it and saw the contract from Brethren Press for publishing my journal. Ruth and I hugged each other, laughing.

There's a possibility that the book will be published in time for the Brethren Annual Conference in 2000. Statistically, the chance that I will live that long is not good. But I have lived long enough to write the journal and to cut and revise the manuscript. This task has been a priority. Editor Julie Garber tells me that journal entries can be included up to the time the book is sent to the printer.

I am so thankful for this prospect. God has opened yet another door for witnessing.

Thursday, March 11.

Through the years I've come to know Psalm 121 nearly by heart. Theologian Artur Weiser, in his commentary, sees verse 1 as the words of a man about to set out on a journey. The man looks at the hills through which he will need to travel (not hills as intimation of God, which has been my interpretation). The traveler anxiously asks, "From whence does my help come?" A second person, perhaps a priest, gives a response in verses 2-8. The Lord, who made heaven and earth, the Lord, who has been the keeper of Israel, will be with him on his journey to protect him: "Help comes from the Lord."

I am about to set out on a journey across the dividing range. The assurance given to that long-ago traveler comes also to me. God's keeping me continues "for evermore."

Saturday, March 13.

Jamie and Julie Edgerton came late this afternoon. Julie looks amazingly good in recovery from having nine-tenths of her stomach removed. They praise God for her rescue from cancer. Jamie says it was a miracle. She had sprained her ankle and began taking pain medication, irritating the ulcer in her stomach. She then had tests that led to the discovery of the cancer. Typically stomach cancer is not detected early enough. The scans showed a two-inch tumor, and only a few days later, she was operated on in Melbourne. In that amount of time, the tumor had disappeared except for a small residual spot.

Jamie told us that as the two of them were in the car ready to leave for the airport on their way to Australia, well-wishers lined the sidewalk. Julie began to cry, and Jim Wallis came over to the car window to say something. Julie replied that her faith was too weak, she didn't have the faith for coping with what was ahead. (She had been thinking that she was going to die.) Jim told her, "That is all right. Your faith doesn't need to be strong. We will be praying for you, and we will hold you up." That assurance was just what Julie needed to hear. She then could let go and be at peace as she prepared for the operation.

Sunday, March 14.

Today we've had the biggest snowstorm of the winter.

I called Don Murray. Things are moving ahead for his play. During the conversation I mentioned Elia Kazan and his role in Hollywood's blacklisting of a lot of people. Don said that he would probably have been blacklisted for being a conscientious objector. But he entered Brethren Volunteer Service, and by the time he returned from Europe, Joseph McCarthy had been discredited. If Don had been blacklisted, his acting career would have gone very differently.

Tuesday, March 16.

In a telephone conversation this evening, Julie Edgerton told us she feels guilty that the prayers for her complete healing have been answered while those for my complete healing have not been. I replied that I could feel guilty—and indeed sometimes I have felt a little guilty—that I have lived so long after diagnosis while others with cancer have died much sooner.

That I have lived this long and am still doing reasonably well is the gracious gift of God, and I don't really know why God has given me so much time. Intercession on my behalf has been a vital factor; but some of the others with cancer must have had comparable intercession. However, I really do not need to feel guilty about receiving what God has given—nor does Julie. If I had been granted only a two-month or three-month span of life remaining, that would have been all right too.

Friday, March 19.

Maren arrived from California a little after midnight last night. She will spend a week of her spring break with us.

A letter came today from Gladys Naylor in McPherson, Kansas. Kurtis has been diagnosed with lymphoma and is receiving chemotherapy. He was director of Brethren Service work in Europe in the early sixties when I was working with the Puidoux Theological Peace Conferences. Of people who have given me so much support in this time, three have received a cancer diagnosis themselves—Marian Witiak, Julie Edgerton, and now Kurtis.

Saturday, March 20.
Daniel came today from Lancaster. Maren's birthday is on the 24th, but since Daniel will not be here then, we had the main celebration this afternoon. My gift for her was another birthday letter. Before and afterward we worked together raking the lawn.

Wednesday, March 24.
Today is Maren's twenty-ninth birthday. She has gone over the book manuscript and done splendid work in spotting quite a number of little points for correction or improvement. She even noticed that I was misspelling rototiller. (I had an *a* for the second *o*.) She commented, "We wouldn't want you to pass on, not knowing how to spell rototiller."

I received a letter from the Masons in Virginia. Steve, a Brethren pastor, wrote that he and Ginny had learned from the newspaper series that I am actually a few years older than they thought. He added, "Pretty soon, you'll be too old to die young!" When people live to a more advanced age, we tend to see their death as a natural and expected thing. My diagnosis shocked a lot of people in a way that it would not have, had it come ten or fifteen years later. I think many people assumed I was younger than I am. At the time of the diagnosis I was fully active and not retired, though I was sixty-six—just retirement age. If I live till the middle of June, I will be sixty-nine—one year away from seventy. I have always thought of seventy years as a rather long life span. Indeed, I have been blessed.

Thursday, March 25.
This is Maren's last day with us. This evening she was talking about Irish immigration to the United States and mentioned the Irish potato famine. She added, "I don't know just when that was."

I volunteered, "It was in the later 1840s."

Maren said, "I don't need an encyclopedia CD-ROM as long as I have my father."

Friday, March 26.
Late this afternoon I rototilled a part of the garden and sowed three rows of seeds—lettuce, spinach, radishes, and kohlrabi—my third garden since the diagnosis. I didn't have time to plant more. I was too tired afterward. I must

be more careful to limit the physical work that I do. But at present there is so much to be done.

There is a chance of snow or rain tonight.

Saturday, March 27.

Joshua Blistein, the son of my former college roommate, came to give us some help. I helped Joshua plant the eleven redbud trees that I had ordered, mostly in spots where I had to take out the diseased flowering dogwoods.

Monday, March 29.

I've continued planting early garden, with no rain to put such work on hold: onion sets, sweet onion plants, dill, arugula, red beets, carrots, potatoes, broccoli, cauliflower, and red and white cabbage plants.

Tuesday, March 30.

Dr. Steve Dejter was in the NCI research protocol with me. In July 1997 he mentioned to me that a doctor from Harvard and Johns Hopkins had told him that he has patients with non-small-cell lung cancer who have been living for years, even without therapy. Dr. Dejter took this as quite encouraging information. But he died in the spring of 1998. I sometimes think about what that doctor told him.

Wednesday, March 31.

The war in Yugoslavia has been weighing heavily on me. As a Brethren Volunteer in refugee camps in 1953–55, I worked with hundreds of people who were forced to flee from their homes at the end of World War II. For a couple of years I was immersed in the pathos of their experience.

Now an estimated quarter of a million refugees are in neighboring countries, and a half million have been dislocated in Kosovo and Montenegro. The tragedy of that can only be taken in person by person and family by family.

In the Old Testament, violence and lying are often said to go together. And this has not changed. In recent years the most impressive justification for the immense U.S. military establishment has been its alleged usefulness for humanitarian purposes. Through various conflicts, that justification has retained some plausibility. But we are now seeing, within God's sovereign judging, the exposure of that lie. President Clinton and those aligned with him are indignant at the charge that the NATO bombing has made matters far worse for the Kosovar Albanians. But matters are worse, so the lying continues. A country that makes military might its first and overriding priority cannot go on and on without reaping terrible consequences. "God is not mocked" (Gal. 6:7). When an evil head of state perpetrates dramatic inhumanities, the self-righteousness of those who oppose him is bolstered. The projection of U.S. power in the world has brought far more deprivation, suffering, and death than what has resulted from the projection of Serbian power in Kosovo. According to U.N. estimates, a million Iraqi civilians, half of them children, have died because of the economic sanctions. This is just one example of how the U.S. has perpetrated a greater inhumanity than that being carried out by Slobodan Milosevic. But America directs its attention entirely toward the wrongdoing of the enemy. We also do well to keep in mind that white Americans again and again drove large numbers of Native Americans from lands that were theirs or had been assigned to them.

Thursday, April 1.
How good this morning to wake up and hear rain on the roof. This rain is what the early garden needs. It will also settle the dirt around the newly planted redbuds and be good for the grass seed Ruth and I planted yesterday.

Good Friday, April 2.
Miriam arrived from New York to spend the Easter weekend with us. Regarding my condition, she commented, "We all like to have certainty. But with you there can be no good certainty apart from a miracle. Uncertainty is much better because the only prospective certainty is a bad certainty." She meant my being dead.

Saturday, April 3.
Today, two years after that Holy Week tree-planting Saturday, we mulched around nearly all the woodlot trees with hay.

Easter Sunday, April 4.
Joyce Hollyday, formerly with *Sojourners* magazine, wrote us, "Despite it all, may you be overcome with Resurrection joy."

At various points in the accounts of the resurrection, the first witnesses needed to be told, "Do not be afraid." It occurs to me that each of us will have acute need to hear that reassuring command, for we will be overwhelmed and dumbfounded by the transition into the beyond.

Monday, April 5.

I have lived to see the lettuce, radishes, and spinach come up through the ground.

Early in the morning of November 5, 1996, before I went to Dr. Caricofe's office to hear what I was sure would be very bad news, I read and pondered Psalm 116. Verse 8 expresses thanksgiving: "For thou hast delivered my soul from death." At first I thought of those words as stating what God in his mercy might do for me. Today when I read this psalm again, I realize that these words have been fulfilled for me in relation to the cancer. I have not been delivered from the cancer. But for two years and five months, as of today, God has held back death and preserved my life.

Thursday to Saturday, April 8-10.

I was able to drive to University Park Church near Washington, D.C., and participate in a meeting of the Christian Peacemaker Teams steering committee for the first time since October 1997. Gene Stoltzfus, CPT director, told us that four years ago several requests had come from the nonviolent student movement in Kosovo, asking CPT to send a team there. At the time CPT simply did not have the people or the resources to do that. Even if such a team would not have made a decisive difference, the involvement would have put CPT in a very different position for relating to what has been happening in the past weeks.

Sunday, April 11.

Brian Baldwin called from death row in Alabama. He said he has been depressed much of the time. His final appeal possibility was turned down without any comment by the U.S. Supreme Court. Probably some law clerk, reflecting the mentality of the present court, scanned the appeal and made the decision. Brian said, "We have not given up." Two of his closest friends on the outside are trying to find new evidence in the case. Before long an execution date will likely be set for him.

Bo Cochran, one of the death row prisoners who sent me a get-well greeting, is now a free man. I need to ask Brian how that came about. Several of the others who wrote on the card have been executed.

Tuesday, April 13.

This morning as I was going through my prayer list and praying for Uncle Harry and Aunt Eileen Miller, I had a strong feeling that I should call them. I tried to call Aunt Eileen but got no answer. When I reached Uncle Harry in the nursing home and asked him how Aunt Eileen was, he told me she had passed away last Tuesday. She too had lung cancer. She was eighty-two. It seems the close of life came rather fast for her. Toward the end she had great difficulty getting her breath. Their burial plots are in the same cemetery where my sister Jane and my parents are buried.

John Baillie in *A Diary of Private Prayer* praises God "for the great and mysterious opportunity of my life." There is so much for each person to contemplate in this regard. Life is opportunity. A central focus for me has been bringing three children into the world. And their lives open out in continuing opportunities.

Wednesday, April 14.
At lunch I listened to Steve Kinzie sing his song "Breathe Together." The refrain closes with the words, "conspiring in the Spirit, till we all run out of breath." Running out of breath is a very apt image for the end of life, especially when one has lung cancer.

Tuesday, April 20.
The report from yesterday's CT scan was not good news. The mass on the left lung has increased some in size and has grown further into the mediastinum (area near the heart). The pleural effusion under the left lung has increased only slightly in size. But now there is a small pleural effusion under the right lung. The two main masses in the liver have increased some in size. But no metastatic spread of disease was found. It appears that the thalidomide is not helping, unless it is working to keep the metastatic spread in check. It seems we will not be making "a believer" out of Dr. Ettinger with regard to thalidomide.

Two of the redbuds in the woodlot are loaded with unopened blooms. The beauties of this spring become more precious now.

Thursday, April 22.
Ruth and I went to the appointment with Dr. Ettinger this afternoon. To our surprise he recommended that I stay on thalidomide for another two months. He thinks there is still some chance that it may stabilize the cancer. If it doesn't after the two months, going back to taxol or entering a Phase I study are options.

At Daniel's suggestion we asked Dr. Ettinger about getting an MRI of the brain. Since I've had the disease a long time, Dr. Ettinger also thinks we should do this.

Sunday, April 25.

In the combined Sunday school class of the Elizabethtown church, I was to talk on "what drives you." I spoke about dealing with cancer, the peace witness of the church, and the centrality of Jesus Christ to what we have to share.

I'd been uneasy about whether I would have enough energy for leading the Sunday school and also preaching. But I was given a good measure of strength. "Why I Believe" seemed to be the right message for this particular Sunday.

Wednesday, April 28.

This morning Dr. Caricofe's office faxed me the radiologist's report of the MRI. There are at least five lesions in the brain. These range in size from 1 cm to 2 cm, which is almost 3/4 of an inch. The lesions are surrounded by some edema (watery fluid in the tissues).

Soon after the cancer diagnosis, I began praying that I would not face metastasis in the brain. I hoped the time would not come when my mind would be wiped out and my body still functioning. I may still be spared that; may it be so. I don't know very much about the physiology of the brain, but when I think about that many lesions of up to 3/4 of an inch, surrounded by edema, I'm astonished that I've had no noticeable mental impairment till now. We also don't know how long the lesions have been there.

Having a clear mind for this long has been a wonderful gift from God, for lung cancer spreads primarily to the liver, bones, and brain. Now I have the threefold spread.

This is very bad news, but we have dealt with bad news often. The assurance deepens that God is with us for coping with whatever is ahead.

Maren confirmed what I had been thinking: It's only because I have lived so long after the diagnosis that I find myself dealing with metastases in the brain. Miriam said that she and Maren had joked that even with all those lesions in my brain I knew when the Irish potato famine was.

We talked with Dr. Ettinger who said in his emphatic way that I should have radiation for the lesions in the brain. If I don't do this, I can expect to have seizures before too long. He said I could expect some hair loss. His recommendation was good news of a sort. At least radiation is feasible, and it's possible that it will help.

Last week I wrote several letters to the editor regarding the war with Yugoslavia. They appeared in yesterday's (Baltimore) *Sun* and today's *Carroll County Times*. The remaining good days may be slipping away fast, but I was able to do that.

The little patches of blooms on our larger redbuds have opened at last. One serviceberry has a branch with blooms. The arrowwood viburnums are loaded with clusters of unopened blooms, as is the quince tree I planted in the spring after the diagnosis. Maybe I'll even live to see an initial quince harvest.

Friday, April 30.

Daniel came at 11:00 last evening, and we had a few minutes together. He left at 4:00 this morning for BWI Airport to fly to New Mexico for a reunion of his medical school class. With all the uncertainties right now, he wanted to be with me again while I am still who I am.

Ruth and I saw Dr. Lee in Frederick, whom I had seen for the radiation of the lower back and the thoracic spine. He said there would need to be whole brain radiation—ten treatments over the next two weeks. I can expect total hair loss, which might be permanent. I may have some fatigue, and there is the possibility of other complications. He advised me not to drive.

At his suggestion we went to Shady Grove for a second opinion. That oncologist said simply that there are "a good many" metastases in the brain. If one or two or three metastases survive the radiation, these might be dealt with by stereotactic radio surgery. She found it quite astonishing that I have not had symptoms of brain malfunction.

The day has been full of blessings, with so many things working out for us in terms of what needs to be done. Ruth said the time was like a date: "Other couples go to Hawaii. We go to the oncologist."

Thinking of all those metastases in my brain, I recalled the line in Shakespeare's sonnet (73): "Bare ruin'd choirs, where late the sweet birds sang." But then for Ruth and those closest to me are the lines:

> This thou perceivest, which makes thy love more strong,
> To love that well which thou must leave ere long.

Monday, May 3.

I had the first whole brain radiation treatment at noon today. Afterward I had a feeling in my head that something had been done.

Irvin Roop came and put up the porch swing that he made for us as a Christmas gift. When the finish is totally dry, we can sit on it and survey our little part of the world.

This evening my forehead is quite red.

Wednesday, May 5.

Today is two and a half years since the diagnosis. So far I have been blessed in not having bad side effects from the radiation to my brain.

When I was a child, my father and the men of the Old German Baptist circle in which we moved wore black broad-rimmed hats. I have never had a hat, except at times a straw hat for very sunny weather. Now with the whole brain radiation, I'm not to have my head (soon to be bald) exposed to the sun for more than several minutes. This evening Doris Ridenour came with five hiking-type hats from two stores in Baltimore. Only one, a white hat made of cotton, was large enough for my head. This is probably the first item of clothing that I have bought in three or four years, though Ruth brings me Mission Store things.

Thursday, May 6.

During this time I have received so much attention and many expressions of esteem. I find that I am thinking too much about how I am being seen by others and how I will be seen after I die. When I think about it, however, what really counts for eternity is God's assessment of me. The day of judgment is drawing near. Affirming love from friends and family comes as intimation of God's love, but I rightly receive it only if I clearly see God's love as the one thing that counts ultimately. I am so far from measuring up to the high esteem in which many hold me. Likewise, before God I don't measure up at all. But I am accepted through the life, death, and rising of the One who "loved me and gave himself for me" (Gal. 2:20).

Friday, May 7.

I received a beautiful letter from Tim McElwee. He wrote out of his sorrow at the prospect of losing me. So much of what we have with any dearly loved person is the accumulation of all past interactions with that person. That treasury from the past issues into and undergirds the relationship in the present. Apart from the past, the present has no breadth and depth. But even if the person is taken out of our present, we still have that treasury of all the shared past. And so it will be for those close to me, when my presence is withdrawn.

Saturday, May 8.

This afternoon a peace pole was dedicated in my honor at the Mid-Atlantic District Office of the Church of the Brethren. I was asked to give a brief response. Though I was tired from the radiation treatments, I was able to go. Since we were in sunshine, I had my new hat on. I began by saying that I was uncomfortable with the dedication in my honor, that I was in the spotlight too much. I gave a summary of the theological grounding of the peace witness of the church and related this to attitudes about the present war.

Monday, May 10.
This afternoon I had the sixth whole brain radiation treatment. The lower margin of the field of radiation is above the eyes, down through the ears to the base of the skull. I lie on my back with my head taped in position. I receive a little less than a half minute of radiation from one side and then the same from the other side.

I have been a little more tired, and I've had a bit of nausea. So far my hair hasn't begun to fall out.

Tuesday, May 11.
Ed Poling, pastor of the Carlisle (Pennsylvania) Church of the Brethren, called this morning and asked if I could preach in a peace emphasis Sunday on October 17. The date seems quite a long way ahead, but I agreed to do it if my health permits.

When I went for the radiation this afternoon, I learned that I am to have twenty treatments instead of ten. Dr. Lee decided to lower the dosage and have more treatments. Doing this is better in case I need to have stereotactic radio surgery as a follow up. When I asked him for a prognosis regarding the metastases in my brain, he said, "Time will tell."

In the waiting room, I was reading in the new study catechism of the Presbyterian Church. It quotes Article I of the Barmen Declaration (by the confessing church under the Nazis): "Jesus Christ as he is attested for us in Holy Scripture is the one Word of God whom we have to hear, and whom we have to trust and obey in life and in death." The article also states that when death comes *not* on account of allegiance to Christ, one can render obedience in one's dying. I hope I have a clear head near the end for doing that.

Thursday, May 13.
A fledgling chimney swift fell into the wood stove in our living room. Ruth let it fly out through the open door. Soon we heard another one. When she

opened the door of the stove, it flew into a window. I caught it with a dish towel, gazed at it closely, and took it to the porch. When I opened my hand, it soared high above the walnut trees, even though it had never flown before.

I happened to read the first paragraph of an article by theologian Jacques Ellul in a series on "How My Mind Has Changed" in *The Christian Century*, November 18, 1970: "In the first place, we must admit that it is difficult for a Christian to talk about himself. Not that it is difficult to lay oneself bare (especially in these days of literary exhibitionism). But a Christian ought to know how little interest attaches to him as a person. And he ought to know that it is better to talk about Jesus Christ than about himself. If, nevertheless, he is led to talk about himself, he must do so not only with strict honesty but above all objectively, in detachment, examining himself without romanticism, as a different object; always aware of the promptings of old human nature and always remembering the warning, 'Do not be conformed to this world.' " The words seemed very relevant to my sharing out of the struggle with cancer.

Friday, May 14.
Paul Grout, our pastor friend from Vermont, had a meeting at Camp Shepherd Spring west of here and came to visit us this evening. He commented, "It's been sad to have you ill, but you have helped us to be less attached to this world—to love this world more, but to be less attached."

Saturday, May 15.
Miriam came from New York yesterday to have the weekend with us. We looked at the red maple near the cattle gate. It barely survived the extreme drought of the summer of 1997. Last spring it sent out a shoot from its base, and I had identified with the little tree in its striving to live. But when Miriam and I checked it, we found that something had eaten off the trunk near ground level. I don't think there is any life. Miriam asked whether this discovery bothered me. The apparent death of the tree may or may not prefigure what is ahead for me. God's grace overarches and embraces whatever negative reports or intimations may come. I planted a small volunteer maple right next to the little maple. A few feet away another little tree seemed to be dead, but then I discovered one small green shoot coming out near the base. Now I am identifying with that tree.

Ruth said to me in German, "All dying is within the dying of Christ"— that is, my dying will be within his. I want to keep this in mind. I thought of

2 Corinthians 5:14: "we are convinced that one has died for all; therefore all have died." All human deaths were taken into that one death he died.

Miriam pointed out to us that her being in law school has come because of my cancer diagnosis. When we received the diagnosis, she was lined up for one or two job interviews in Moscow for work that would have kept her there at least a year. She dropped all that to return to the U.S. and decided on law school as the best route in the time of waiting.

Tuesday, May 18.
When I washed my hair this morning, it came out in globs. The one radiation technician told me that I have kept my hair much longer than most people do. Soon, with some face paint, I can play the clown.

Saturday, May 22.
Paula Bowser, pastor of the Glade Valley Church of the Brethren, wrote, "I praise God that, though you have a 'life-threatening disease,' you are living a 'disease-threatening life'!"

Frances Loberg called this afternoon from Oregon. She mentioned that I was very much on her mind one weekend some time ago. She tried several times to call us, but did not reach anyone. She found out later that I had been in the hospital that weekend with pneumonia.

Sunday, May 23.
I have been feeling quite fatigued from the radiation. Most of my hair has fallen out. The radiation that is aimed at the fast-growing cells in the brain hits the fast-growing cells that cover the top, sides, and back of the skull.

I've been feeling more numbness in my feet and a little more in my hands. This is presumably from the thalidomide. I have to be more careful walking.

Tuesday, May 25.
This morning I read about the healing of Simon Peter's mother-in-law. Jesus "stood over her and rebuked the fever, and it left her" (Luke 4:39). As the radiation this afternoon was streaming through my head, I repeated the prayer, "Rebuke!"

On the way to my treatment, I saw a man from the power company, working at an electric pole. This reminded me of the first person I ever saw dying. I was six. Several men were working at a power pole close to my grandparents' farm house. Our family lived catty-corner across the road.

Something went wrong. Probably the electricity was not turned off. Orie Brumbaugh, a first cousin of my mother, was electrocuted. I recall seeing his purple, unconscious face on a pillow my grandmother brought. The power company claimed—successfully, I think—that it was simply a heart attack.

A letter came from Cordell and Marlene Bowman at the Darvell Bruderhof in England. They sent a *Boston Globe* article about Cassie Bernall, the Columbine High School student who was killed after answering "Yes" to the gunman's question, "Do you believe in God?" Her youth group was studying Bruderhof leader Johann Christoph Arnold's *Seeking Peace.* "The last assignment Cassie completed on this earth" was the reading of the chapter that was to have been discussed the evening of the day she died—"No Life Without Death." The Bowmans pointed out that many in the youth group of two hundred (forty of them Columbine High School students) presumably read the long excerpt from my article, "Living with Dying," that comes several chapters later. How strange to have that tie with young people close to the massacre.

Wednesday, May 26.

Donald Bloesch called from Iowa. He and his wife continue to pray each evening for my deliverance, my healing. I said, "Deliverance will be given in one way or another." When I mentioned this to Ruth, she hugged me and said, "I don't pray every evening for your healing, but my life is a prayer for you."

It occurs to me that an element in my thinking about the church has been very wrong. I've seen the Anabaptist/Brethren tradition as rightly understanding the teaching of Jesus on certain points. Actually, I've tended to see those right understandings as having a certain merit or justified position before God. But what is right in the Church of the Brethren (or any other denomination, for that matter) has come by the grace of God. But so much is wrong, faltering, and unfaithful. Only by the amazing mercy of God revealed in Jesus can any denomination continue in relationship to God. No less than the individual Christian, a denomination should be drawn into the plea, "Kyrie eleison."

Thursday, May 27.

A man from a local nursery drove in this morning. He said he was delivering a weeping cherry tree as a gift from the New Market woman I had met during earlier radiation treatments in Frederick. We had talked together in the waiting room and I had sent her some things to read; she felt that this helped her to a spiritual breakthrough. (She has been told that her ovarian cancer is now in remission.) How beautiful and touching that she would give me this seven-foot tree. The tree will specifically memorialize God's graciously bringing good out of evil.

When Ruth came home from school, she laboriously dug the hole and planted the tree behind the house and a little to the west. I picked the first half dozen strawberries.

Friday, May 28.
This afternoon I completed the last of the twenty whole brain radiation treatments. The literature says it may take several weeks to get over the side effects.

Friday, June 4.
My friend Steve Kinzie, who lives in California, arrived the day before yesterday and left this morning. Each evening he sang songs for us. How good it was at this time to have my favorite singer sing to us. One song had the refrain: "Never, never may it be, / that death shall have the victory." That prayer has so many dimensions, but I thought of it relating especially to my situation.

Monday, June 7.
Most of the ten European alders in the woodlot have some brown leaves. This may be from some sort of virus. I was telling Maren that it is good to plant several kinds of trees rather than just one species: "If you have only one kind and a disease develops, you have a really big problem."

Maren added, "As Dr. Caricofe would say." She was referring to his first comment to me after the chest x-rays.

Sunday, June 13.
This afternoon Daniel came with a van load of his friends from Lancaster, mostly medical residents. He wanted them to see where he had grown up. We had strawberries and homemade ice cream for them. I was grateful for the opportunity to be with this group of his friends.

Late this evening Brian Baldwin called from death row in Alabama. He was very hopeful. He said that the next morning the governor was going to a nursing home to see an ailing, seventy-five-year-old deputy sheriff, who had signed a statement and given a video deposition that he had seen Brian beaten and tortured into signing a confession—really the only evidence the prosecution produced against him. Brian assured me that when he gets out, he will come and see us.

Monday, June 14.

This afternoon Daniel came again from Lancaster. With two of the children at home, we celebrated my birthday two days early. It's God's miracle that I can celebrate my third birthday since the diagnosis.

The family had lovely gifts for me. Mutter had knit a gray skull cap, which fits well and looks very good on me. Gottfried gave me a music CD. Maren played forty-nine hymns on her viola and gave them to me on a cassette. Ruth had sent my hymnal out to her and borrowed another copy from the Pipe Creek meetinghouse so that I would not notice. I said, "These will be good to listen to if I am fading away." Indeed, Maren had that in mind. Daniel and Ruth got me practical household gifts. Miriam and Chuck had brought from Florence a dark blue hat with a floppy brim that slants down some. It's a splendid addition to my newly acquired assortment of headgear.

As dusk deepened, Ruth, Daniel, Maren, and I sat on the porch talking about the memorial service. The service will of course have an orientation toward me and my life, but we do not want it to "dwell on" me. Ruth suggested that there might be a bulletin insert to share the significant things in my life. I said, "I've always liked bulletin inserts. Maybe I could have my last peace bulletin insert."

Wednesday, June 16.

This is my actual birthday. Ruth and Maren picked seventeen quarts of strawberries this morning—an appropriate beginning for the day, except that I didn't join them.

A letter came yesterday from Brian Baldwin's main support group in Alabama. His execution is set for June 18, just after Thursday midnight. He no doubt knew this when he called on Sunday but chose not to mention it. I faxed a letter to Governor Don Spiegelman. Then Maren changed the letter some and sent it as her letter.

I had not been in touch with Phil Berrigan and Elizabeth McAlister since the diagnosis. But when I received the article that told about Cassie Bernall reading a chapter in the Bruderhof book *Seeking Peace* shortly before she was shot in Columbine High School, I checked that chapter and found that it dealt mainly with the very costly witness of Phil and Elizabeth. I thought they might not know about their tie to the tragedy, and I wrote them.

It was good today to read Phil's reply. He thanked me for my witness and wished me well. "You have our daily prayers." He wrote: "Your enclosure about Cassie Bernall is very moving. Not enough is made of the connection between our imperialist savagery in Iraq and Yugoslavia and the shoot-out in Colorado. It's the Big Guns/Little Guns connection."

Calls and letters came. In the evening Ruth, Maren, and I stemmed strawberries.

Thursday, June 17.

This morning I called an information number for Brian Baldwin in Alabama. The governor has refused to grant a stay of execution. There's only a remote possibility that Brian will not be executed tonight. Brian had told me that the governor was going to visit the deputy sheriff in the nursing home on Monday. When Maren and I talked about this, we decided that the governor himself would probably not do that. But the man in Alabama told me that the governor, with four aides, had indeed gone. No other witnesses were present. The politician intent on the killing found ways to pressure or manipulate the aging, sick man into retracting his statement and deposition about Brian's having been beaten.

Ten years ago on July 13-14, 1989, I was there in the same prison and moved with our friend and death row inmate Ronnie Dunkins through the infernal process. In the hours before he was strapped to the electric chair, the evil of this premeditated killing was almost palpable in the prison air. For a considerable time before and during that murder by the state, the men on death row down the corridor were pounding on things and shouting—a despairing protest.

Friday, June 18.

Yesterday Ruth tried to call Brian but could not get through to him. Just after midnight last night I was lay awake praying for Brian. I had forgotten the one-hour time difference. The phone rang. It was Brian. He had probably been given some telephone time for calling family and friends. Ruth asked him, "Are you ready?"

And he said, "Yes."

He thanked us for being such "good parents" to him, and I told him, "I may not have much more time on earth, but we can meet over there and praise God together."

We learned that he was executed at 1:29 a.m., Eastern time. During the execution the governor was on the telephone with the warden—not a standard procedure, I'm rather sure.

I've been thinking of the cry of the great multitude in heaven: "Hallelujah! For the Lord our God the Almighty reigns." In recent months the powers of evil and their human agents have been on a rampage. But before long God will finalize their defeat.

Tuesday, June 22.

A year ago Ruth had neighbors and local friends in for my birthday. Some said then that they were looking forward to celebrating my next birthday with me. So we invited much the same group for this evening. We made two freezers of homemade ice cream. Ruth picked the strawberries and baked shortcakes. It was a carry-in. Thirty-four came. I was very tired and somewhat dispirited, but later in the evening I revived a little.

Saturday, June 26.

Last evening was the graduation for the resident doctors who had completed the three-year program in family practice at Lancaster General Hospital. Daniel was a part of it, although he needs to do an additional half year because of his transfer from Augusta, Maine, to Lancaster. But Ruth and I were able to take in this event. It was good to see how appreciated Daniel is. One doctor, in working out a slide program that was shown after dinner, had described each resident to his young children and asked them to pick an animal to correlate with the person. Daniel was a bear.

Monday, June 28.

Daniel left this morning for a four-week obstetric rotation in Louisiana.

For more than a week, I've been very fatigued, rather nauseated, and without appetite. (I've been forcing myself to eat substantial meals.) I'd had these symptoms during the latter part of the radiation and afterward, but they have become worse. On Friday we checked with Dr. Lee, the radiation oncologist. He doesn't think that I would still be having side effects from the whole brain radiation. Also on Friday we went to Dr. Caricofe. He had blood work done, but the results showed nothing that would explain how I have been feeling.

Friday, July 2.

Yesterday morning I had a CT scan of the chest, abdomen, and pelvis. I felt miserable the rest of the day. The report came this afternoon. The main tumor in the left lung has remained stable. There is a new 1 cm nodule in the right lung and some increase in the size of the pleural effusions. The largest tumor in the liver has increased from 4 cm to 10 cm. It seems that an inguinal lymph node is now affected. Dr. Caricofe recommends that I go ahead and use up the week's supply of thalidomide that I have on hand. He thinks that it may have helped some even though it has not held the cancer in check. When we talked with Daniel this evening, he did not see the report as that bad.

I'm thankful there has been time for doing so many "undone things." In fact, today I completed the editing of the journal manuscript through February 1999. I got the printed copy, the disk, and a letter ready to send to Julie Garber at Brethren Press. I still need to go over the entries written since February.

A line that keeps coming to me is "My times are in thy hand" (Ps. 31:15).

Late in the afternoon a front passed through, and we received 1.1 inches of rain—the most rain we've had at one time in a number of weeks—a sign of God's providential care. We been sharing our surplus of vegetables.

Monday, July 5.

Today is two years and eight months since the diagnosis. I am four months away from three years— and six months away from the year 2000.

Since getting the CT scan report, I'm intensely aware that my remaining time may be rather short, though God could continue to amaze us by giving me more time. I still want to resist that agent of death within my body as long as I can.

When I am feeling bad with fatigue and nausea, my spirits are weighed down, but I should be thanking God that I am feeling as well as I am.

Wednesday, July 7.

This morning I had another MRI of the brain. We do not have the radiologist's report yet.

When I say the wrong words, get mixed up, or forget something I think I should remember, I wonder whether these things come from the lesions in the brain, although I think for the most part they don't.

After the MRI I threw myself into correspondence that needed to be taken care of. I am feeling the pressure of many things still to do and probably not much time left for doing them. I don't think I have felt this sort of pressure before. After a couple of hours, the feeling passed. I don't want to be driven like that. Time enough will be given. I could have been killed in an accident, with no time at all for undone things.

Scott Duffey, our pastor in Westminster, visited us this evening even though he is on a three-month sabbatical. He asked whether I "fantasize" about what comes after the transition. I said that my main thought on this is that I will be met, but I have little idea how that will be.

Thursday, July 8.
My thalidomide ran out today. I was glad to be taking the tablets for the last time, but if the drug were helping I would be very glad to continue.

Friday, July 9.
The MRI report came today while we were in Dr. Caricofe's office. He could help us process the news, the grimmest we have received since the first weeks. The tumors in the brain have increased some in size, and there are more of them. The radiation treatments had been such a big expenditure of time, effort, and technology, with no good result, except that there is less edema around the lesions.

Ever since the diagnosis, we've wondered: How long do I have to live? But now another question replaces that one: How long will I have the normal functioning of my mind?

I've been recalling Bible verses about peace, as well as Romans 8:39: Nothing can "separate us from the love of God in Christ Jesus our Lord."

Saturday, July 10.
Don and Phyllis Miller arrived here from Indiana Thursday evening and left this morning for some other visits in the East. I was very moved as they were leaving. Don and I lived so much of our first twenty-five years together.

Frauke and Heiner Westphal came late this afternoon. I asked Frauke what I could expect in terms of symptoms, given the latest MRI report. She emphasized that it is such a miracle that my mind is still functioning normally. But as for what is ahead: seizures, headaches, nausea, small bleedings in the brain that can cause pressure and strokelike symptoms— partial loss of the use of a hand, slurred speech. She advised Ruth not to return to teaching in late August but to take an unpaid leave of absence.

She said we should do as much together as we can. In a phone call this evening, Daniel said that I could have a major stroke.

Ruth was looking at me with intense emotion: "I have to drink you in while I still can." We embrace each other again and again.

Maren called from Berkeley. She said that she is giving consideration to taking the fall semester off in order to be back here. She said that if she does go on for a Ph.D., one semester off should not make that much difference. But if Ruth takes an unpaid leave of absence for dependent care, there would be less need for Maren to be here. In any case, her offer is a beautiful sign of her love and support.

Sunday, July 11.

This morning Ruth played a cassette by the Canadian Mennonite singer Louella Klassen Friesen. The tape has songs she sang for her brother Kenn Klassen as he was dying of pancreatic cancer. The concluding song has the refrain, "Give us hope to the end." This seemed just the right word for us, and Ruth and I embraced each other as we listened to it.

Paul and Phyllis Dodd came by this afternoon with three of their children. As we talked, Phyllis asked, "Aren't you scared?" I may not have answered directly. I am finding it harder now to give an involved answer. Though bad things may be coming soon, I don't feel afraid—a sign of God's grace released to me through the prayers of many friends.

Monday, July 12.

I am trying to figure out which jobs should be done first. I spent much of the day sorting through books to be given away.

This evening we had our first corn on the cob.

On Wednesday we are to see a Johns Hopkins neurosurgeon, and on Thursday we have an appointment with Dr. Ettinger. The time has probably come to not have further therapy.

Tuesday, July 13.

Ulrich Wolf-Barnett, pastor of the German Lutheran Church in Washington, came out to have lunch with us. Ruth asked him to give us communion. It was so good again to eat the bread and drink the cup.

Wednesday, July 14.

We had our appointment with Dr. Jeffrey Williams, a neurosurgeon at Johns Hopkins. We learned that the radiologist who had read the last MRI of the brain had given a wrong report when he said that the lesions had increased in number and size. Dr. Williams double-checked the pictures and told us that the lesions instead were smaller and the edema around them was less, though there are still too many lesions for stereotactic radio surgery to be feasible.

We had been thinking the lesions would soon cause seizures or strokes. But the doctor does not see that as an immediate threat. Although this was wonderfully encouraging news for us, I was so fatigued that I felt little energy for being thankful.

Ruth has been bearing me up emotionally. When people visit or call, I don't have the resilience for sharing the faith. I don't see much fulfilment of the promise, "Power is made perfect in weakness" (2 Cor. 12:9).

Thursday, July 15.

At last we had our appointment with Dr. Ettinger. He was very caring and considerate. He said we are looking at dying and death. He sees my fatigue and nausea as coming from "progression of disease" and thinks that I am too weak to be put on any other sort of chemo. When Ruth asked him about the time remaining, he said "three to six months, at the outside." "You'll decide that you have had enough, that it's time to go home to your heavenly Father, and you'll go to sleep and not wake up." That certainly is a comforting picture of how the end might come.

Monday, July 19.

At various times since the diagnosis, Ruth has spoken of having hospice care. Today we had an intake interview. Laura Welty, the nurse who came, was splendid to deal with. I have the feeling that the timing is about right. They don't work with people for longer than six months. My mother had hospice care in 1983 and my father in 1993. Ruth now feels the need for backup support for the first time. We have received an oxygen tank to be stored here, in case I would have sudden need of oxygen.

Wednesday, July 21.

Letters came today from Maren and Daniel. Daniel poured out his heart expressing things he wanted to tell me while there is still time. A letter lends itself to greater openness. He sent the letter two-day priority so it would get here before he arrives back from Louisiana.

Thursday, July 22.

The last couple of days I haven't felt quite so fatigued, and I've used some time to lay out the order of the memorial service. I have felt uneasy that this task hadn't been accomplished.

Friday, July 23.

Tim McElwee came for an hour. It was another of the farewell visits. He mentioned that twenty-five years ago he entered a BVS discipleship training unit that I was leading, and that experience shaped his life from there on. He reminded me that twenty-five years is a good part of his forty-four years.

As we were bidding each other good-bye, I was touching both of his hands and was suddenly overcome by a sense that this is what Jesus meant when he pointed to the rock in speaking with Peter. And then I immediately thought that this is what needs to be passed on—is being passed on— through many people.

Saturday, July 24.

Miriam came last evening to have the weekend with us. Today is our thirty-fourth wedding anniversary.

Sunday, July 25.

Daniel arrived home from Louisiana late yesterday. This morning the four of us walked through the woodlot and were struck especially by the clusters of indigo-blue berries of the arrowwood viburnums. Later, when we were talking about the memorial service, we had the idea that if we dry a good quantity of these berries, we could have a bowl at the memorial service from which people could take two or three to plant. We will need to find out if the seed needs to be frozen in order to germinate. We all liked the symbolism.

Monday, July 26.

Ruth looked at me intensely and said: "You must decrease, and Jesus must increase. You will be less for us but he will be more in us." She made this comment because of my struggle to get words written down right. I have trouble working on the computer now, so Ruth has begun typing these entries; Miriam also typed some entries over the weekend.

Friday, July 30.

All the children are here.

Daniel's friend Pearl had sent a gift for me. It was water from the convent of Lourdes where huge numbers of people have gone to receive healing. We decided that tonight would be as good a night as any for using the water. When I took my bath, Daniel poured the little flask over my head and shoulders. He said a few words of blessing over the water as he poured it. My main reaction was shock at the water being as cold as it was.

Saturday, July 31.

Yesterday a call came from someone whom Ruth didn't recognize. It turned out to be David Heim, an editor at *The Christian Century*. I think Stanley Hauerwas, a theology professor at Duke, must have recommended me to write an eschatological article dealing with the year 2000. But now I don't have the energy to write a full-fledged article, and I would not be good at bringing out the current cultural things related to the year 2000. David was open to the possibility of using some later sections of *Reckoning with Apocalypse*. I am to send him a copy of the book. It occurred to me that Jeff Bach, who teaches at Bethany Seminary, might do the rounding out for Y2K. I was able to reach him by phone, and he was delighted to work on the project. He will draw together passages and motifs from the book and aim for an article that relates to the year 2000. I'm actually quite hopeful now that the article will be published.

Later in the evening, Miriam discovered she had been omitting the "h" in eschatology in the correspondence I had dictated to her related to the assignment. Miriam commented that I would not want a letter going to Stanley Hauerwas with *eschatology* spelled wrong.

Sunday, August 1.

On the way home from church, the rest of the family was singing Sojourners-type songs that we so often sang together when we were driving here or there in earlier years. It was a pleasant reminder of how much singing we had done when we traveled as a growing family. Ruth asked me whether I had any article in mind that I still want to write. I said, "Not really." If the "Why I Believe" article turns out to be the last one, I could feel very good about that. But maybe some other article will still be given.

Thursday, August 5.

Ruth has begun to sing the children's prayer protection song for me each
evening. She often sang this song for the children when they were small and
has continued to sing it as a prayer for them in later years.

Breit aus die Flügel beide
O Jesu meine Freude
Und nimm dies Kindlein ein
Will Satan Dich verschlingen
So lass die Englein singen
Dies Kind soll unverletzet sein.

Spread wide both your wings,
O Jesus, my joy,
And take this child in.
Should Satan want to devour you
Then let the angels sing:
This child shall not be harmed.

I am stirred every time she sings it to me. It is like a special plea against
the powers of darkness impinging on our present situation.

I feel very weak much of the time. I frequently lie on the couch during
the day. Some of the time I sleep; or I'm just resting. Most mornings I try to
get out to take a walk with Ruth and Maren, even as far as Haines' shed on
Stem Road. We have been able to do this some evenings as well. I think it
was Monday evening that a red fox ran across the lane only a few yards
ahead of us. It's the closest I had seen a red fox in daylight for many years.

Maren and I have gotten into a pattern. She sits at my word processor. I
lie on a mat and dictate journal entries. With her help and Miriam's, I've
been able to catch up. The two of them have also helped me make long
instruction lists for the family regarding such things as gardening, keeping
up and winterizing the place, and taking care of the spring house. I'm glad
that most of these are taken care of, because making these lists was one of
my priorities.

We had received the unsettling news that our Aetna health insurance
would not cover many of our Carroll Hospice expenses, because Frederick
Hospice is the regional "preferred provider." But Frederick Hospice does not
even serve Carroll County. Through the help of people in Ruth's school
district office, Aetna finally agreed to cover Carroll Hospice. We are glad to
not have to cope with this additional concern.

It has been two years and nine months since the diagnosis—and three months left to complete three years. My energy level remains very low, but my family tells me that my mind is clearer and brighter than it had been several weeks ago. I have recognized the deficiencies a little. The improvement has meant a great deal to them, though. Probably the edema in the brain has dissipated some. I still continue dictating these journal entries, because that's easier than using the word processor myself.

Monday, August 9.

For quite a long while, Ruth and I have been following a German devotional book for reading scripture. With my energy so low, I became lax in reading my daily prayer lists, until Ruth suggested that we do this together. While Maren is here, the three of us have been doing it together. Ruth reads the names as we pray together.

I have also decided to sleep downstairs at night. I'm steadier on my feet than I've been some of the time in recent weeks, but I don't want to fall, especially on the stairs.

Tuesday, August 10.

Dale Brown had a meeting at the Brethren Service Center in New Windsor and came to have the evening meal with us. He made a special point of telling me: "You have been able to be a witness to many people. But I want to tell you that because of this you should not feel that you dare not become low or depressed. If you become that way, that will be all right." I was touched that he would make a special effort to assure me that I don't need to be a model of faith and hope at the end. So much grace has been given to me, keeping me in good spirits through these months, that if later I receive less of that grace, that will be all right too.

Thursday, August 12.

I have felt the urgency to go through my books, mainly those in my old third floor office—a very big project. Maren and I made a limited start on this again last week. But in the past few days, climbing the two flights of stairs has become even more difficult, so we developed a different pattern. Daniel and Maren would bring the boxes down from the office to the living room. I would put them into categories: those to remain in the family, those for the district, those to be sent to the Comenius faculty in Prague, and those for younger pastors and other friends. Being able to do this downstairs helped a great deal. Today we were able to complete this project with a great sense of accomplishment.

It has occurred to me a number of times that the room in our addition and our living room give beautiful spaces to die in. I can look up and see the exposed beams and the white between the beams. A week or so ago I had Daniel measure the distance between the beams directly above me when I am lying down on the couch in the living room. I didn't think they were set exactly the same distance apart; indeed, they are set at slightly different distances.

Though I am so fatigued that I could lie down most of the time, I assume that it is good for me to be walking around some, inside and outside. The hospice nurse says that if I want to give up on walking, that would be simply one way of winding down. But I would like to keep walking if I can. Every afternoon Maren puts my socks and shoes on, and she and Ruth and I make a little walk through the woodlot and down the lane. I'm often tired when returning, but I also feel I have accomplished something.

Saturday, August 14.
Since the completion of the book project, Maren and I have turned to catching up on the baskets of correspondence that have accumulated over the past months. I am unable to answer everyone because of my very limited energy, but there are a few people whom I feel the need to write while I am still able. I lie on the couch and dictate; Maren writes the letters by hand.

Sunday, August 15.
Ruth and Daniel moved another bed down into the addition room yesterday, so Ruth and I can both be sleeping in the same room again. Today we also made the decision to listen to scripture tapes at home rather than going to the worship service in Westminster. My energy level is too limited. In the afternoon I went outside, and Ruth showed me a mockingbird nest in the mock orange bush by the garage. The little fledglings are already quite large.

Monday, August 16.
Larry and Ann Fourman made a special trip from Indiana to see me for the last time. Before we had a closing prayer, Larry mentioned visiting Phil Weller, an old Pipe Creek elder, a little before his death years ago. Phil was extremely agitated and mentioned that he had had a vision of the devil. The next day when Larry visited Phil, Larry saw right away that a change had

come over Phil. He was as peaceful as he had been agitated the day before. Phil explained the change to Larry. He said he had seen Jesus, ready to welcome him to heaven. At first I found it strange that Larry would tell this story, but then I saw the wisdom in it. Larry was telling me that near the end I might feel myself in the grip of evil. Maybe I will not, but if I do, that will be all right, for the love of Jesus will be stronger.

Tuesday, August 17.

Daniel has applied to work in a Lancaster poverty clinic starting in January, after he finishes his residency. He had his main interview this afternoon. It seemed to go very well. We are grateful to him for taking us into account in his planning. It would be good if it worked out for him to be located so close geographically to Ruth.

I have felt very weak all day and have a good deal of difficulty breathing. A little after eight p.m., we decided to try the oxygen tank again. We had tried it once before, several weeks ago, and had not found any benefit. But this time I found that the oxygen helped significantly in easing my breathing.

Wednesday, August 18.

I thought of sleeping without the oxygen last night, but I rapidly found that this was too much of a strain. So I am on the oxygen all the time now. The plastic tubing from the oxygen tank is long enough that I can go anywhere here in the house that I need to go, but I do not have much energy for walking around.

Ruth tells me that the baby mockingbirds have flown.

Thursday, August 19.

Yesterday morning we received a call from Jeff Bach, who had written a draft of the article for *The Christian Century*. He faxed it to us, and this morning I read the piece. It is the first reading on my own that I have done in several weeks. Mainly I have relied on Ruth and Maren reading to me, but I felt that I needed to be able to read this on my own.

Both Maren and I were impressed with Jeff's knack for synthesizing and consolidating the material. Jeff mentioned the need to cut the article and welcomed suggestions, so I turned that over to Maren. I simply do not have the mental energy to engage in this sort of conceptual work. Maren worked much of the day on recasting the piece. After I read the revised article, we faxed a copy back to Jeff.

Friday, August 20.

We have needed to increase the oxygen. For the first time, I felt a slight sense of discomfort in my left chest area, presumably from the tumor pushing against something there. But in the afternoon I did not notice it anymore.

Janet and Bill Heltzel brought us a lovely dinner. They have been such models of Christian helpfulness. We ate in the living room. Ruth fixed up a tray for me so I could eat in the easy chair. I find this less tiring than sitting at the table.

Saturday, August 21.

Maren requested that I bless her before she returns to California tomorrow. So this morning I asked for my Bible and a blank sheet of paper. I spent some time writing down blessings and scripture passages, resting several times. Shortly before noon, Maren sat down on a stool in front of the easy chair and I was able to give her my blessing, with Ruth helping to support my arm. Then I anointed her forehead with oil. What a gift that we could share this beautiful time yet. I think of this as a blessing for all three children.

In the early afternoon, Daniel arrived from Lancaster. He is taking a week of vacation to be with us here. A little while later Miriam and Chuck arrived. They are on their way to Atlanta, where Chuck starts teaching next week. They will leave early tomorrow morning and take Maren to the airport. It is marvelous to have the whole family here together another time.

Sunday, August 22.

We again had worship with tapes here at home. We listened especially to Max McLean reading from the Gospel of Luke. In the late afternoon Ruth got the idea that I could take the oxygen line and walk into the front yard. Daniel took the portable oxygen tank, and I walked all the way to the rail fence. While I felt a sense of achievement, I also thought that perhaps I would not be doing this again. I was quite exhausted when I came back inside.

Daniel found a large stack of cards on which I had written quotations. These were from all sorts of authors and sources. It's fascinating to revisit my intellectual past. One quotation gave the simple story that when Martin Niemoëller was eight years old, he went with his father to visit a weaver who was dying of tuberculosis. The weaver had woven the words, "What would Jesus say?" I was moved by this as an indication of what I would still like to express at the end of my life.

Maren and Jeff Bach exchanged e-mails concerning the final editing they had been doing to the text of the article for *The Christian Century*. Jeff is submitting the article.

Monday, August 23.

Dawn Ottoni Wilhelm at Princeton is writing a doctoral thesis on prophetic preaching and is trying to get sermons that will give her a basis for this study. She had written to me some time ago about sending a few of my sermons. When I felt very weak, I did not think I could help. But Daniel spent most of today going through tapes and typescripts of some sermons. We were able to send her a few sermons that may be helpful. I found it invigorating to be able to do this. The stimulus came partly from reading two old sermons later in the day.

Friday, August 27.

Miriam arrived last night. This evening my sister, Ann, came with her husband, Mike, and their daughters Mande, Hopi, and Nicole, and Mande's little son, Gavin. They will spend the weekend with us. Our families have not been together like this for many years. I am grateful that I have not had a downturn mentally that would prevent me from being able to interact with them.

I have not given much thought to the possibility that I might die quite unexpectedly in my sleep. I should think about this more.

Saturday, August 28.

This afternoon Ruth suggested that I accompany the family outside for a tour of the garden. I managed to walk outside, and Daniel then pushed me through the grass in a wheelchair with the portable oxygen tank strapped to it. From my chair it was delightful to see some of the late garden that I had planted earlier in the summer. The spinach has not done too well, but the lettuce and broccoli are coming on. I also saw the fruit trees and the heartnuts, and watched Gavin eat red raspberries. After I went inside, the rest of the family kept harvesting. I don't have much of an appetite anymore for most fruits and vegetables, but it is splendid that others can enjoy them.

Ann's family is wonderfully musical and has always done a lot of singing together. They have been singing hymns for me.

Sunday, August 29.

This morning Maren told us that she had heard from Jeff Bach that *The Christian Century* will be publishing the article. We do not yet know when the article will appear. If it is published soon, I might live to see it.

We had a worship time this morning, listening to music and scripture tapes and reading Bible quotations from the cards Daniel had found. Afterward we listened to an old reel-to-reel tape recording. My parents, Ann, and Jane had made it for me for Christmas in 1953, when I was doing peace work in Germany.

This afternoon Daniel took Nicole to the airport and headed back to Lancaster. In the evening I bade farewell to Ann, Mike, Mande, Gavin, and Hopi. Understanding that we will not see each other again in this world has made our time together even richer and more intense than other times.

Monday, August 30.

Ruth made the comment: "You will be in the choir and sing even if you can't snap your fingers." She was referring to an incident in grade school when the class was to snap their fingers to the rhythm of "Up on the Housetop." I was unable to snap my fingers so I did not try. The teacher was upset with me and made me go with her to the two youngest classes she was teaching and dismissed me from music altogether. I took no further part in music in school. The incident had a profound influence on my openness to music after that time. It's taken years to recover from this. Now I am listening to music for much of each day.

Ruth also said, "You will take something of me with you and you will leave something of yourself here with me." So many letters and calls have continued to come from people who are walking with us in this time. To represent that outpouring of compassion, I am including part of a letter from Deborah Hunsinger, who teaches at Princeton Theological Seminary:

> We were so moved to receive your recent letter, Dale. You have been so faithful throughout this walk through the valley of the shadow of death—keeping us apprised enough so that we can walk with you at a distance—through our constant prayers for you. I almost always ask God to grant you joy in each day that you are given—joy in Him and in the faith that he has so graciously given you, joy in your beloved family, who has been such an inspiration to me over the years, and joy in the present

miracle of each new day. And as I pray for you I find that the very gifts I ask for you, God also grants them to me. The deeper I dive into the mystery of prayer, the more mysterious it becomes. I also ask Him to free you from all anxiety and care, to enable you to trust in Him completely, and to keep all fear from your heart. Sometimes I sing St. Patrick's prayer for you:

> Christ be with thee, Christ beside thee, Christ before thee, Christ to guide thee, Christ in rising, Christ in sleeping, Christ in working, Christ in speaking. Christ beneath thee, Christ above thee, Christ in quiet, Christ in danger, Christ in the hearts of all who love thee, Christ in the mouth of friend and stranger.

I also pray for the members of your family and all who love you. Please let me know whether you need prayers for anything in particular beyond these. It is a privilege and an honor to share this holy time with you in this way.

Tuesday, August 31.

Ruth made the comment that she is brimming with thankfulness for every day that we are given.

Thursday, September 2.

Miriam arrived last night. This morning I asked her to get my Brethren manual, which I have used for many years in pastoral work. She read me the scriptures suggested for graveside services. Then I had her jot down notes for the service, which I envision as being very simple. Maren called with the wonderful news that Crossroad has decided to let *Reckoning with Apocalypse* continue in print. The earlier news that the book would not remain in print had weighed on me. Now I am hopeful that *The Christian Century* article and the accessibility of the book through Crossroad should provide *Reckoning with Apocalypse* new opportunities, perhaps beyond what it had earlier. God grants blessing upon blessing.

We had turned to Lisa Spence, of the local agricultural extension service, for advice about tree seeds to pass out at the memorial service. We liked the symbolism of this. We had hoped to use our dried arrowwood viburnum seeds, but they apparently don't do very well. Lisa explored various possibilities for us, but there were problems with all of them. Today she called to report that she could get us tiny balsam fir seedlings that people could take home to plant after the memorial. We will get 250 of these. Miriam showed me a photo of a balsam fir; it is a beautiful tree. The catalog says it is well-suited for Christmas tree use. But I hope that if people use the firs for that purpose, they will dig the trees up and replant them, not cut them down.

In the last weeks I have sometimes had some abdominal pain. Early this evening it hit me quite hard. I started with the first dose of Roxinal, a pain medication with morphine that hospice had given us for such a time. I have had short periods of severe pain in the past, but no pain that has been this extended. Ruth and Miriam rubbed my abdomen and sang to me to try to help me through the pain. We seem to be entering a new era in terms of difficulty.

⟫●⟪

Friday, September 3.

Dale, thinking back on the many blessings of the day before, told the family, "I've been wondering for months how the journal would end. This seems like a good ending." That night he began hyperventilating. Ruth and Miriam sang hymns to him again. With an increased dose of morphine, his breathing eventually settled again. At about 3:00 the next morning, Daniel arrived from Lancaster; Dale was sleeping. When we went to administer the 4 a.m. dose of morphine, the expression on his face was peaceful. Dale was gone.

Ruth, Daniel, and Miriam washed the body and placed it into the pine box that Ken Koons had prepared many months ago. Maren and Chuck arrived in the early afternoon. We sang and held devotions by the body. After reading Dale's prayer list and saying the Lord's Prayer together—the prayer we always said before any of us went on a journey—we sealed the box.

In the evening, a few friends arrived, including Wilbur Wright with his pickup truck. They helped us load the box onto the back of the truck. As Wilbur drove the truck through the woodlot, the gathered friends and family followed, some on foot, some in cars, through pouring rain from tropical storm Dennis. At the end of the lane, Ruth got into the cab with Wilbur.

Daniel, Miriam, Chuck, and Maren climbed into the back with the pine box, and we rode over to the Pipe Creek Cemetery. We held a simple graveside service there, with the scriptures Dale had chosen.

Even though I walk through the valley of the shadow of death, I fear no evil; for thou art with me; thy rod and thy staff, they comfort me.

Psalm 23: 4

But we would not have you ignorant, brethren, concerning those who are asleep, that you may not grieve as others do who have no hope. For since we believe that Jesus died and rose again, even so, through Jesus, God will bring with him those who have fallen asleep.

1 Thessalonians 4:13-14

A Photo Journal

The photographs in this section were taken by Ken Koons for a series of articles written by Scott Blanchard that appeared in the *Carroll County Times* in December 1998. They are used here with the permission of the *Carroll County Times*.

Following his cancer diagnosis, Dale finds strength from scriptures that are "given to him."

Dale writes journal entries in his third-floor office.

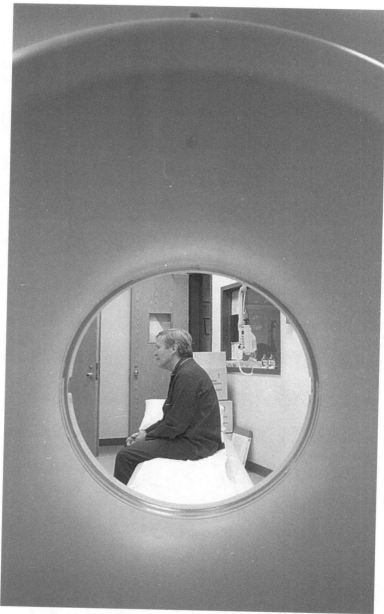

Dale prepares to undergo a CT scan as part of his participation
in a study conducted by the National Cancer Institute.

Ruth supports the family as an art teacher for the Carroll County public school system.

Dale, accompanied by daughters, Maren and Miriam, marches for peace at the Pentagon.
They walk with David Braune (left).

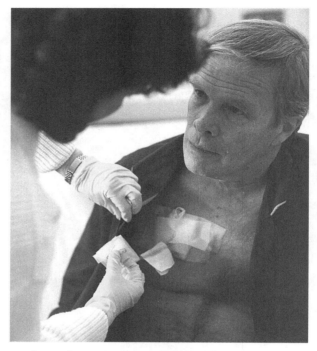

An oncology nurse prepares Dale for a chemo treatment.

Dale stacks wood that he doesn't believe he will live long enough to burn. (Winter 1997)

Dale's failing health prompts him to give away his two steers. (March 1997)

Waiting at the hospital Ruth feels the strain of dealing with her husband's illness.

Dale is exhilarated by "doing just a little of the tree planting himself" in the memorial wood lot. (March 29, 1997)

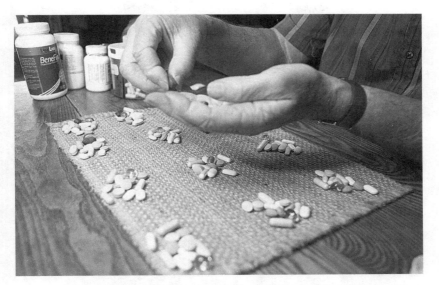

Dale counts out a four-day supply of pills—a regimen of vitamins and nutritional supplements that he believed helped to lengthen his life.

Dale is thankful to be able to work in the garden yet another year. (June 1998)

Dale preaches at Pipe Creek Church of the Brethren. (September 1998)

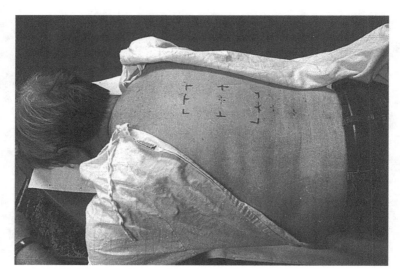

Dale awaits a radiation treatment for the cancer that has spread
to the middle and upper part of his spine. (November 1998)

Ruth discovers the first bloom of the Christmas rose in their flower garden.
(December 1998)

Just hours after a chemo treatment, Dale relinquishes the task of digging the Christmas tree to Daniel and son-in-law Chuck Pazdernik. (December 1998)

The family enjoys tea and Christmas cookies after digging the Christmas tree.

Dale prepares for the time when Ruth will have to do heavy
chores alone, such as installing storm windows by herself.

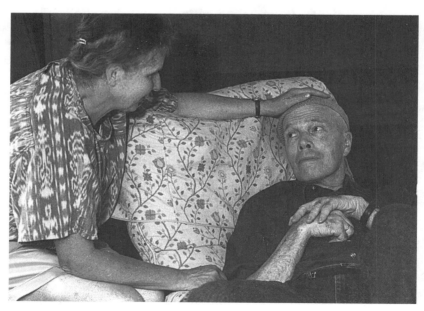

Ruth chats with Dale. (July 1999)

As Dale's strength wanes, even addressing envelopes
becomes an arduous task. (late July 1999)

Miriam and her husband, Chuck, prepare for the walk to the gravesite. (September 4, 1999)

Dale rests after sorting books with Maren. He dies less than a month later on September 4, 1999.

Dale's family accompanies him one last time past the memorial woodlot that was planted just two years before his death.

Dale is buried atop the hill of Pipe Creek Cemetery in Union Bridge, Maryland on September 4, 1999.
(From left to right: Daniel, Maren, Ruth, Miriam, Chuck)

Writings by and about Dale Aukerman

A memorial service was held for Dale Aukerman on September 12, 1999, at the Westminster Church of the Brethren. Paul Grout, pastor of the Genesis Fellowship in Putney, Vermont, spoke at the service. These are his words.

We gather together to remember one who was among us, one whom we loved. We gather together to hold one another, to give and receive comfort. We gather together to worship in thanksgiving to God for life, in thanksgiving for the life of our beloved. We gather together praising the God who holds us, who holds now eternally the one we have loved.

We gather together, we stop. The pace and flow of our lives have stopped for a time. Life cannot just continue as it has. We must stop now to mourn a loss and, even in our sorrow, to celebrate a life. The too often frantic pace of our lives is broken for a time, and for a moment we stop to wonder: What has meaning? What lasts?

Love lasts. Our love for him, and in a way we are only beginning to comprehend his love for us. A husband's love lasts, as does a wife's. A father's love lasts, as does a child's. God's love lasts.

We gather together, we stop. We recognize how we have been touched. We open ourselves to what God would say to us, to how God would restore us.

There is one primary thing I will ask of us—that we receive this time as an opportunity to discover again what it means to be human, to be fully human as God creates us in his image to be.

I have had such great respect for Dale's integrity, how he sought to conform every aspect of his life to his faith. He sought with such intentional purpose to live out what he believed. Every thought, every word he spoke, seemed to come under the scrutiny of his ethic.

Before Dale prayed he paused; whenever he assumed responsibility to pray aloud publicly, the pause could seem interminably long. To be honest, I frequently found this pause anxiety-producing, especially when sharing in a meal at the Aukermans. In this time of anticipatory silence, I would be asking myself: Did I miss something? Maybe I'm supposed to be praying, maybe everybody's waiting for me to pray, . . . Maybe I should just start. I think the mashed potatoes are getting cold. If we were holding hands around the table, my hands would begin to sweat and after a time to twitch involuntarily.

As a pastor, I feel the need to move things along. Silences can put us ill at ease. Dale seemed a little out of touch with a culture that likes to keep things moving; no standard ready-made prayer for him. It was as if he were waiting on the Holy Spirit, seeking the mind of Christ even in this ritual moment.

The same kind of thing happened if you asked Dale a question. The pause before his answer could be exasperatingly long. In this period of waiting for an answer, my mind would often drift. When Dale's answer would finally come, I might be sailing off the island of Majorca in the Mediterranean. I would snap back to attention and listen intently to his answer in hopes that I could quickly remember the question I had asked.

Our theology and opinions get shaped in particular ways over the years so that over time we can quickly regurgitate "correct" answers to almost any question. My sense was that in pausing Dale was not searching his mind for an answer, he was seeking the mind of Christ.

It, of course, made perfect sense that as the end of his life drew near this too would be approached with the same sense of pause, intentionality, and integrity. The simple, beautiful, wooden coffin lay ready in the garage loft. A daily examination of what was worth doing, what made sense if time left was short, began with a new intensity.

The structure and content of this memorial service was planned. I received an outline over a month ago. Dale had asked if I would preach. I know that you're thinking, I bet he sent Grout an outline of the message. No, but he attempted to determine the focus of my words when he first asked me to speak. Some time ago, fairly early on in the battle, while I was visiting Dale, he took me aside and said: "Paul, Ruth and I would like you to preach at my memorial service. We want this because we know that we can trust you to lift up Jesus Christ and not Dale Aukerman."

But now as I stand before you I have a problem. I understood what Dale was saying and I agree. It's just that I'm not so very sure of what was Dale and what was Jesus. Was it Dale who visited Ronnie Dunkins on death row, or was it Christ? Was it Dale who witnessed the execution or Christ? Was it Dale who wept, or was it Christ?

Jesus Christ protested against a country that had lost its way.

Jesus Christ was arrested in Washington.

Was I standing next to Dale, or was I standing with Christ at the barbed wire fence between us and the armed soldiers guarding horrible weapons of unimaginable destructive power?

Did Dale's truth-telling keep him from rising in our denomination, or was Christ kept from rising?

Sitting at the Aukerman table, I recognized Christ in the breaking of the bread.

Christ comes to us through the Holy Spirit, he comes to us through the least in society, he comes to us through scripture, and Christ comes to us in one another.

> *From now on, therefore, we regard no one from a human point of view; even though we once knew Christ from a human point of view, we know him no longer in that way. So if anyone is in Christ, there is a new creation: everything old has passed away; see, everything has become new!*
>
> 2 Corinthians 5:16-17

> *And it is no longer I who live, but it is Christ who lives in me. And the life I now live in the flesh I live by faith in the Son of God, who loved me and gave himself for me.*
>
> Galatians 2:20

> *Now by this we may be sure that we know him, if we obey his commandments. Whoever says, "I have come to know him," but does not obey his commandments, is a liar, and in such a person the truth does not exist; but whoever obeys his word, truly in this person the love of God has reached perfection. By this we may be sure that we are in him; whoever says, "I abide in him," ought to walk just as he walked.*
>
> 1 John 2:3-6

In giving ourselves over to Christ, the Holy Spirit dwells within us. His life resounds within us. We pattern our lives either after Jesus Christ or after someone or something else. Even our language, our particular dialect, betrays our unconscious patterning. Social scientists can usually tell which area of the country we grew up in by listening to us speak. Our attitude, thought process, and action are more dictated by the world than we often realize.

A friend told a story of an incident that occurred in his hometown. A man had an accident that permanently damaged one of his legs. For the rest of his life he would walk with a noticeable limp. The man married and this union produced a healthy baby boy. The child grew up in the small town among family, friends, neighbors, and a close knit church community. No one noticed anything wrong until the boy went to school. His kindergarten teacher was from another town and had never seen the boy before his first day of school. At the end of that day, the teacher went to the school nurse and asked what had happened to the child, causing him to walk with a limp. Of course, the boy so admired and loved his father that he wanted to be just like him in every way.

Our lives will be patterned; intentionally or unintentionally they will be patterned. Dale Aukerman sought to pattern his life after Jesus. We saw this in the way he walked.

The church in North America is in great numerical decline. So many young people are rejecting the church. But what are they rejecting? What are they seeing? We have thought that they were rejecting Christ, but is that so? Is it possible they are rejecting our religion because they have not seen Christ in it? Is it possible that young people when looking at the church are not seeing anything very different than what they see when looking at the world? Are they seeing the same bickering, smallness, and emptiness they see in the world? Are they seeing lives caught up in the same frantic pace the world is caught up in? Are they seeing the same values, the same self-seeking they see in the world? Are they, in fact, seeing us correctly and saying, "No thank you"?

Do we understand the degree of damage to the human soul that has been done in our culture? Do we truly understand "Who" people need to see to be restored to health?

People need to know and they need now to be taught how to be human, as God created us to be, in his image. We can only become fully human as we encounter and pattern our lives after Jesus Christ. In Christ we see all that we hope for in God. In Christ we see all that God hopes for in us. He restores our souls. In him we become God's own children. In him we become fully human.

Dale Aukerman was not a great man. Do not diminish his life by designating him so. Dale Aukerman was not a good man. He would never claim for himself a designation that Christ rejected for himself. If Dale was great and good, he was an exception, and we don't have to deal personally with his life. This is what we saw: we saw the One in Dale to whom he gave his life. To be sure, we saw Dale, a unique person, unique to all others on earth, but we saw this too: a human being, a soul alive, made alive in Christ.

The enormity of our loss is great. The only thing greater is the enormity of God's love. Nothing can separate us from that love. Experience now the completeness of our humanity that comes through Christ. He restores our souls. Experience Christ's sorrow as he weeps with us. Experience Christ's joy as he laughs with us. Forgive as he forgives. Love as he loves. Experience God's creation. Praise God for the earth, the sky, the sun, the rain, everything working together, a part of God's divine plan.

Worship in recognition of God's goodness. Go to the least and find Jesus. Love the church, the church local, denominational, universal. If the church has hurt you, love the church even more deeply. Love as Christ loved.

Love all people, seeking their healing. Love your enemies. Love being human. It is lonely being human. Husbands grow ill. Fathers die. Our dear ones are taken away. We see oppression. We see injustice. This is a lonely seeing. Christ removes none of this loneliness from us. He walks with us through it. He enters the depths of our souls as we allow him entrance. Loneliness will always be a part of us, the loneliness of being human. But in the breathtaking beauty of his presence, we will never be alone.

Reflections by Don Murray

Don Murray, writer and actor, became Brethren partly through his association with Dale Aukerman in Brethren Service in the 1950s. He writes about Dale in these journal entries in his autobiography, Actors and Other Angels, *reprinted here with permission.*

New Windsor, Maryland

December 5, 1952.

Our Brethren Service training unit of some dozen young women and half again as many men is housed in a dormitory, the men's floor above the women's. We sleep in double-decker beds, about eight to a room. The bunks are only six feet long, so my feet hang over the edge.

The working day is spent half in physical labor and half in classes. The labor is packing clothing and occasional food and medical supplies for shipment overseas.

The classes are the best general education I've ever had: sociology, European history, Brethren history and the basis of their nonviolent action.

December 9, 1952.

The Actress arrived two nights ago, drunk, swearing, and making fun of the "religious nuts." Today she packed clothes with the volunteers. One found cigarettes in a pocket. Knowing that she smoked, they held a brief debate over which was the greater error—to give them to the Actress or to throw them away. They voted to give them to her, feeling that she'd buy some anyway, and the greater error was waste. I haven't seen her smoke since, and tonight she said, "I love these people. They're completely sincere in their beliefs but have a sense of humor about everything. If I wasn't Bat Mitzvahed, I think I'd join them."

February 1953.

There's a counselor here who trained in a unit prior to ours. His name is Dale Aukerman. He's about twenty years old, five-foot nine or so, with wide-set eyes and the broad shoulders of a football linebacker. He's a brilliant student, having completed a four-year college course in just one. He is very quiet, walking noiselessly, like an Indian. He has this aura of aesthetic mysticism about him. He keeps holding up the ideas and actions of our group to the light of the teachings and example of Jesus. It would be comfortable to dismiss him as a religious fanatic so I could get him out of my conscience, but I keep seeing him as a modern-day John Hess instead.

There was a young divinity student visiting the service center who kept telling us that feeding and clothing people was a harmful waste: "Their spirits have to be clothed in righteousness and fed with salvation." The guy was a humorless, self-righteous bore, and I wished that he'd been sent on his way, but I had to admire the Brethren for their tolerance in letting him stay and express beliefs that were in direct opposition to the activities of the center and to the very foundation of Brethren service. Dale had the best answers for the dissident in the life and teachings of Jesus: "Jesus fed and healed the people and said, 'He who does this to these, the least of my Brethren, does it for me also.' "

Dale is an enigma to me. He's very bright and roundly educated, but he believes in Jesus not only as a great teacher and humanitarian, but as a personality that has transcended physical death and has a presence here today. This is Jesus Christ, the Savior. He believes that by recognizing the Savior in Jesus, as well as by trying to follow his teaching and example, we can be free of our debilitating submergence in destructive preoccupations. In this sense, we are "saved."

I relish conversations with Dale, because he has such extensive knowledge in history, art and religion, but I find his religious ideas a bit spooky. I have a materialistic and mathematical mind: You do this and that is the probable result. But he seems to believe that there is a "God" who moves people and events and that there is a heavenly existence, which is in addition to the "heavenly" state that we experience when saved from destructive activities. He seems to be saying that this is the existence that Jesus refers to as "my Father's house."

A Brethren who altered my philosophical and religious concepts and enabled me to better understand and feel a union with Dale's is Bob Richards, "the Polevaulting Parson," who won gold in two Olympics. He gave a series of evangelical sermons at the Westminster Church of the Brethren. The salient theme of Bob's sermon seemed to be Jesus as a man of flesh and blood, who felt the same degree of pleasure and pain that all of us feel, but gave up the things most of us find most pleasurable and endured the greatest pain imaginable as a way to help us find a joy beyond pleasure, an eternal ecstacy. Unlike most evangelists, Bob didn't rant and rave against sinners and solicit money, but, like most, he invited people to come forward to be "saved."

After hearing two sermons, I had a strong urge to go forward but resisted the impulse as giving in to hypnotic emotionalism. But after his third sermon, I did go forward. . . .

What change had happened within me that came of being "saved"?

I found myself reading the Bible more often, with the realization that I was enjoying it more fully and the impression that I understood it more deeply. The opening words of the Gospel of John, which had confused and annoyed me before, gave me enlightenment and comfort now: "In the beginning was the Word, and the Word was with God. . . . all things were made through him. . . . in him was life, and the life was the light of men [God created life on earth and has knowledge and wisdom for man]. . . . And the Word became flesh and dwelt among us [God came to life with that knowledge and wisdom in the person of Jesus]."

I feel now that I have more of an understanding of and kinship with Dale Aukerman.

Kassel, Germany

August 1953.

Working in construction of the building that will be Brethren Service headquarters in Germany, I find that the hardest job is to endure the boredom of the job. Mixing mortar, chiseling stone, and painting have some artistry. Even digging foundations is rewarding for the exercise. But now I spend all day sitting on a pile of old bricks from a bombed-out building, chipping the dry mortar off their sides so they can be used again. I've been doing this for over a week now, and I find myself looking forward to my dental appointment as a relief from the tedium.

Last night's dental visit dissuaded me from any idea that pain is preferable to boredom. I had root canal work where the nerve is removed from a tooth. Back in the states, we get Novocain anesthetic for a simple filling. Here there was none for digging out a nerve. I didn't think the human mechanism could endure such pain. I kept thinking that my body would just shut down and die or that I'd at least pass out, but neither happened. I was fully wake through three and a half hours of agony.

This morning I got out of bed before dawn. The soreness of my mouth was overridden by a general nervousness throughout my body. I couldn't sleep and didn't want to sit or eat, so I went out to the building site to resume work on the old bricks just as light was spilling through the windows and holes of the bombed-out buildings along my way. I was ironically amused at the idea that pain was preferable to boredom, but after less than an hour of sitting on the brick pile chipping away at the clinging dry mortar, boredom made the nervousness more severe. I felt a sensation of tickling under the skin, like having your nails dragged along a blackboard. I looked for any excuse to drop the brick cleaning: carrying water and cement bags to the masons who laid the bricks, piling my cleaned bricks into a wheelbarrow to replenish their supply. After a lunch that I longed for but couldn't chew, I was relieved to be given a different task. Big paper bags, some three and a half feet tall and two and a half feet wide, were filled with clumps of goat hair. My job was to pick the hairs off the skin with my fingers, just a few at a time, and drop them into a bucket where they awaited insertion into a mortar that was stuffed between the roof tiles as weather proofing and insulation. Next to this, the brick-cleaning job seemed a luxury.

My companion in this Chinese torture of the building trade was Dale Aukerman. He hadn't eaten lunch either, but not out of any disability. He never ate lunch. "With half the world starving, two meals a day is enough."

I could never say something like that without coming off like a self-righteous crank, but from him this was just a simple statement of his own truth. Dale has been at this horrendous job for over a week, and there isn't a hint of self-pity or discontent. He just pads around the attic in his bare feet, with that smooth, animal-like gait of his, working through lunchtime and beyond the quitting whistle.

As I watched him, a bit in awe and wonder, I thought: This guy would be the perfect companion for a wacky scheme of mine. I outlined my idea for him: to enter Russia at Leningrad, which is the closest city to the free world of Finland, and from there walk to Moscow, living and working with the Russian people as we went, sleeping in barns, haylofts, or open fields (in the summer, of course). Napoleon proved that a Moscow journey in winter is not such a great idea). We'd demonstrate that there was no enmity or basic differences between the people of communist Russia and democratic United States. Dale liked the idea, and we began throwing back and forth the things we'd need to do to make it work. We'd have to learn Russian, but since we were both fluent in German, we figured that after about three months and some textbooks from America, we could achieve that. We decided to contact the American Embassy and Russian Consulate in Vienna for permission to go as soon as our service period was over.

Vienna, Austria

April 1955.

If we don't get permission from our own country, we'll go anyway, but we can't go without a Soviet visa. We won't have much of a peace walk in a Siberian prison, and one day in New York's "tombs" as a conscientious objector was enough jail to last me a lifetime.

The Soviet Embassy was ironically ornate, with rococo moldings and ceilings decorated with reubenesque nymphs and angels. The walls supported two huge, highly romanticized portraits, one of Stalin, the other of Lenin. Only one of their staff seemed to speak English, an aesthetic looking blonde man of about thirty. He was dressed in a simple gray suit of Sears Roebuck quality and had a soft, shy manner. He listened patiently, if a bit nervously, to our proposal to walk from Leningrad to Moscow "not in any official government or church capacity, but as two individual Americans meeting with individual Russians in a gesture of peace and common humanity in this Atomic Age."

If there was a sign blinking "spies" somewhere in his head, he didn't give us any hint of it as he handed over reams of forms for us to fill out, which he promised to forward to Moscow. Once the papers were received we could expect a reply within a little more than a month. Dale and I separated and I went up to Kassel, Germany.

—————◆————

November 1999.

Since coming home in May of 1955, though hospitalized with pleurisy, hernia, and cancer, I've recovered from the physical woes of Europe. Dale and I never got an answer to our request for a visa and, although I've been around the world a couple of times, I've never set foot in Russia. Dale has traversed the world too—much more constructively and courageously than I have—and has faced much worse physical woes.

We've seen each other a number of times, though not nearly often enough, and exchanged considerable correspondence in which his erudition and good sense have been helpful to me in my career and life in general. We've both been fortunate in sharing life with courageous and inspiring wives, Ruth and Bettie.

Two visits with Dale and Ruth come most vividly and warmly to mind. In the early seventies, Bettie and I visited New Windsor. Our four-year-old son,

Michael, was happily playing with some contemporaries at the service center when we led him away to visit the Aukermans. In very un-peace church-style, Mick punched, kicked, and cried when I tried to carry him into the house. He dug his toes into one door jam and his fingers into the other. I couldn't drag him inside without injuring him, so we left him in the car to fuss until he fell asleep. When he finally came inside, he found a Tarzan rope swing hanging from the living room ceiling in front of the big fireplace— and like-aged Daniel Aukerman. They swung and played like life-long buddies all afternoon while Bettie and I enjoyed lively discussions with Ruth and Dale over their delicious homegrown food. While driving away, Bettie commented that all the epicurean tables of Hollywood, New York, and Europe pale next to the offerings at the Aukerman house, and the company was as vital, stimulating, and interesting as the accumulation of minds we'd enjoyed in the sum of all those places. Mick said simply: "This was the best day of my life!"

The last time I saw Dale and Ruth was at the 50th Anniversary of Brethren Service. Dale was deep into his illness now but only Ruth, his children, and a few close friends would have observed that. He came to the celebration with a surgeon's mask over his nose and mouth to ward off infection, but he participated in that same quiet, observant manner that he'd shown in Brethren Service. His gait was more cautious now, but it still had enough of the smooth glide that had reminded me of an Indian or a majestic animal forty-seven years ago. I spent several stimulating, inspiring days with Ruth and Dale, along with their son, Dr. Daniel Aukerman, and a few friends. We capped the visit with a love feast at the Westminster Church where, all those decades ago, I'd heard the sermons of Bob Richards and stepped forward to be "saved." Dale and Ruth thanked me for the visit, but I thank them constantly for the blessing of their company and friendship through the years. I'll concur with Mike that those were some of the "best days of my life."

I've been deeply enriched by the friendship of dozens of Brethren and enjoyed the company of hundreds more. I'd like to pay homage to all of you through Dale. And, though the Brethren have too much genuine humility to accept the tribute, I can't help thinking of a line that I spoke in Maxwell Anderson's classic play, *Winterset*: "He was a man like men would be if gods were men."

In Brotherhood,
Don Murray

Living with Dying
By Dale Aukerman

My wife, Ruth, and I were finishing a meal in a Chinese restaurant. I broke open a fortune cookie and read the words, "Your deepest wish will be fulfilled." As someone likely to die quite soon, I smiled at getting this as my fortune. The first thought that came to me was, yes, the wish that I would continue to live much longer with my loved ones.

But later I got to reflecting. That was not at all right. What I want most should have to do not with longer life, but with living for the glory of God and toward the coming of God's kingdom. With that as my deepest desire, I can look confidently to God to help me toward its fulfillment, whether my remaining time on earth is very short or relatively long. The shallow fortune cookie prediction would turn out to be true.

On November 5, 1996, I found out that I had a tumor three and a half inches across on my left lung. Later tests showed that the cancer had spread to the liver, the right hip, and two spots in the spine. I learned that I could figure on living two to six months, with a median survival prospect of four months.

It's amazing the reorientation of outlook that can come when you find out that you may have only a couple of months to live. Each day and each close relationship became much more precious than before. Every morning I would think of which new day of the month it was—this further day given by God. With fresh intentness I gazed at my family, my home, and God's creation, knowing that my time for seeing all this might very soon be at an end. In the anointing service held not long after the diagnosis, I confessed that I had not been giving God nearly enough attention. Through the cancer God certainly gained much more of my attention.

When my sister Jane died of an especially lethal form of cancer at the age of 14, my mother saw this as God's will: God chose to take her, and who were we as human beings to challenge that? For some people this type of view gives comfort. I see such things somewhat differently. I don't think God sends cancer or heart disease or Alzheimer's. When a drunken driver swerves into another car and kills a number of people, I don't believe that is God's will.

So much in the world is not what God intended and not what God wants. Around us are the threatening powers of death, rebel powers within God's creation. In 2 Corinthians 12:7, Paul writes of his troubling ailment, that thorn in the flesh. He calls it "a messenger of Satan." God has messengers, agents that represent his dominion. Things like cancer are agents of the contrary power that enforces the dominion of death.

Take lung cancer as an example. Some people smoke and bring on lung cancer. I'm in the seven percent of victims who have never been smokers. But I've not taken up the useless question, "Why me?" Such illness can come to anyone. Embracing modern technology, we have messed up the environment with all sorts of pollutants. I live downwind from a cement plant that through the years has burned some terrible things in its kilns. A millionth of a gram of plutonium is enough to cause lung cancer in a person. All of us have in our bodies some plutonium from nuclear weapons production, testing, and use. In so many ways, humanity aligns itself with the powers and agents of death.

But God is with us as the One who stands against death. In more ways than we can notice or comprehend, God turns back the powers of death. As a boy I came near to being killed under a farm wagon. Several years later I almost died from what may have been arsenic poisoning. I've had close calls in automobiles. A few years ago I was attacked in a truck by a steer with horns. He charged twice, then stopped and walked out of the truck. After six cycles of chemotherapy, a regimen of nutritional supplements, and so much praying by a host of friends, I had another CAT scan, which showed that the tumor on my lung had shrunk to less than one-fourth of its earlier size. Two of the doctors spoke of that as a miracle. In an amazing way, contrary to the medical probabilities, God has held back death from me and given longer life.

God brings into existence every living creature and every one of us. God is also the Sustainer, holding up into existence each creature and each of us. All of us have had times of rescue from death. All of us have experienced God's power of healing many times—even from something so common as a cold. As just one dimension, the immune system of the human body is an incredible array of defenses against attack. God keeps us in life by turning back the forces of death.

After my diagnosis I started to pray much more for people with cancer. A number of those on my prayer list have died. For some God brings about full healing from a disease such as cancer. For others God graciously gives a considerable length of time before the end. There are those who die so soon.

Death was not part of God's original intention for humanity. But all of us have sinned, and for each of us the time comes when God no longer holds back death, and one by one we seem to be given over to that dark power.

In Ephesians 1:19-22, Paul writes of "the immeasurable greatness of [God's] power" by which "he raised [Christ] from the dead and made him sit at his right hand in the heavenly places." We read: God "has put all things under" the feet of Christ. That is, God has brought Christ to victorious dominion over all rebel powers. This is a biblical image for triumphant conquest and subjugating rule. The One who died and rose again is the victor over cancer, heart disease, AIDS, Alzheimer's, schizophrenia, abuse of children. He is the victor over exploitation of the poor, over the mindless blighting of God's good earth, over the madness of military spending and nuclear weapons.

But we may ask: If Christ already has the victory over such things, why are they so much in evidence? Why do they seem to have such encompassing dominion? In a war there may be one decisive battle that determines which side will win. Because of that battle, the one side is sure to go on to complete triumph, even though the other side still has troops in the field and the struggle continues. It's only a matter of time until that side is utterly vanquished. When we look to Jesus Christ, executed on a Roman cross and risen from a rock-hewn tomb, we put our trust in the One through whom all the powers of darkness have been defeated. Their grip on humanity has been broken. It is just a matter of time until they will be totally vanquished and swept from the field.

Our hope as Christians does not have to do first of all with gaining eternal life after death. The towering hope given in the New Testament is that God's glorious kingdom will come, the invisible risen Lord will appear in splendor to recreate all that God has made, everything evil and destructive will be done away with. That is, history will turn out right. The human story will receive its God-given ending. God at some point will take total control of the stream of human events and bring in the unimaginable wonder of the New Age. We hope in God for the fulfillment of all that God has promised, and, quite secondarily, we hope to have our own tiny part in that for all eternity.

One friend who asked to pray with me for my healing was very insistent that I must have "100 percent faith" that God would deal with me completely and, if I did, that healing would certainly come. I was grateful for her concern and prayer, but I can't agree with that approach. In that view, we have the determining role: If we can reach such a degree of certainty, this brings God's healing. It can become almost like a magic formula that gives us control.

In contrast, a key passage for me has been the story in Mark 1:40-45: "A leper came to [Jesus] beseeching him, and kneeling said to him, 'If you will, you can make me clean.' " The leper had strong faith that Jesus could heal him, but he was not supposing that his faith would automatically induce Jesus to perform such a healing. The leper saw Jesus as the One who would freely and graciously decide whether to give healing. We read: "Moved with pity, [Jesus] stretched out his hand and touched him, and said to him, 'I will: be clean.' And immediately the leprosy left him, and he was made clean.

A number of best-selling books about healing have been published that have a message something like this: Have positive thoughts, picture your illness as eliminated, be confident you're going to be healed, and the chances are very good that you will be. I think there is some truth in this approach. The outlook of a sick person certainly is important. But the popular literature gives it the central role. The idea is that we ourselves have that positive power to bring healing for ourselves.

But biblical faith is basically different from such a view. If as Christians we grope toward healing, we recognize that God has the central role. Our part is quite significant, and God makes use of it. However, we look to God for healing, and not to the power of positive thoughts that we evoke within ourselves.

Another key passage for me has been the one in Mark 5:24b-34 in which the woman, coming through the dense crowd, touched the garment of Jesus, and healing power flowed into her. I want to be in touch with Jesus so that power from him can flow into me for healing or for coping with whatever comes.

God has given me a measure of healing, and we rejoice in that. God may give me or any stricken person full healing from a deadly disease, and that is cause for yet greater rejoicing. But when God does not and the agent of death sooner or later seems to win out, we can still rejoice. For death's triumph is swallowed up in Christ's victory. At some point each of us is given over to death, but that infernal grip cannot hold us. God lifts us out of it to be with our risen Lord.

When we found out that I might have only a few weeks to live, there came the urgent question of priorities. What was important enough to give time to? My pattern of reading shifted. As for the daily newspaper, I would look at the headlines and check the weather. Time seemed too precious for more than that. We didn't have the television on for maybe three months. I read the cards and letters from friends, but very little else that came in the mail. Reading the Bible was what seemed so crucially important.

God speaks to us in many ways. For me the most personal and vital way is through the words of scripture. It is sometimes said that a verse in one's devotional reading can jump out at a person to be God's "marching orders for the day." Continually during the past months I've been given such verses. These messages from God are a decisive help when we are cornered by death, but we need them so much also in what seem less critical times.

I have kept returning to verses having to do with fear. It has many ways of getting a hold on us, even through lesser threats. God's word is given in Isaiah 41:10: "Fear not, for I am with you, be not dismayed, for I am your God." Jesus, walking on the water, said to the trembling disciples in the boat (and to me): "Take heart, it is I; have no fear" (Matt. 14:27). The risen Christ speaks in Revelation 1:17-18: "Fear not, I am the first and the last, and the living one; I died, and behold I am alive for evermore, and I have the keys of Death and Hades." Even if death comes close to stalk us or a loved one, we don't have to be afraid. The Lord is risen indeed. He has defeated death and will soon put an end to it.

Throughout my adult life I have been much involved in peace witness and peacemaking. During these past months I've cherished verses about peace. Isaiah 26:3 gives the promise: "Thou dost keep him in perfect peace, whose mind is stayed on thee, because he trusts in thee." The risen Lord said to the fearful disciples in the upper room: "Peace be with you" (John 20:20, 21). As I was being thrust in and out of the MRI tunnel, I would think of the verse "the peace of God, which passes all understanding, will keep your hearts and your minds in Christ Jesus" (Phil. 4:7). This peace, in the biblical understanding, is more than inner tranquility of spirit. It is wholeness of life and relationships given by God over against all that fragments and destroys. God's gift of peace can bear us up even when we walk through the valley of deep darkness. Other verses that have stood out and accompanied me have to do with rejoicing. Psalm 70:4 gives the appeal: "May all who seek thee rejoice and be glad in thee." Jesus said to his despairing followers in the upper room shortly before his arrest: "These things I have spoken to you, that my joy may be in you, and that your joy may be full" (John 15:11). Paul gave the exhortation: "Rejoice in the Lord always: again I will say, rejoice" (Phil. 4:4).

When my sister Jane died, we who were closest to her were grief-stricken. But there was something in us stronger than that. We could rejoice because Jesus raised from the dead had changed everything for us and for all humanity. Our experience was that of the Easter hymn:

> Lo! Jesus meets us.
> Risen from the tomb.
> Lovingly he greets us,
> Scatters fear and gloom.

I talked in Bridgewater, Virginia, with William Beahm, retired dean of Bethany Seminary, a little before he died of prostate cancer. One thing he said was, "Be thankful when your plumbing works." There is so much we take for granted and don't give thanks for. He also said, "Death is as close as the truck in the oncoming lane of traffic." I think he meant: Ordinarily the huge semi in the oncoming lane goes on by; but something can happen, and there is a head-on collision. The possibility of death is that close, and none of us knows when for us the possibility *will* become the actual thing.

We are given these years of life on earth as testing and preparation within God's scrutinizing view. Each day is precious. Don't waste time. Keep examining your priorities. Cherish your loved ones and hug them often. Feed on God's word and take with you each day words that spring out at you as God's special promise or command. In times that aren't so hard, give God your deepest attention, and when the hardest times come, God will be right there with you.

Take heart. Fear not. Rejoice in the Lord. "And the peace of God, which passes all understanding, will keep your hearts and your minds in Christ Jesus."

This article first appeared in the April 1998 issue of Messenger *magazine. Copyright © 1998 Church of the Brethren General Board, Elgin, IL.*

Why I Believe
By Dale Aukerman

After returning from a radiation treatment, I made the comment, "If this about God and Jesus is true, there is life beyond death."

A friend, who is not a committed Christian, pointed to my use of the word *if* and asked me, "Do you have doubts?"

I replied something like this: The possibility that the Christian faith is an illusion can hardly be dismissed. But I don't find myself pulled back and forth between faith and doubt. I have a deep assurance, a strong certainty, that the gospel about God and Jesus is true.

We can rather easily coast along in our faith. We have come to believe certain things, and we almost casually go on believing them. But if we suddenly find ourselves face to face with dying, we come up against ultimate questions. Is death the end? When we die, are we kept within the gracious care of God, or do we sink away into nothingness? After I received the diagnosis of advanced lung cancer, I needed to deal with those questions more intensely than I ever had before.

In a meditation titled "Message in the Stars," Frederick Buechner asks, "If God really exists, why in Heaven's name does God not prove that he exists instead of leaving us here in our terrible uncertainty?. . . What would happen if God did set about demonstrating his existence in some dramatic and irrefutable way?"

Buechner then presents a story. One night people look up at the sky and see the words emblazoned in the Milky Way, I REALLY EXIST. The message in the sky has a tremendous impact on earth. There is terror and awe. Many repent. Persons near death are filled with hope. Wars and crimes cease. Church services overflow into football stadiums. The message continues. Several years pass, and then one evening a child with a wad of bubble gum in his cheek looks up and says, "So what if God exists? What difference does *that* make?" In the twinkling of an eye, the message fades away for good.

If God were to give that sort of proof of his existence, that would not meet our deepest need. We would know that God exists, but this knowledge might not make much difference. God has given us something far better than a message in the stars.

Why do I believe? Most of all because of Jesus. There are many reasons and factors that enter into my having faith in God, but Jesus is at the center.

In the first chapter of the Gospel of John, we read about two disciples of John the Baptist who started walking after Jesus. "Jesus turned . . . and said to them, 'What do you seek?' And they said to him, 'Rabbi, where are you staying?' He said to them, 'Come and see.' They came and saw where he was staying; and they stayed with him that day."

The call of Jesus to his disciples was, "Come, stay with me, and see." Day after day and month after month the disciples rubbed shoulders with him, they heard him preach, they saw him deal with the masses, they watched as he confronted adversaries.

The disciples were drawn to Jesus. They saw him as a most extraordinary person. He amazed and puzzled them. Only gradually did they come to understand just how extraordinary this person was. Here are some of the ways:

- At the close of the Sermon on the Mount, we read: "The crowds were astonished at his teaching, for he taught them as one who had authority, and not as the scribes" (Matt. 7:28-29). Jesus was not offering opinions. He was not saying in effect, "This is the way I see things." He spoke as one who felt himself to be in direct touch with ultimate reality. He claimed to have definitive knowledge of God, and he communicated it.
- We see it as essential for right living that a person recognize and own up to the wrongdoing in his or her life. But Jesus said to his opponents, "Which of you convicts me of sin?" (John 8:46). Jesus saw human beings as sinners, but he did not include himself in that.
- In the Gospel of John, we find several statements of Jesus like the one in 7:29, referring to God: "I know him, for I come from him, and he sent me." That outlook is implied throughout the Gospels. Jesus saw himself as the one uniquely sent to reveal God and to do his work. He believed himself to be the central person for all the human story.
- Even the officers of the chief priests and Pharisees reported, "There has never been anybody who has spoken like him" (John 7:46 JB). The disciples reached that conclusion too, but they went beyond it. As Jesus taught them after the Last Supper, they told him, "Now we know that you know all things . . . ; by this we believe that you came from God" (16:30).

Something like what the disciples concluded has been my experience. Something like that can be anyone's experience. We can come to the Gospel stories. We can listen, watch, and ponder. Like the disciples, we can reach conclusions about this man Jesus.

No one else ever saw so deeply and truly into the human situation or spoke with such authority. No one else ever expressed so well in teaching and life what right human living is. More radically than anyone else in history, Jesus called into question prevailing assumptions that through the millennia have shaped individuals and societies. Decisive for his life and teaching was his total rejection of lethal violence.

Around us are all sorts of religions and views of life. What makes sense? What holds together? What rings true?

I am convinced that Jesus spoke truth as no one else ever has. What he said and did came out of his unique relationship with God. Far beyond anyone else he had a grasp of what the human situation is and who God is. I trust his understanding.

Some of the critics of Jesus said he was mad (John 10:20). There were even friends of his who said, "He is beside himself" (Mark 3:21). There have been mentally ill people and occasional imposters who have made claims similar to those of Jesus. Either Jesus was who he claimed to be, or he was deranged, or an impostor. Only one explanation makes sense: that he was who he presented himself to be.

I give myself to the faith that God is like Jesus. As this carpenter from Nazareth said to Philip, "He who has seen me has seen the Father" (John 14:9). Jesus is the key to the mystery of who God is. There can be no more marvelous view of God than this, that God is like Jesus. God loves with the love that Jesus has put into our view.

The depth of that love is to be seen most of all in Jesus going to the cross. He took the hate, the ridicule, the abandonment, the excruciating agony. Jesus believed that his going to his death by execution on a cross was the will of God. In what Jesus did we see God's love for humanity acted out.

Jesus died on that Roman cross. His body was placed in a rock-hewn tomb. It seemed that his enemies had triumphed. His disciples had fled. All their hopes had been crushed. They had seen the defeat of what they thought was the coming of God's kingdom. They were utterly distraught.

But then something happened. Jesus came back to be with his disciples again. He came back, not as he had been earlier, but as far more. His body still had the nail prints, but it was a spiritual body. The disciples could know beyond all doubt that right there with them was the one who had come from God, the one whom God had raised up to be Lord of all. The Word that was with God and was God had taken human form and dwelt among them (John 1:1, 14).

The risen Jesus greeted the women at the tomb. The earliest account of the resurrection was given by Paul in 1 Corinthians 15:4-8: "He was raised on the third day in accordance with the scriptures, and . . . he appeared to Cephas [Peter], then to the twelve. Then he appeared to more than five hundred brethren at one time, most of whom are still alive, though some have fallen asleep. Then he appeared to James, then to all the apostles. Last of all, as to one untimely born, he appeared also to me."

At that time many of the closest friends of Jesus were still alive. They could vouch for having seen and experienced the risen Lord. Paul was saying that several hundred people were still alive as witnesses to testify to the reality of a resurrection appearance. One person can have a hallucination. Paul's vision on the road to Damascus could be dismissed in that way. But 11 people or 500 do not all at the same time have a common hallucination.

Near the close of Matthew's Gospel, we read that the chief priests gave money to the soldiers who had been guarding the tomb and said, "Tell the people, 'His disciples came by night and stole him away while we were asleep' " (Matt. 28:13). Through the centuries there have been all sorts of attempts to explain away the resurrection of Jesus. But if his followers had carried out a hoax, why would they have lived and died as they did? It could have been a delusion, but too many people were involved.

One explanation has it that soon after the crucifixion the disciples came to the insight that the love, goodness, and truth that Jesus had lived out was what they could still live for. It would have been like followers of Martin Luther King deciding after his assassination that they must carry on his work. But there is nothing in the Gospel accounts or elsewhere to indicate that this is what happened.

What else but the resurrection could have transformed the shattered group of disciples into a band ready to challenge the Jerusalem authorities and face prison and death as they bore witness to this Lord? What else but the resurrection of Jesus could have transformed the Peter who fled from Gethsemane and three times denied knowing Jesus into the Peter who preached at Pentecost? What else but the resurrection could have been the impetus for the emergence of the Christian church, which within decades spread across the Roman Empire?

We are asked to believe that the One who lived a superlatively loving life beyond any other was raised from the dead. We are asked to believe in the rising of this One who claimed a role in relation to God such as no other sane person ever did. Is it that hard to believe that the One who lived the most extraordinary life in all of history would triumph over death and come back to be with his friends? Not if there is the God to whom Jesus pointed.

I think of myself as having heard the invitation of Jesus, "Come and see." I've gone with the disciples on a journey with this Itinerant Preacher. Through their accounts I have been given a closeup view of who he was. I have come to the same conclusions about him that they reached. I also have their testimony about his rising from death. The resurrection of Jesus is central to why I believe and what I believe. God has not written a message in the stars, but he has given exactly the message we need in the life, death, and rising of Jesus.

But it's not just that I am convinced in my mind that Jesus is risen. I have found again and again that this living Lord comes to me. I have not seen the risen Jesus with my eyes or touched him with my hands as the disciples did. But throughout my life he has met me, directed me, rebuked me, inspired me.

When I talk with persons without Christian faith who might be interested in checking it out, I often say something like this: "There are the accounts about Jesus. Read them, immerse yourself in them, come to your own conclusions. We have the accounts of the resurrection of Jesus. Ponder them. These questions about Jesus are the most important questions you can ask and answer. If you are really seeking to find out the truth concerning Jesus, an amazing thing can happen. Jesus will no longer be simply a historical person in those events nearly 2,000 years ago. This Lord will step out of those stories to meet you and to lay hold on your life."

An internationally known evangelist was giving a series of messages on a university campus. In the discussion time, a student challenged him with skeptical questions. Several days later the evangelist met the student at breakfast. The student said, "I still don't believe what you are saying. But since we talked, I have read through the New Testament." The evangelist replied, "You're on the way." Those who seek that ardently will find.

I believe in God most of all because of what I have seen in Jesus. I believe that he comprehended the truth about our human situation, and I yield myself to his understanding. I believe that God gives eternal life beyond death, because Jesus promised us that.

I don't know what is ahead for me. But I hope to be sustained in the faith that the disciples declared on the first Easter evening, "The Lord has risen indeed!" (Luke 24:34).

An excerpt from Reckoning with Apocalypse: Terminal Politics and Christian Hope
By Dale Aukerman

Christians should not be taken in by the ethereal (and unbiblical) individualizing of the Christian hope: A person dies, and the consolation is that this life somehow continues with God in heaven. Rather, they are to hold fast to those Hebrew prophecies about vines and fig trees, lions and lambs, and to the plea Jesus entrusted to the Messianic community, "Thy kingdom come, thy will be done on earth as it is in heaven." God will bring shalom on earth, the earth recreated. What draws near will not be the multiplication of a narrow, private happening but a cosmic event embracing all God's people. With the New Earth will come the perfected wholeness and harmony of all that does not hold out unendingly against God.

"Behold, he is coming with the clouds, and every eye will see him, every one who pierced him; and all tribes of the earth will wail on account of him" (Rev. 1:7). But this (at least in its major strains) will be no wail of despairing consternation. The allusion is to Zechariah 12:10: "When they look on him whom they have pierced, they shall mourn for him, as one mourns for an only child, and weep bitterly over him, as one weeps over a first-born." All people will see the unfathomable marvel of who Jesus was and is and take in the all-embracing pathos of what was done to him. They shall mourn for him as the One dearest and most beloved, mourn for what all have inflicted on him and on all others; and they that mourn shall be comforted by this One who was pierced to death and is first-born from the dead. . . .

The prospect that humans may devastate the planet and even terminate human history can be seen as the climactic threat to the sovereignty of the living God. . . . Seemingly, global nuclear holocaust or desolation of the earth brought on in other technological ways would be the most determinative action in history. . . .

The crucifixion of Jesus brings some explication. There most of all, humans were permitted the power and "freedom" to move against God, to crush the inauguration of God's Rule in Jesus, to do away with God who had come so near. That move did not impose the insurgent human will upon God but was taken up by God's incomparably more determinative countermove of atonement and resurrection. What human defiance of God imposed, God in Jesus took freely to himself for the rescue of all. That countermove remains more determinative of the human future than any possible insurgency, even that of human self-destruction, because God is bringing it toward consummation in the unveiling of the One still hidden. Only the rising of Jesus of Nazareth has more power and momentum than the sway of death that is tightening so perceptibly around our planet. God who remained graciously sovereign when the corpse of the incarnate Son was entombed would be equally omnipotent even in the aftermath of the ultimate war or other terminal madness and near the full revealing of his power. "The Lord is risen indeed!" Death's dominion is at an end. The fullness of God's Rule is breaking in. What God has begun on earth he will complete.

An excerpt from Darkening Valley: A Biblical Perspective on Nuclear War
By Dale Aukerman

The resilient hope we have been pointing to can be very easily cheapened—and often is: If nuclear war comes, I have the assurance anyway of going to heaven; even if nuclear war comes, God can be counted on to clean up the planetary mess. There is this cheapening unless one's life is drawn into his resurrection advance against the defeated but still rampaging last enemy. Only when, in the momentum of that resurrection advance, we face death, press in upon death, and cry out its annihilation, can we, without shallowness, point to life beyond and to a new earth, after whatever human folly may bring upon this one.

The time in my own life when the power and the splendor of Jesus' rising was most real to me was when my sister Jane died of cancer at fourteen. There pressing upon the ugly, dismal awfulness of death's triumph was something far stronger that brought us who were most bereaved into the glad exhilaration of hope in the Risen One. Christians throughout the centuries have discovered that precisely when death demonstrates its power, they are borne up by the might of the One who is concluding his victory over death. . . .

In this perspective too, it is clear that any alignment with lethal violence turns a disciple into a defector from that resurrection advance, into one who would promote death's claim and dominion. A stance of living Christ's resurrection life as combat against death and its sway is the ground and essence of Christian nonviolence. . . .

We are to look to Jesus, who "for the joy that was set before him endured the cross, despising the shame, and is seated at the right hand of the throne of God" (Heb. 12:2). Converging into that cross was God's empathy with all his suffering creatures, Christ's standing as victim through all the years and days with those whose plight he took and still takes as his own; converging into it also would be the nuclear crucifixion of our Lord with the multitudes of the least of the earth. But the destination, the end-fulfilment beyond all that, is the joy, the new glory, the harmony of all within the Father's caring. . . .

We believe that, twisted and erring as we are, the Risen Lord raises us out of that. Ours is the confidence that he will lift us out of death's abyss. Blessed are those who, in the midst of whatever may come, live in yet more ardent faith that the Risen One, at the moment of God's choosing, will lift a resurrected earth, a new humanity, out of the shambles of the old. . . .

Copyright ©1989 by Dale Aukerman. Herald Press, Scottdale, PA.

Dale walks through the memorial woodlot on May 6, 1999, thankful to be able to see the redbuds bloom. Though redbuds normally bloom only in the spring, this particular tree bore several branches of blooms a week after Dale's death on September 4, 1999.

Dale Aukerman
June 16, 1930 – September 4, 1999